HOUSING ASSOCIATIONS – REHOUSING WOMEN LEAVING DOMESTIC VIOLENCE

New challenges and good practice

Cathy Davis

The POLICY PRESS

First published in Great Britain in July 2003 by

The Policy Press
University of Bristol
Fourth Floor, Beacon House
Queen's Road
Bristol BS8 1QU
UK

Tel +44 (0)117 331 4054
Fax +44 (0)117 331 4093
e-mail tpp-info@bristol.ac.uk
www.policypress.org.uk

British Library Cataloguing in Publication Data

A catalogue record for this book is available from the British Library

ISBN 1 86134 489 9 paperback

Cathy Davis is a Research Fellow at the Social Work Research Centre, University of Salford.

Cover design by Qube Design Associates, Bristol.
Printed and bound in Great Britain by Bell & Bain Ltd, Glasgow.

For Olive Davis

Contents

Preface

Domestic violence is in the news again and is more prominent in government attention to legislation and practice. This study brings domestic violence back down to the personal level – to women (and men) who experience it, and housing staff who are faced with the daily reality of deciding whether or not to help.

My decision in the mid-1990s to explore housing association practice in the context of the 'enabling' or 'strategic' role of local authorities proved to be prescient. The world of social housing continues to fragment. Local authorities may now deal with homelessness 'in house' or contract it out to a diverse range of housing associations and companies: relatively 'new' stock transfer associations and arms-length management organisations or 'older' housing associations, some organised in complex group structures. The provision of longer-term support when required also continues to be difficult to obtain despite the current emphasis on 'inclusivity' in housing management services and the as yet unknown long-term impact of the new Supporting People funding arrangements.

Chapter One sets out the study's particular context in more detail. The historical background to the development of the homelessness legislation and changing practice is described in Chapter Two. The local authority's 'enabling' role is explored in Chapter Three, especially as it relates to homelessness and domestic violence. The work of one local authority is described in detail – the chapter looks at the impact of legislative change, policy development and practice issues. Together, these three chapters provide the detailed background for understanding the role of housing associations.

Three housing associations then take centre stage for the remainder of the book (Chapters Four to Eight). Each chapter looks at association work from different perspectives: senior staff, frontline staff, and women who have been rehoused. Organisational change and current management practice are evaluated for their potential impacts on applicants and tenants who have experienced domestic violence. The reception service, the processes of applying for housing, housing assessment and housing allocation – as well as longer-term housing management – are all considered. Women's experiences and views of the three associations form the penultimate Chapter Seven. Their day-to-day lives provide a counterpoint to some of the attitudes of professional staff expressed in the earlier chapters.

The book concludes with Chapter Eight, which draws together some of the themes which have emerged. A particular emphasis here is on the need for a reinvigorated and revalued 'public service' ethos within housing associations. Regrettably, they are now becoming far more 'private sector' in outlook, priorities and practice than they were in the past. If this broader perspective develops, housing associations (and local authorities) will be able to more fully and more sensitively respond to the women and men who need help with housing because of domestic violence.

Acknowledgements

This book would not have been possible without the help of a great many people. Most of them must remain anonymous, but I would like to thank them here.

First, thanks go to the women who were rehoused by associations and who agreed to be interviewed for this study. Thanks also to the women of the interpreting service who interpreted on behalf of those women who preferred to talk to me in languages other than English.

The staff of the case study associations, the staff with whom I piloted interview schedules, and the staff in the local authority and refuges and hostels in this study: all of these must remain anonymous so that the location of the women who were rehoused is protected. Their interviews also covered a lot of internal organisational issues that would otherwise not have been possible to discuss. I am very grateful for the time they gave to me and their openness in talking about what to many of them were difficult and complicated issues.

The Department of Social Policy and Social Work and the Centre for Housing Policy at the University of York provided timely financial and academic support. The anonymous referees for this book should also be thanked for their positive and supportive comments.

Particular thanks go to Alan, Carol-Ann, Dot, Khalda, John, Geoff, Sheila – and to my mother Olive, who gave me the idea of finding out what had happened to women in the 1950s and 1960s. They all provided help and support to me at different times and in various ways so that the research and this book could be completed.

Finally, a big 'thank you' to the staff at The Policy Press who had the faith and the expertise to help me turn this research into a book which I hope will be used by housing management staff as well as the academic community.

Dr Cathy Davis
University of Salford

Working together: local authority and housing association responses to domestic violence

Introduction

For the past 25 years it has been recognised in the UK that many women need access to short and long-term rented council housing to enable them to leave violent men. Since the 1977 Housing (Homeless Persons) Act, local authorities have had an important role to play in providing accommodation to women who have become homeless because of domestic violence. However, their role is now changing. Some of these changes were initiated by former Conservative governments, although they are being developed further under the current Labour administration (DETR and DSS, 2000). By focusing on the work of privatised and independent housing associations, this book examines the realities for homeless women of the fragmentation of direct state provision of council housing.

On average, between 10% and 25% of the total number of households accepted as statutory homeless each year by local authorities are women who are homeless as a result of domestic violence (DoE, DETR and ODPM, Quarterly returns for each year [ODPM, 2002c]; see also Chapter Two). Throughout the 1990s, the local authority in the study reported in this book annually accepted approximately 2,000 homeless people as statutory homeless. By the mid-1990s, 30% were women fleeing domestic violence. 14% of those were black or Asian. This authority was known to respond sympathetically to any person who was homeless because of domestic violence or the risk of violence, whether or not they had dependent children. One question I asked in this research was whether the 1996 Housing Act affected this approach. This study's findings provide the grounding for any future evaluation of the impact of the more generous provisions of the 2002 Homelessness Act.

Three different housing associations were case studies for this research: one small black housing association (Tulip HA), one city-wide housing association (Bluebell HA), and one multi-regional housing association (Foxglove HA). Each one worked within the boundaries of the local authority which was included in the wider case study. This enabled me to look at the local authority service provided to homeless women and the impact of local authority 'enabling' on the services provided by these three associations. Housing association staff of various professional levels were interviewed, as were women tenants who had been rehoused by these associations because of domestic violence. A wide range of local authority and hostel staff were also interviewed. Each interview was tape-recorded. The interviews, as well as further documentary evidence and statistics, were then analysed and used as data sources to build a picture of how each association's housing management service was changing and the impact this had on homeless women.

All of the staff quoted in this study are referred to by their job titles. The women who were interviewed have been given different names and identifying information changed. The associations were assured that they would not be identified; the local authority is also anonymous.

This introductory chapter is divided into three parts that provide a broad overview for the rest of the book. First, the role of local authorities is outlined, concentrating on what they have achieved in responding directly to women who have become homeless because of domestic violence. Women have been treated in contradictory ways because their experience flies in the face of dominant housing policy and practice preferences towards the nuclear family that have been commonplace within local authority housing departments (Watson, 1986, 1988; Watson with Austerberry, 1986). The more recent 'enabling' role of local authorities is then described. Here, the study concentrates on three possible ways in which a local authority might 'enable' change in housing associations: nominations, domestic violence policy development, and inter-agency working.

Second, the changing position of housing associations is described, and some of the pressures on their housing management services since the 1988 Housing Act are outlined. Housing associations were relatively small organisations before 1988, providing rented housing which complemented local authority provision. They have since grown significantly (with the support of successive Conservative and Labour governments) because of new house building and stock transfers in over 140 local authorities (Malpass and Mullins, 2002). In the past, associations have rehoused fewer homeless people than local authorities, partly because of their size and partly because they have not had a statutory responsibility for homelessness. They have also had a variable reputation in relation to race equality issues. An issue explored in this study was whether or not association staff were influenced more by institutional traditions and internal managerial priorities than by a household's homeless status under the relevant homeless legislation.

The final part of this introductory chapter describes the issues that homeless women have highlighted in approaching local authorities for help. There have been few accounts of women's views of housing associations, although there might be similarities between women's view of local authorities and their views of housing associations since they have similar housing management cultures. Women interviewed for this study commented on the help that they received when they were homeless, their current home and neighbourhood, and their 'new life' in general. They provided challenging insights into issues of personal safety and 'social capital building'.

The local authority role

Housing homeless women

Most research about housing and domestic violence has concentrated on the perspectives of homeless women who have applied to local authorities for help (Binney et al, 1981; Homer et al, 1984; Charles with Jones, 1993; Malos et al, 1993). More recently, Charles with Jones (1993) and Bull (1993) have explored the views of local authority staff to understand *why* particular decisions were made. For example, in local authorities where few vacancies occurred each year, both studies identified practices that staff were using to deter women from applying. These included insisting that women pursue all other available legal remedies to resolve their housing problems before considering their housing application. Staff also made judgements about the violence that women endured, especially in relation to what was 'serious enough' to merit rehousing. They required 'proof' of the violence such as copies of former injunctions and ouster orders. Charles with Jones (1993) found that staff in a number of rural Welsh authorities were reluctant to accept women whom they regarded as 'incomers'. This practice was encouraged by local councillors. The 'local connection' provisions were often used to refer women to other authorities, whether or not they wanted to live there. Not every local authority was like this. Others were more sympathetic, partly (but not wholly) because they had more vacancies each year. In these authorities, staff were more likely to accept what they were told by the woman and were less likely to expect women to use other means to resolve their housing difficulties.

These differences in local authority responses were possible because of the discretion available to staff in the homeless legislation to assist or prevent an application. There have been two potential restraints on the use of discretion, but their impact has been variable. First, the *Code of Guidance* (DoE, DH and WO, 1977-96; ODPM, 2002a, 2002b) was available to local authorities to help with the interpretation of the legislation. Although over time the Code has become more sensitive to the situation of women experiencing violence, it continues to have no statutory force. Local authorities have only been expected to 'have regard' to its suggestions in reaching a decision. Interpretation of the legislation has also been affected by the courts, and a body of case law that has built up over the years, some of which has specifically related to women who have become homeless because of domestic violence. For example, *R v LB Ealing, ex parte Sidhu* [1982] determined that refuges could not be regarded as a solution to homelessness since they were temporary accommodation. This decision remained relevant at the time I undertook this study as refuges could not be considered by local authorities as 'suitable' accommodation to discharge their duties under the 1996 Housing Act (Arden and Hunter, 1997).

The role of local authorities as direct providers of housing

Although most local authorities could usually balance waiting-list priorities with obligations to homeless households, their role from the late 1980s as direct housing providers became increasingly difficult to sustain politically. From 1979, successive Conservative governments pursued the objective of reducing or ending this role in a number of ways. First, the right to buy introduced with the 1980 Housing Act led gradually to significant losses of desirable family accommodation. Second, local authorities' new house building was gradually reduced to virtually nothing during the 1980s. Third, the 1988 Housing Act introduced the possibility of council tenants selecting alternative landlords and council estates being taken out of the sector for improvement through Housing Action Trusts. Finally, there was an increased emphasis on local authorities transferring their housing (wholly or in part) to housing companies or housing associations so that they could concentrate their efforts on developing their 'enabling' role (1989 Local Government and Housing Act). Exactly what 'enabling' entailed was never clearly defined (Goodlad, 1994), but the message was clear: local authorities should not see themselves as long-term landlords.

Many local authorities – and those in London especially – reported that they were finding it increasingly difficult to rehouse the statutory homeless, especially homeless families (AMA, 1990). Although they were concerned about reductions in new council and housing association house building and improvement, most local authorities believed that homeless people should have priority and that the homeless legislation was an important safety net. Some wanted the legislation to be extended (IoH, 1988; AMA, 1990).

The Conservative government initially had no plans to respond to increasing homelessness (DoE, 1987, 1989) and chose to ignore local authority views. Four years later, the national domestic political situation had changed. The government decided that the homeless legislation was encouraging and supporting the existence of an 'underclass' and that the legislation would have to be changed to give priority to traditional nuclear families. It issued a Consultation Paper proposing reductions in the rights of homeless people to permanent accommodation (DoE, 1994). It was widely opposed by local authorities (AMA with the Association of District Councils, 1995). Many challenged the government's justification for the proposals: that lone parents (especially unmarried single mothers) were 'jumping the housing queue' by using the existing homeless legislation to obtain housing priority (DoE, 1995a, 1995b). There was overwhelming professional opposition (IoH, 1995) but the government proceeded to legislate, and the 1996 Housing Act replaced the 1985 Housing Act (Part III).[1]

The 1996 Housing Act

The 1996 Housing Act reduced local authorities' statutory obligations towards certain 'priority groups' of homeless people. Local authorities no longer had to provide permanent council accommodation (or housing association accommodation through nominations). They could provide time-limited temporary accommodation – and then only if and when the local authority considered that there was no housing in the private sector which might be available for applicants (1996 Housing Act, s 193.1, 197.1). A maximum period of two years' stay might be extended if an applicant's circumstances remained unchanged.

The legislation had two main aims. First, it reinforced local authorities' 'residual' role by reducing their statutory responsibilities. Second, these changes fitted into Conservative 'family policy'. The government sought to stigmatise homeless lone parents and exclude them from permanent social housing by claiming that their supposed abuse of the legislation had forced the government to act (DoE, 1994; Phoenix, 1996, pp 177-8). These claims attracted considerable publicity. They became part of an orchestrated debate in certain national newspapers, on the television and in housing policy circles about the possible existence of an 'underclass' in Britain. There was a concern that welfare state policies (such as the provision of 'subsidised' social rented housing to lone parents) were helping in its construction (Murray, 1990; Dennis and Erdos, 1993; Roseneil and Mann, 1996; Field, 1998).

For the first time, the 1996 Housing Act determined that the assessment of an applicant's homeless status (Part VII) would be separate from the assessment of priority for permanent housing (Part VI). A permanent council home would only be available through the local authority housing register (as the waiting list was renamed). The housing register priorities which local authorities were statutorily obliged to adopt were set out centrally in government regulations (DoE, 1996). The government emphasised that it saw the social rented sector ('subsidised housing for rent') as catering for "couples seeking to establish a good home in which to start and raise a family" (DoE, 1994, para 3:1). Council housing was not available for what *the government* saw as queue-jumping lone parents, intent on leapfrogging the waiting list by claiming to be homeless. Homelessness was not initially a housing register priority. Homeless applicants had to be assessed and given priority on the basis of circumstances *other* than homelessness.

Homelessness continued to be a major problem in London and the South of England. Local authorities responded more or less sympathetically – the 1996 Housing Act only assisted those authorities that wanted to be 'tough'. In other parts of the country, the numbers of statutory homeless households actually fell in the latter part of the decade although it was impossible to tell whether this was directly because of the 1996 Housing Act or because fewer people were applying. This reduced the pressure on many local authorities to find other landlords (such as housing associations) to rehouse them. In the North and the

Midlands, voids and low demand also became a notable problem for local authorities and housing associations. In these parts of the country, local authorities could easily rehouse homeless households themselves even though they might not now have a high priority on the housing register. Nevertheless, women might be offered the poorest quality housing in areas where no one wanted to stay, and since most authorities only made homeless households one offer, their choice was very constrained.

The new Labour government in 1997 changed government guidance to local authorities (via the housing regulations). They were now expected to include homeless people as a 'preference group' within their housing registers. A subsequent Green Paper (DETR and DSS, 2000) suggested a number of proposals to extend the priority groups within the 1996 Housing Act (Part VII). This might have helped single women leaving domestic violence, but the Homes Bill that followed was lost when it ran out of time at the end of the parliamentary session 2001/02.[2]

The 'enabling role'

Since 1997 there have been a number of important changes within local government. One has been that the local authority's role as 'enabler' has been transmuted into that of the 'strategic authority' (DETR and DSS, 2000), although in fact the terms are interchangeable in New Labour discourse. Local authorities are now also expected to promote the social, economic and environmental well-being of their areas (2000 Local Government Act, Part 1). Nevertheless, consensus remains lacking in relation to what 'enabling' in housing actually entails. Suggestions include the promotion of the private sector, collecting information about housing needs and monitoring other organisations' work in the field (Goodlad, 1994). A slightly wider perspective was adopted for this study.

Discussions about local authority 'enabling' have often concentrated on the development process, considering the pros and cons of stock transfers to associations or ways of assisting association house building through public/ private partnerships and consortia. In the present study, management rather than development issues were the primary consideration. One management issue was that of nominations to the new association housing estates which were built in the mid-1990s with the help of the local authority. Were homeless women nominated and rehoused into new association housing?

The second aspect of 'enabling' was the development of the local authority's domestic violence policy for housing services and the extent of its impact on policy development within associations. Having a formal policy was important. As Mullender has argued:

> Coherent policies and consistent guidelines represent a major advance over individual workers either ignoring the problem entirely, or taking inappropriate action, or happening to be able to give useful assistance but without consistent support from their agency. (Mullender, 1996, p 82)

A domestic violence policy (or set of 'good practice' guidelines) might 'raise the profile' of domestic violence and encourage a consistent approach from staff. Nevertheless, there were likely to be limitations to this. The reality in housing departments was of a changing internal culture and shifting organisational priorities because of the increasing impact of competition and managerialist practice (Pollitt, 1990; Hood, 1991). Some staff might be keen, although others might be indifferent or hostile towards the problem or have alternative priorities (Lipsky, 1980). How effective, then, might a policy be in these environments?

Third, the extent to which the local authority encouraged inter-agency cooperation between itself and local associations in responding to women in this situation was also relevant in evaluating the 'enabling' role. The local authority might use a domestic violence forum to pursue particular objectives, especially if it grant-aided the work or employed forum staff directly (Home Office and Welsh Office, 1995). In other policy areas such as community care, practical cooperation between organisations on specific projects had a long history. Inter-agency work on homelessness and domestic violence did not appear so well organised or established, possibly because no single organisation was ultimately responsible for service provision (Hague et al, 1996; Kennedy et al, 2001). Networking, information exchange between staff, and occasionally multi-agency awareness training, had been the main work of domestic violence forums (Hague et al, 1996). Some had tried to ensure that different organisations' responses to women were effectively coordinated. In this study, the effectiveness of inter-agency cooperation between the local authority and housing associations was considered in the context of the organisational changes they had undergone and the increasingly competitive environment in which they all worked.

The housing association role

Homelessness and housing associations before 1988

Before the 1988 Housing Act, some associations had a reputation for being selective in relation to new tenants while some local authorities were known to have nominated only their 'better' tenants to association property (Audit Commission, 1989; CRE, 1989b;). Associations attracted criticism from local authorities in the late 1980s because their new government-supported pre-eminence in social house building came despite their comparatively poor record in rehousing homeless people (AMA, 1990). Housing associations traditionally housed far fewer homeless people than local authorities. They had fewer vacancies so were unable to provide accommodation quickly enough. They were less likely to have family homes to rent or property in the areas that people wanted. Both of these features illustrated the difficulties of a much smaller sector, numerically and spatially (Binney et al, 1981; Niner, 1989; Malos et al, 1993). They also appear to have played a small part in rehousing homeless women who had left violence. The only exceptions in published research being some areas of the North East and in Wales (Homer et al, 1984; Charles with Jones, 1993). Some local authorities were very conservative and reluctant to rehouse 'outsiders'. Housing associations did this instead.

The Audit Commission (1989) identified three problems that associations had to tackle to improve their services to homeless people. The first related to differences in the housing managed by associations compared to local authorities. Most statutory homeless households were families, so associations would have to start to build for families in the future. Second, the Audit Commission identified a widespread unwillingness in associations to accept nominations of people who were statutory homeless because they might cause 'management difficulties': this would need to change. Finally, even in the late 1980s, some associations were identified as letting property with rents that were too expensive for ordinary working households. Associations would have to charge 'affordable' rents if they were going to assist local authorities.

Homelessness and housing associations after 1988

Following the 1988 Housing Act, associations became increasingly reliant on private finance to fund new building and were exposed to the risks of the market for the first time. House building in the early 1990s relied on associations being able to change working practices to become more 'efficient' and to deal with financial risk. The ways in which associations were managed as organisations and the nature of their housing management services were also changing in response to this pressure by the mid-1990s. As a parallel and complimentary phenomenon, 'new public management' ideas were becoming popular at this time in central and local government (Pollitt, 1990; Hood, 1991).

The Housing Corporation responded to concerns about associations' rehousing practices by insisting that from 1991/92, associations should specifically target a proportion of their new lettings to rehouse statutory homeless households. The aim was to increase the pressure on associations to rehouse increasing numbers of statutory homeless households. Nevertheless, it later proved difficult to find out whether or not the 'paper' commitments of associations had been realised in practice because they were not effectively monitored by the Housing Corporation on this issue. The initiative was abandoned after three years but the associations studied here were still feeling its impact in the late 1990s.

One reason for the initiative's demise was growing controversy about whom associations were rehousing, fuelled partly by a poorly researched but influential report which claimed that local authorities had been 'dumping' 'difficult' tenants on to housing associations which were ill-prepared for the task of managing them (Page, 1993). These management difficulties had not been found in other research (Cole et al, 1996) but the reputations of associations were damaged by the ensuing public debate. This involved government ministers expressing concern about members of 'the underclass' (especially lone parents) being allocated new housing. In this way, the Conservative government played a very active part in creating the ideological climate in which it was considered legitimate by some associations in the late 1990s to begin to question waiting-list priorities based on 'housing need.'

When this study started in 1997/98, the building programmes of housing associations had been curtailed compared to the growth years of the early and mid-1990s. By the mid-1990s, the role of associations in rehousing homeless households was also in doubt. Some housing managers became more cautious about housing lone parents, and there was more discussion in housing management circles about the need to provide 'support', especially for people who had been homeless in the past (LFHA, 1995). At the same time, there appeared to be more interest in finding ways in which associations might be able to create 'balanced communities' through selective allocations. Research was completed on local letting schemes; but they were not the panacea which some associations sought (Griffiths et al, 1996).

In summary, research to date and historical developments indicated that the association staff studied here were likely to be concerned in varying degrees about financial risk, controlling costs, maximising income and responding to competition. They might be relatively inexperienced in dealing with homelessness, domestic violence and managing large new estates. In considering applications from homeless women, they might be affected by the homelessness legislation and a range of attitudes and values. These might include dominant conservative ideas and assumptions relating to gender roles within the family and concerns about lone parents creating an 'underclass'. Class-specific issues (especially in relation to ideas about 'deserving' or 'genuine' applicants) were also likely to be evident given the history of housing management and homelessness (see Chapter Two). Ideas and practices associated with 'race' and housing issues might also emerge. Institutional racism, the 'racialisation of space' and racial stereotyping might affect the rehousing process. In this study it was possible to look at these issues from a range of perspectives given that the specific local authority and three different associations, as well as a range of women, were involved.

The views of women who were rehoused

Local authorities have been most likely to rehouse women who have become homeless because of violence (Binney et al, 1981; Mama, 1989; Malos et al, 1993). Consequently, most research has concentrated on examining their role. One notable exception has been Charles with Jones (1993), who examined the role of Welsh local authorities and housing associations. More broad-based research on rehousing following relationship breakdown has also identified important issues for women when they have been rehoused by local authorities. For example, see McCarthy and Simpson (1991) and Bull (1993).

The assessment of homeless women's circumstances and the quality of the housing they have received have been recurrent issues. Many women have lived for years in temporary housing in some areas before being made an offer of a permanent home. This has especially been the case in southern England or rural authorities in England and Wales. The quality of accommodation offered by local authorities has been variable. A small number of women have been offered very poor housing in unsafe areas (Binney et al, 1981; Charles with Jones, 1993; Malos et al, 1993). Most women who have been offered housing association accommodation have been satisfied, since, generally, it has been better quality (Charles with Jones, 1993; Malos et al, 1993). Would this also be the case in the housing associations studied here?

For women who were rehoused, it seemed likely that safety and poverty would be significant issues. A long-term concern of women has been the need to be able to maintain personal safety for themselves and their children (Binney et al, 1981; Charles with Jones, 1993; Kirkwood, 1993). Although some women have been confident and happy to leave a refuge, others have expressed great anxiety about moving into permanent accommodation because they have feared being found by their violent ex-partner. Some have preferred to be rehoused nearby to maintain contacts with friends and staff (Binney et al, 1981; Charles with Jones, 1993). Where and how women obtained help and support and what they thought of the quality of that assistance were important questions for this study. The introduction of the Supporting People arrangements for funding hostels and support services emphasise the need to assist people in the community, and women's views have relevance to this shift in focus.

Poverty has created difficulties for women in re-establishing a home for themselves. Most women who have been rehoused by local authorities have been working class. Their financial options have been very constrained. Women who have been better-off financially have tended to be able to find alternatives to refuge accommodation, bed and breakfast or other hostels (Pahl, 1985, p 81) and have been less likely to apply for social housing, although it is not possible to be sure about this.[3] How would the determination of associations to reduce risk and become more 'efficient' affect women with few resources themselves?

Conclusion

This chapter has outlined briefly the main areas that formed the background to this study. The study was undertaken between 1997 and 2000. It provides a rare and detailed insight into the implementation of the 1996 Housing Act. It looked specifically at the relationships between the local authority and housing associations as well as considering the ways in which management services in associations were changing, and the effects of those changes on homeless women leaving domestic violence.

Chapter Two reviews the research literature to reveal the historical development of housing services in local authorities and housing associations for women who have become homeless because of domestic violence. The chapter concentrates on homeless and waiting-list procedures, identifying the variable impact of familism on women's access to housing.

Chapter Three is the first of the volume's substantive chapters, based directly on the research. It describes the case study local authority's role in some detail, outlining the homelessness procedures as well as elements of the 'enabling' work which were relevant to understanding the relationship between the authority and local associations.

Chapters Four to Six describe the three case study housing associations' role in rehousing women. These chapters present a broad overview of these associations' position in the housing market and the pressures on their housing management services. This is followed by more detailed analysis of their assessment and allocation processes.

Chapter Seven is based on interviews undertaken with women who had been rehoused. With one exception, they had become tenants of the associations in this study. The chapter explores how they coped with homelessness and the help they received, what they thought about where they now lived and how they maintained their own and their children's personal safety.

Chapter Eight concludes this book with an evaluation of the role that associations are now playing in rehousing women who have left violent men. It comments on the way in which association management responses seem to rely in part on assessments of 'housing need' and in part on stereotypical attitudes towards the family and women's role within it. That being said, the associations in this study were constrained by the expectation that they would be financially efficient and would control or minimise risk. The study illustrates the complex relationship between these different ways of considering homeless women who have left violent men.

Notes

[1] See Arden and Hunter (1997) for a more detailed historical account.

[2] The new 2002 Homelessness Act has built on this and its likely impact is considered in Chapter Eight.

[3] For example, studies have shown that women's position in owner-occupation is more tenuous than men's, and relationship breakdown may precipitate a transition from owner-occupation into the social rented sector for financial reasons. See Smith (1990) and McCarthy and Simpson (1991).

TWO

Finding a new home from the council or a housing association

Introduction

Two aspects of housing management are reviewed in this chapter to better understand their impact on women leaving domestic violence: first, the variable implementation of the homeless legislation and, second, the operation of waiting lists. Research published in England, Scotland and Wales since the 1950s is examined with the aim of understanding the wider historical background against which current developments are occurring and to identify those themes that have proved remarkably resilient over time. Most research has concentrated on how the homelessness legislation has been implemented. Research on council and housing association waiting lists also has been included here since they became more important as a route to rehousing following the 1996 Housing Act. The current government's enthusiasm for introducing more 'choice' into the housing register and waiting-list systems currently in use will also affect homeless people in ways which have not yet been seen (DETR and DSS, 2000).

The review begins with a discussion of the impact of familism on council house assessment and allocation. Familism describes processes and practices which have explicitly or implicitly attributed merit and priority to the white nuclear family form. Housing management staff have used to varying degrees particular attitudes towards the nuclear family as a baseline or 'ideal type' against which to use their discretion in assessing applications and allocating property through the homeless legislation and waiting-list practices. These have adversely influenced the nature of the housing service offered to women trying to find a new home away from violent partners/ex-partners because they have not conformed to the 'ideal type' nuclear family.

What follows is a more detailed look at the way women who are homeless because of domestic violence have been helped by housing staff. The first section deals with the period during which the 1948 National Assistance Act was in force. This is important, since some have argued that the 1996 Housing Act marked a return to this minimal approach. The second section considers research completed relatively soon after the enactment of the 1977 Housing (Homeless Persons) Act. And the third section evaluates research completed following the consolidation of the 1977 Act into the 1985 Housing Act.

The review then focuses on housing associations' responses to homelessness. Most research has examined the work of local authorities because they continue to have the statutory responsibility for the homeless. However, during the 1990s, associations were expected to house more homeless families. Much more pressure was placed on them to do this in the first half rather than the last half of the decade. Doubts emerged later about rehousing large numbers of homeless families in new association estates. These affected the opportunities for homeless people in the last few years of the 1990s.

The chapter then concludes with a brief evaluation of the reasons why the Conservative government abolished the homelessness and waiting-list provisions contained in the 1985 Housing Act (Part III) and replaced them with the 1996 Housing Act, despite widespread opposition. A number of themes drawn from the history of local authority and housing association intervention in the field of domestic violence are then carried forward into the rest of the book.

Familism and housing management in local authorities

Familism has affected housing management in different ways. It has influenced the type of housing built by local authorities (for example, their preference for family homes) and housing design and layout (Roberts, 1991). It has also strongly influenced staff judgements about different types of households and has been important in influencing the assessment of housing applications and allocation of property. Judgements have also been made in relation to class distinctions and supposed 'racial' differences, as well as the more gender-specific features of different households. These practices went unchallenged until the 1980s and reduced the opportunities available to a range of different households to obtain good quality council housing in desirable locations.

The historical roots of familism are probably twofold: Fabianism and late 19th-century attempts to re-moralise the poor (Mann, 1992). In the housing management context, the clearest expressions of familism were in the 1950s and 1960s. Housing managers were officially encouraged to 'educate' people to make them 'respectable' or 'good' tenants during this early period. Welfare department staff did this with homeless families (CHAC, 1949, 1955). However, in the face of a growing housing crisis, the government tried to change housing staff preferences for 'respectable' or 'deserving' applicants. For example, the Central Housing Advisory Committee (CHAC) encouraged local authorities to rehouse applicants on the basis of 'housing need'. It expressed particular concern for lone parents who were often treated by local authorities as 'undeserving' applicants despite the poor housing conditions in which many then lived (CHAC, 1969). How much has housing management practice changed since then?

In the 30 years that have passed, change has been slow. In the 1970s, housing managers were found to have no consistent ideology based on their occupational position. Norman (1975, p 80) suggested that managers simply had a set of operational stereotypes that they used to judge applications. Flett (1979) discovered that local authority lettings staff created moral boundaries for themselves beyond which they placed applicants of whom they disapproved, such as lone parents or black people. These applicants received poorer quality housing offers than those regarded favourably.

Since then it has become clear that housing management continues to be weakly professionalised and difficult to improve (Clapham et al, 1990; Cole and Furbey, 1994). Local authorities tend to ignore generalised good practice recommendations and staff continue to be vulnerable to local political pressure from elected councillors or the local press (Welsh Women's Aid, 1986; Bull, 1993). A survey of local authority practice in the late 1980s found that the range of applicants considered by local authorities *had* shifted during the decade to include more lone parents and single people. This was possibly because of the changing market position of council housing rather than the deliberate intentions of housing managers. Moral judgements about 'deserving' and 'non-deserving' applicants were still found. Nearly a half of the local authorities that responded still assessed the standard of housekeeping in applicant's homes and over a third considered the decorative state (IoH, 1990).

Assessing housing applications and allocating homes

A number of feminist writers in the 1980s identified the significance of the nuclear family to women's access to council housing (see, for example, Austerberry and Watson, 1983; Watson, 1986). Other writers had spotted this before, although they had not emphasised gender differences in relation to its significance. Rather, *their* interest had been broader: they looked at the ways in which ideas about an applicant household's 'respectability' (including the contribution made by the mother/wife) were constructed by staff to help them make allocation decisions. The emphasis on the housing of nuclear families (and if necessary disciplining and controlling them) was an example of the influence of Fabian ideas about the efficient reproduction of the workforce. The house types built and management practices reinforced this. For example, the number of bedrooms in most local authority housing meant that large families or single person households were effectively excluded or marginalised from most council housing.

Early research described how allocations staff and housing visitors created and maintained class distinctions between applicants and tenants to help them decide who should be allocated better-quality property (Tucker, 1966; Damer, 1974; Norman, 1975; Gray, 1976). Staff seemed to rely heavily on an evaluation of the presumed class position of the household. If the application was from a couple, their starting point was usually the breadwinner's income and status. (It was presumed that the breadwinner was a man.) Staff considered women mainly through their skill as housewives and mothers (CHAC, 1969; Henderson and Karn, 1987; Mama, 1989). This put lone parents in a difficult position since they did not match this 'ideal' household.

The process was not straightforward; instead, class and gender distinctions mixed in odd ways. Tucker illustrated how complicated this grading might be. Using his experience of Bristol as an example, he described how class distinctions, hygiene and home management were very strong considerations in assessing families. A grading of "Very Fair" meant that an applicant had been assessed as either "clean and working class or dirty but above working class". "Very Good" meant an applicant had both "cleanliness and class". In a household other than a nuclear family, where the household's class position was ambiguous, cleanliness in itself was "only good for a Good". Households given low grades were more likely to be black families, "problem families" or those who were "rehoused with low gradings ... after some behaviour or financial misdemeanour" (Tucker, 1966, p 52).

Relatively few black or Asian households applied for council housing at this time. They may have believed they were not eligible, the housing might not have been attractive to them, or staff attitudes may have discouraged them (Flett, 1979). When they did apply, they were sometimes treated less favourably than their white counterparts because of direct or indirect racial discrimination. The latter was the outcome of the ways in which staff built up mental pictures of 'respectable' or 'good' applicants and tenants. These often downgraded the circumstances of black and Asian applicants (Burney, 1967; Flett, 1984; Henderson and Karn, 1987).

Local authority staff in the 1960s and 1970s regarded lone parents as 'problem families' because they were poor and might have had difficulties paying the rent. However, there was more to it than that. Research in Birmingham discovered that staff received complaints from neighbours if they rehoused lone parents in good property (Henderson and Karn, 1984). Female lone parents were considered to be potentially or actually promiscuous whether they were divorced, a widow or had never married (Henderson and Karn, 1987). These views were also found in other authorities by different researchers (Daniel, 1968; Gray, 1976). There were specific racial implications associated with these attitudes (Daniel, 1968; Parker and Dugmore, 1976; Henderson and Karn, 1987; Mama, 1989). For example, treating lone parents in this way affected some ethnic groups more than others depending on the variable incidence of lone parenthood in different ethnic communities and the dominant racial stereotypes relating to women from those different communities (Bryan et al, 1985; Rao, 1990). Many black lone parents found themselves disadvantaged in a number of ways: through class distinctions, assumptions about their role as mothers, and racial discrimination. Many remained in the private rented sector in the 1960s and 1970s (Committee on One-Parent Families, 1974).

By the late 1980s, the Institute of Housing (IoH) found that the situation was changing: local authorities had increased the numbers of lone parents they rehoused (IoH, 1990). Twelve per cent of applicants on local authority waiting lists across the country were found to be lone parents. (This was confirmed by Prescott-Clarke et al, 1994.) However, the quality and location of housing offered to them was still a potential problem. Single people (including single women who were divorced, widowed or never married) remained marginalised in relation to local authority housing because of the sector's emphasis on providing housing for families. In some parts of the country, local authorities had few properties for single people and were not considered a realistic rehousing option. Nevertheless, most single people wanted to live independently in their own home and many wanted to rent a council or housing association property because private renting was insecure and expensive (Drake et al, 1981; Anderson et al, 1993). Nevertheless, having to apply and wait may have deterred some people. Other restrictions such as age limits meant that single applicants often waited much longer than families before they qualified for the active waiting list. The position for homeless single people was even more difficult and complicated.

In summary, familist ideology revealed itself most clearly in the exercise of discretion by staff in local authorities. Familism influenced staff views about different kinds of household (nuclear, lone, extended or single) and how 'respectable' or 'deserving' an applicant's household might be. At different times, discretion has been exercised negatively in relation to applications from women who were lone parents or single for different reasons. These may include their marital status (Gray, 1976; Henderson and Karn, 1987) or income (CHAC, 1969; Committee on One-Parent Families, 1974) or colour (Burney, 1967; Mama, 1989). They may relate to their housekeeping standards (Henderson and Karn, 1987; IoH, 1990), the number of children a woman had (Gill, 1977), or the nature of the relationship with the father(s) of a woman's children (Parker and Dugmore, 1976; Simpson, 1981). Her immigration status (Simpson, 1981; Mama, 1989; Arden and Hunter, 1997) and if English was her first language (Parker and Dugmore, 1976; Simpson, 1981) could also be important.

As Tucker (1966) had shown, these features might interrelate in different ways for different applicants. Discretion enabled staff to decide who should receive the best (and worst) offers of accommodation. Lone parents were often poorly served by these practices compared to nuclear families. Black lone parents, however, were often allocated even poorer accommodation than their white counterparts (CRE, 1984a). Single women were even less fortunate.

Up until the 1970s, there was little direct reference to how staff views about domestic violence affected assessment and allocation processes. This issue was usually notable by its absence but there were exceptions. Tucker (1966) believed that a history of domestic violence was treated as an indicator of a 'problem family'. Even though influential government committees, pressure groups and changing demography have since resulted in a less vindictive approach to lone parents, discretion remains an essential element in assessing housing applications. Staff often remain reluctant to intervene or take sides in relationship breakdown even when violence is involved. For example, Bull (1993) found that relationship breakdown and domestic violence were dealt with in a variety of ways by local authorities through the waiting-list or homeless legislation and that the use of discretion and the expectation that family law remedies (not rehousing) would suffice was still common.

The next section of this review examines how homeless women have been helped – or hindered – by local authorities implementing the homeless legislation. Familist priorities were formally structured into this legislation in different ways although local authorities have not *always* used these in their implementation of the legislation. This will become clear in the following discussion.

Rehousing homeless women who have left domestic violence

Before 1977, local authorities provided minimal help to homeless women who had left violent partners, whether or not they had dependent children with them. Following the 1977 Housing (Homeless Persons) Act, local authorities had a statutory responsibility to rehouse certain groups of homeless people. These included women who were homeless because of domestic violence if they had dependent children or were 'vulnerable'. Local authority responses were not uniform. The legislation was structured in such a way that women with children were more likely to be considered as statutory homeless than women with no children (another example of the priority accorded to families in social policy legislation). In some authorities, however, staff were concerned to ensure that women complied with specific conditions before offering permanent housing. This was an example of the way in which local authority staff distinguished between 'deserving' and 'undeserving' families – a distinction that ultimately derived, as we have seen, from familist ideas. The 1996 Housing Act marked a return to pre-1977 days, although it was possible that its implementation by local authorities might differ from government intentions structuring the legislation itself. The 2002 Homelessness Act signalled a return to a more sympathetic response by local authorities and housing associations across England and Wales.

The 1948 National Assistance Act, Part 3, Para 21 (1) (B)

Local authority responsibilities to homeless people were very limited until 1977. The 1948 National Assistance Act obliged local authorities to:

> [provide] temporary accommodation for persons who are in urgent need thereof, being need arising in circumstances which could not reasonably have been foreseen or in such circumstances as the authority may in any particular case determine. (Section 2)

Local authority welfare departments provided temporary accommodation in certain circumstances. Very few homeless single people received help. If the adult (or adults) in the family could show that they were not responsible for their homelessness and that they fell into one of the 'priority groups' – such as the elderly or families with young children – they might be given temporary accommodation. 'Battered women' were not considered a priority group (Greve et al, 1971). Sixty per cent of local authorities refused to help anyone outside the priority groups. A woman with children who had left her violent partner would often be sent back. She would not be considered homeless and would be held partly responsible for the violence (Greve, 1964; Glastonbury, 1971; Greve et al, 1971; Freeman, 1979).

Two differing views about the causes of homelessness were prevalent during this time in organisations that worked with homeless people. Many considered that families were responsible for their situation; others saw homelessness as predominantly structural – that is, due to a lack of appropriate housing for poor people. These different views were evident among welfare department staff, but worries about the behaviour of 'irresponsible families' were far more commonplace among housing staff (Greve et al, 1971, pp 82-5). Officially, re-education was emphasised with the expectation that welfare and housing staff would cooperate in this process: the former would provide the education while the latter would provide the housing.[1] However, the relationship between these staff was often difficult and not conducive to working in this way (Greve, 1964; Tucker, 1966; Flett, 1979).

Many women never sought help from local authorities, but nor did all women stay in the family home (Hague and Wilson, 1996). Well before the 1970s, women's need for housing and the attitudes and practices of local authorities were at odds. Research into homelessness in the 1950s and 1960s identified domestic violence as a problem although at the time it was called 'marital discord' or a 'family dispute'. It was not singled out for special attention. At the time, Greve (1964), Greve et al (1971) and Glastonbury (1971) reported that housing managers were not happy rehousing homeless families. With the growth of the women's movement, domestic violence was 'rediscovered' in the early 1970s in the sense that it began to be named publicly (Timms, 1975; Dobash and Dobash, 1979; Hague and Wilson, 1996). However, its subsequent recognition as a social problem was far from straightforward.

Women with dependent children

A picture may be drawn of the whole country for this early period. Greve (1964) first researched 16 local authorities between 1957 and 1961, eight of which were in London. He then completed more research in London (Greve et al, 1971) for the period 1966-69. This included surveys of households in temporary accommodation in eight London boroughs, applicants to all London boroughs over four weeks in 1969, and a small survey of housing associations. Glastonbury (1971) investigated the extent and nature of homelessness in South Wales (Swansea, Cardiff and Glamorgan) and the West of England (Gloucestershire, Bristol and Somerset), covering a variety of local authorities and industrial settings in 1969.

Glastonbury and Greve each identified similar difficulties for homeless women with children. They both discovered that a very significant proportion of admissions to temporary accommodation were households leaving 'domestic friction', but that official homeless figures were an underestimate of the problem. Fewer than a third of applications for emergency accommodation were accepted from women who had left a violent partner (Greve et al, 1971). Staff made judgements about whether or not an applicant was "blameworthy" (Glastonbury, 1971, p 17) and tailored help accordingly. Croydon, for example, would not admit "any blameworthy families (homeless due to quarrels, rent arrears, etc.)" (Greve et al, 1971, p 126) unless they had children under five years old. Their stay was limited to six months.

Glastonbury discovered that 116 of the 493 families that he interviewed in temporary accommodation in 1969 had been affected by domestic violence. Seventy-five families (13.7% of the total) gave domestic violence as the main reason for their homelessness (Glastonbury, 1971, p 70). In London, Greve found that lone parents accepted for temporary accommodation because of 'marital friction' in 1969 had stabilised at about 18% in the inner boroughs of London (325 out of 1803) (Greve et al, 1971, p 109). This was a reduction compared to the data he had analysed for 1959 and 1961. He thought that the figures had decreased because local authorities had become more restrictive in the face of overwhelming numbers of applications from people who needed emergency help with housing rather than because 'marital disputes' had declined. Nevertheless, many women, faced with very poor hostel conditions and unsympathetic staff, decided to leave after a short time. Greve et al (1971) found that 37% of lone parents who were given temporary accommodation because of 'domestic disputes' stayed for less than a week. Over a half had left within a month (Greve et al, 1971, p 81). Greve et al were not gender-specific, but it is likely that most of the heads of these families were women.

Women were often blamed for the violence and, if not, the violence was minimised or disregarded. 'Educating' women (presumably about *their* behaviour) was the preferred social work option at this time. Often nothing was done practically to help the women concerned (Borland, 1976; Scottish Education Department, 1982; Maynard, 1985). Some women were ambivalent about what they wanted in the longer term. Lone parenthood was an extremely difficult option to pursue at the time (Wynn, 1964; Marsden, 1969), but the most common response to women's homelessness was to send them back immediately to their violent partner rather than offer a temporary hostel place and time to think.

In their small community survey, Marsden and Owens (1975) found that none of the women who had tried to leave violent partners identified the housing department as a source of help. This was confirmed by Pahl (1985, p 80) and by Binney et al (1981), who reported on women's experiences of trying to leave violent partners mainly in the time before the enactment of the 1977 Housing (Homeless Persons) Act. Pahl's (1978, 1985) longitudinal studies of the Canterbury Women's Centre found that half of the 42 women she interviewed wanted to live independently in a council house, yet only one third achieved this. Although it is not made explicit in each of these studies, it is likely that most of the women they interviewed were white. The situation for black women was more difficult because of the direct racism they were likely to encounter from staff in this period (Committee on One-Parent Families, 1974; Runnymede Trust, 1975; Flett, 1979).

By the early 1970s, homelessness was increasing and becoming more of a public issue (Bailey and Ruddock, 1972; Shelter, 1976; Thompson, 1988). It had become clear to the Department of the Environment (DoE) that it would be administratively more appropriate to transfer the legal and practical responsibility for dealing with homelessness from welfare to housing staff.[2] This change in approach had been recommended by a number of official committees. A joint circular (DoE, 1974) was intended to re-emphasise the government's view. It formally recommended that housing departments take on the responsibility for providing suitable accommodation. However, a DoE survey in April 1975 found that only 30% of housing departments had accepted sole responsibility for dealing with homelessness. Another 30% accepted the main responsibility for the problem, working in tandem with social welfare departments (Richards, 1981; Evans and Duncan, 1988). Clearly, something had to be done.

Single women

If this picture seems bleak, the situation facing single women who were homeless because of domestic violence was bleaker still. The Department of Health and Social Security (DHSS) only provided reception and resettlement centres for people without a settled way of life. Some local authorities managed large hostels but most of these were for men. As Drake et al commented (1981, p 9), the "single homeless as a group were widely perceived as people with problems". This gradually changed during the 1970s possibly because of the impact of research findings and pressure from campaigning groups (Drake et al, 1981). The extent of the change is not clear since local authority staff were often indifferent. Glastonbury expressed concern:

> No one ... seemed to bother much about the unattached women who appeared from time to time and asked for hostel accommodation. As far as the local authority was concerned, this was generally a problem to be passed on to someone else .... Only brief interest was shown in these people and it was often tinged with regrets at the inconvenience they caused by coming along wanting accommodation in the middle of the night. Rarely was there any follow-up, rarely any referral back to the woman's town of origin for further information. (Glastonbury, 1971, p 152)

Glastonbury had interviewed a number of homeless single women of different ages (some with mental health problems) who had experienced violence. For example, one woman was trying to leave her violent husband (Glastonbury,

1971, p 72) and another left home because she was expected to stimulate her father before his intercourse with her mother (1971, p 75).

The DHSS national survey of 1972 provided a picture of the hostels, lodging houses and shelters for single men and women across the country (Digby, 1976). It built on another national survey undertaken in 1965 (National Assistance Board, 1966). Unlike the 1972 survey, the survey of 1965 had not distinguished between men and women; therefore, their particular circumstances could not be described separately. The 1972 survey revealed that most lodging houses and large hostels were for men. Many large hostels were owned and managed by local authorities. There was much less accommodation available for women and most of it was run by the voluntary sector. Just under one third of the women interviewed said that 'marital problems' were the reason for their homelessness.

A more comprehensive picture was drawn by Drake et al (1981) for the mid-1970s. They interviewed 521 single homeless people in seven local authorities in 1978: Manchester, Stoke-on-Trent, Bedford, Brighton and the London boroughs of Camden, Tower Hamlets and Haringey. Twenty-three per cent of the interviewees were women – more than Digby (1976) had interviewed. They managed to do this by including small hotels and sleeping on friends' floors/spare rooms within their definition of homelessness. Both 18% of men and 18% of women reported that they had left their last settled address because of a 'marital dispute' though there was no further analysis of exactly what that meant (Drake et al, 1981, p 57). Most homeless single people were sharing with friends or living in hostels or lodgings. Local authority accommodation was insignificant, at less than 1% (1981, p 54).

The extreme marginalisation of homeless single people was clear. Single women had to rely on family or friends for help. Otherwise, they had to fall back on the voluntary or private sectors – and not the local authority. Lone parents fared little better, although some refused to return to violent partners (Marsden and Owens, 1975; May, 1978). Only a voluntary sector response at that time from women's groups could provide specific practical help and an alternative view of what was happening to women (Miller, 1975; Timms, 1975; Marcovitch, 1976; Melville, 1977; Weir, 1977).

A different understanding of male violence and the reasons for its occurrence was necessary to begin to challenge the dominance of familism and the continued perpetuation of a model of homelessness which blamed the victims, by emphasising their personal inadequacy and need for 'education'. Nevertheless, even among women's groups there was no unanimity about why violence occurred and what should be done.[3]

The 1977 Housing (Homeless Persons) Act

Concern about 'battering' and 'battered women' became a media issue from the early 1970s. Publicity was generated by Erin Pizzey[4] (1974) and feminists involved in the Women's Movement, as well as a number of highly publicised child battering cases. As far as practical help was concerned, the first refuges for women leaving violence were established from 1971 onwards. The earliest were established as part of women's centres, but the idea of establishing a specific refuge quickly emerged (Pahl, 1978; Pizzey, 1974; Sutton, 1978). They were open to any woman who needed to escape from violence.

Against this background, the Private Member's Bill, which became the 1977 Housing (Homeless Persons) Act, was introduced in the parliamentary session 1976/77 (Richards, 1981; Thompson, 1988). There was now a sufficient groundswell of opinion to ensure that homeless women with children were included as a 'priority need' in the new legislation. Unfortunately, homeless single women were treated differently. The predominant view was that single women could find alternative accommodation more easily than lone parents (Richards, 1981). They would only be considered in priority need if they were 'vulnerable'. The *Code of Guidance* to the legislation (DoE, DH and WO, 1977) (which local authorities were to use as additional help in interpreting the Act) recommended that single women who were homeless because of domestic violence should be regarded as 'vulnerable' and in priority need. However, the Code did not have statutory force.

The 1977 Housing (Homeless Persons) Act has been called "an Act of compromise" (Thompson, 1988), but all-party support came at a price. Local authority housing departments now had statutory obligations to certain groups of homeless people but they had also been given various opportunities to use discretion in their decision-making: a concession granted to reduce opposition to the bill during its passage through parliament (Richards, 1981; Thompson, 1988). For example, authorities could decide whether or not an applicant was 'intentionally' homeless. The Code's guidance recommended that women leaving violent men should not be considered to be intentionally homeless. Nevertheless, the different ways in which some authorities exercised discretion and chose to ignore the Code's guidance proved to be a major difficulty for women leaving violent men. This was the case in the years immediately after the Act's enactment (Joint Charities Group, 1978) as well as later (Binney et al, 1981; Malos et al, 1993).

Women with dependent children

The new legislation seemingly provided a straightforward route to permanent council housing for homeless women with children. That had been Parliament's intention. Yet it was evident from research that there continued to be difficulties for women in getting advice and finding alternative housing (Freeman, 1979; Borkowski et al, 1983). The most extensive research on how the Act was working was undertaken by Binney et al (1981). They contacted 150 refuges in England and Wales and interviewed a national sample of 636 women between 1977 and 1978. One of the priorities of 'battered women seeking help' was to find another home. The majority had left their violent partner before and then returned (on average, three times). Women gave a number of reasons for doing this, the most usual being "problems with accommodation" and "to give [their] partner another chance" (Binney et al, 1981, p 6).

Over 500 women were trying to find alternative accommodation: 418 had applied to a local authority and, of these, 184 (44%) were offered and accepted a council home (Binney et al, 1981). Fifty-seven others moved to housing association or privately-rented property. These figures were an improvement on the rehousing rate discovered by Pahl (1978, 1985) especially in relation to council housing. The researchers found that the main difficulties which women faced were local authority staff attitudes towards domestic violence and whether or not they were accepted as statutory homeless. Extra conditions imposed on them when they were offered a council tenancy, such as paying off any outstanding rent arrears, might also be problematic. The researchers discovered that lobbying by Women's Aid helped women to obtain council tenancies.

Research in a Cleveland refuge in the first half of 1982 revealed a bleaker picture. As many women as possible were contacted who had used the refuge for at least three nights in the period January 1977 to December 1981 (Homer et al, 1984). Eighty women came forward and were interviewed. Twenty-nine of these (36.2%) had been rehoused by a local authority. This was proportionately fewer women than in the national study conducted by Binney et al (1981) over approximately the same period (where 44% of the sample had been rehoused by the local authority). Only six women (7.5%) in this group had been rehoused by housing associations. The 80 women identified similar problems to those noted in Binney et al (1981):

- staff in a number of local authorities refused to consider women as homeless;
- the women were regarded as potential waiting-list applicants;
- some local authorities expected women to provide independent proof of violence beyond what might be considered reasonable;
- staff in some authorities added conditions, even if the woman was considered to be statutory homeless, such as expecting a woman to divorce before rehousing her.

The researchers also looked at what had happened to all of the women (393) who had used the Cleveland refuge between 1 January 1977 and 30 June 1982. Fewer had been rehoused by local authorities (50, or 12.8%). Sixty-six (16.8%) had been rehoused by housing associations (Homer et al, 1984, p 130). Unfortunately, no analysis of these data was provided. The researchers made the point that the long period of time covered by their study presented difficulties in analysing the responses, particularly those from local authorities. There had been changes in legislation, in local authority practices and growing Women's Aid influence over this time. The presumption to be drawn was that the situation had improved.

In summary, it seemed that the new legislation had improved the chances of women with children obtaining a permanent council tenancy. Advice was now available to authorities in dealing with the problem through the *Code of*

Guidance and other publications. Nevertheless, while some authorities were implementing the legislation without difficulty, others were still unhappy at the prospect of rehousing homeless families and used various strategies to reduce or avoid their responsibilities. Homer et al (1984) illustrated the situation in Cleveland: only 13% of women using the refuge over six years had been rehoused by local authorities, and 17% by housing associations. Women were often forced to make other arrangements, including returning to their violent partner. Having said that, not all women who used a refuge wanted to find another home. Many needed time to think over their situation; some then returned to their violent partner or moved in with friends or relatives.

Single women

Although there was no statutory obligation, the *Code of Guidance* recommended that authorities

> should secure that whenever possible accommodation is available for battered women without children who are at risk of violent pursuit or, if they return home, at risk of further violence. (DoE, DH and WO, 1977, para 2.13)

In the late 1970s and early 1980s there was very little information available to see whether authorities were helping homeless single women.

Austerberry and Watson (1983) interviewed 102 women who lived in a variety of hostels in London between 1980 and 1981. Each was over 25 years of age. (The researchers had excluded younger women since they were believed to have different experiences and options.) Only 15 women had ever heard of the Housing (Homeless Persons) Act. They found that some women might have been considered to be 'vulnerable' under the Act although none had been accepted as such by a local authority, including women who had left domestic violence (Austerberry and Watson, 1983, p 44). One difficulty they identified – which was also found later by Thomas and Niner (1989) – was that women did not know what their rights were and were often demoralised by their experiences to such an extent that they accepted staff views without question. Unless hostel staff could advise them, they would continue to be at a disadvantage. Austerberry and Watson (1983) found that Women's Aid staff in refuges had helped single women but few single women stayed in refuges. The numbers of children living in refuges and the obvious differences between single women's lives and those of women with children may have been too great to bridge (Pahl, 1978, 1985; Binney et al, 1981).

The 1985 Housing Act (Part III)

The 1977 Housing (Homeless Persons) Act, along with a number of other pieces of legislation, was consolidated into the 1985 Housing Act. Part III of the Act dealt with homelessness and was subsequently amended by the 1986

Housing and Planning Act. A useful postal survey of all local authorities in England and Wales was carried out in the period 1986/87 to find out how authorities were implementing this part of the Act (Evans and Duncan, 1988). A response rate of nearly 90% was obtained. The survey was quantitative and included questions about how the local authority responded to domestic violence. It revealed that a woman's situation might be assessed in different ways, although it did not explore the reasons for this.

About half of the local authorities that responded expected a woman to return to her former home and take legal action to remove her partner (temporarily or permanently). She would only be considered homeless when these attempts failed. (This was contrary to the advice in the *Code of Guidance*.) Only 78% of local authorities accepted a woman as homeless if she was living in a refuge. Proof of violence was an issue in some local authorities: 36% of authorities required independent proof of violence. Forty-one per cent accepted what a woman told them as the truth, although they felt that independent proof was useful. Goss (1983) had found a similar situation in six London boroughs. However, Niner (1989) emphasised that there were likely to be differences between what local authorities reported officially and what staff did in practice. In the nine local authorities she had visited to evaluate their homelessness services, she found that all of the authorities

> accepted as homeless those subject to violence within the home or those in fear of such violence. However, since the authorities seemed to vary considerably in the supporting evidence they required, particularly in cases where violence had not yet occurred, such agreement on paper was misleading in practice. (Niner, 1989, p 28)

More positively, 80% in the survey (Evans and Duncan, 1988) said that they would accept a single woman who had left violence as being in priority need because of 'vulnerability'. However, other research found a more variable picture than this (Welsh Women's Aid, 1986; Niner, 1989).

Women with dependent children

Three important research reports were published in 1993 (Bull, 1993; Charles with Jones, 1993; Malos et al, 1993). Slightly earlier and more broadly-based research contributed to the overall picture (Brailey, 1986; Welsh Women's Aid, 1986; Mama, 1989; McGibbon et al, 1989). At this time, it became possible to group local authority responses to homeless women based on their responses to particular parts of the legislation.

Malos et al (1993) provided a detailed study of four local authorities – one in Wales and three in England. Eighty women (20 in each area) were interviewed. Sixty-two women had dependent children with them. Fifty-two of them (65%) were rehoused within six months: 39 by local authorities and 13 by housing associations. Only three were nominated. This was a much higher rehousing rate than had been reported in previous research. Staff were also interviewed in three of the four local authorities, in local housing associations and in the refuge(s) in each area. The researchers found a difference between policy and practice in the local authorities (see also, Evans and Duncan, 1988; Bull, 1993) but by concentrating on actual practice they identified three groups of authorities (Malos et al, 1993, p 25). The first were generous (often using policy guidelines and manuals); the second were legal, keeping within the spirit of the law and the *Code of Guidance* (though sometimes being selective or inconsistent). Finally, the third were restrictive, adopting an approach of minimal compliance with the legislation. The situation was further complicated because some local authorities were inconsistent in their approach.

Local authorities responded differently to similar circumstances. Women were more likely to be taken seriously if they had experienced physical violence. Some local authorities accepted a woman's statement and her wish to live independently. On the other hand, the most restrictive were more likely to expect women to take legal action against their violent partners. For example, many authorities continued to expect women to use injunctions to exclude violent partners from their previous home whether or not they thought this was realistic or safe (Barron, 1990; Law Commission, 1992). If they refused this advice, women would be considered intentionally homeless.

Some black women raised the issue of local authority staff imposing their own views about marriage on applicants, especially when they insisted that women start divorce proceedings (Malos et al, 1993, pp 52-3). This practice had been identified by white women in research in Wales (Welsh Women's Aid, 1986) and in London, where Muslim women raised this issue (Mama, 1989). Mama had argued that making divorce a condition of rehousing affected black women from traditional backgrounds. The local authority concerned

> was imposing very limited and parochial notions of marriage and the family on people from complex and varied familial and marital systems. It amounts to using people's cultures against them to exclude them from housing. (Mama, 1989, p 124)

This showed how institutional practice might affect women differently depending on their 'race' and religion. Henderson and Karn (1987) and many others (Smith and Whalley, 1975; Parker and Dugmore, 1976; Simpson, 1981; CRE, 1984a, 1984b, 1985, 1989a, 1989b, 1993) had shown before that the systematic effects of formal procedures and the use of staff discretion might produce racially differentiated housing outcomes.

Malos et al (1993) also found that there were differences in the ways in which women had been interviewed. Most thought they had been interviewed sensitively. A smaller number had a different recollection. They thought that staff believed that they were 'undeserving' (especially in the rural Welsh authority). Few black women had experienced overt racist behaviour or attitudes. The staff who worked in a London borough were overtly nasty towards *every* woman they interviewed. This was deliberately designed to deter applications in this authority:

> A majority described their interviews as humiliating and degrading experiences. Women variously summarised the experience as one of being treated like dirt or feeling as if they were regarded as coming out of the gutter. One woman described being bombarded with questions which were repeated over and over until her head spun. (Malos et al, 1993, p 52)

Bull (1993) examined the housing consequences of relationship breakdown more generally. She undertook a telephone survey in 1989 of 52 local authorities and examined policy and practice in six case study local authorities. She discovered a wide diversity of policy and practice in relation to relationship breakdown in both homeless and waiting-list assessment. There were few examples of written policy. When talking of the local authority's policy, officers variously referred to committee papers, internal notes and guides, procedure manuals, written policy documents or the received wisdom or common understanding of "how things are done" (Bull, 1993, p 33). There was strong support for the use of discretion. This often created uncertainty for women and for advice agencies about how discretion might be applied although staff thought of it as using 'professional judgement' in decision making.

> This was viewed to be particularly important in developing a sense of the *genuineness* of particular cases. (Bull, 1993, p 35, emphasis added)

Like Malos et al (1993), Bull found that an important issue was whether a woman had to pursue legal options in relation to her former home. Most of the local authorities in the telephone survey initially advised women to get an injunction and return home. Almost half said that they would consider a woman to be intentionally homeless if she did not follow this advice. The only exceptions might be where there was 'extreme' or 'severe' violence or where women's religious or cultural beliefs prohibited divorce (Bull, 1993, p 48). Staff in more liberal authorities could exercise discretion about this. In less liberal authorities, injunctions were

> usually part of an overall requirement that an applicant should demonstrate serious attempts to return to their property or prove that their case was *genuine*. (Bull, 1993, p 49, emphasis added)

Charles with Jones (1993) and Charles (1994) found similar difficulties for women in their research into 37 Welsh local authorities and 30 housing associations. The rehousing rate in Wales was poor: 140 women (and their children) who lived in refuges during the period 1990/91 were rehoused by a local authority or housing association. This represented 12% of the 1,219 women who moved out of refuges in Wales in that year. One hundred women were rehoused by local authorities (92 were statutory homeless); forty women were rehoused by associations (but only ten were nominated). More women returned to their former home to rejoin a violent partner (30.5%) or returned with an exclusion order or because their violent partner had moved out (15.3%). Twenty-eight per cent moved to different temporary accommodation from which they eventually may have been rehoused by the local authority (Charles with Jones, 1993, pp 49-51).

Councillor involvement and control of the lettings process (for waiting-list and homeless applicants) in some local authorities in North Wales was widespread. This had been found in other studies of local authority allocation practice. For example, research by the Institute of Housing (IoH, 1990) had discovered that councillors had a significant influence over individual allocations in Wales (43.3% of authorities), in the East Midlands (34.8%), Yorkshire and Humberside (33.3%) and the South West (33.3%).

Bull (1993) noted that most local authorities in the telephone survey had commented about the 'local connection' provision in the legislation that could be set aside in the situation of women leaving violence. They thought this could be detrimental to local people.

> There was a concern which was often generated by elected members about opening the floodgates. (Bull, 1993, p 54).

Charles with Jones (1993, p 78) showed how women's rehousing opportunities from refuges in four local authorities were affected by local councillors' involvement in allocations. Officers drew up shortlists for councillors to consider. It appeared that their main concern was to reduce the numbers of 'incomers' being rehoused, including women who had fled violence. The researchers felt that strong distinctions between 'deserving' and 'undeserving' applicants underpinned this practice, reinforced by language differences in some areas. This was another variation on the theme of 'Englishness' that Flett (1979) had identified as part of the moral boundary used by some officers to help them in their discretionary decision making in relation to applications from black and Asian people. In this instance, however, it was 'Welshness' which was identified and it was councillors who were making the decisions to include some applicants and exclude others on the basis of applicant's 'local-ness' or belonging to the area and their ethnic origin.

To conclude, the local authority practice in this period was variable. This was due to the discretion inherent in the 1985 Housing Act and different local authority staff and councillor attitudes towards women, domestic violence, the family and housing. Although local authorities might be grouped into three types – generous (or sympathetic), legal and minimal compliance – the majority preferred to see first whether or not civil remedies were available to a woman with a violent partner.

Why did they do this? There were a number of possible reasons. They might have thought that women were trying to jump the queue by inventing violence. They wanted to make sure a woman being rehoused by them was truly 'deserving'. Officers may not have understood or appreciated the level of violence and the situation of women trying to escape it. They might be wary of intervening officially in what could be considered a private matter, best sorted out in the family itself (or if necessary by the law). Finally, officers might be expected by local authority policy to minimise the local authority's rehousing responsibilities towards homeless people. Homeless women who had left violence might be regarded as relatively 'undeserving' compared to waiting-list applicants.

Not all authorities were as stringent as some of the minimal compliance authorities described by Mama (1989) or Malos et al (1993), although sympathetic authorities were rare. The rehousing rate had improved for women following the 1977 legislation but it was still patchy across the country. It was clear from Bull's research that a more sympathetic approach was not directly linked to the easy availability of vacancies. Also, more stringent approaches had not developed in response to overwhelming demand from homeless or waiting-list applicants. The nature of housing demand in the area may partly explain local authorities' responses, but there were other factors. Some local authorities had housing management cultures where support for local 'respectable' families was strong (including councillor support). Lone parents who had experienced domestic violence did not match their idea of 'respectability'. In others, officers wanted to identify 'genuine' applicants to avoid any suggestion that the system was being 'abused'. More generally, councillors wanted to avoid the possible political repercussions associated with rehousing 'outsiders'.

Single women

It was widely believed in the 1980s that single homelessness had increased (Anderson et al, 1993). It also seemed that women might be more likely to obtain housing from local authorities during this time. Evans and Duncan (1988) found that 80% of local authorities considered single homeless women as 'vulnerable' when they had left domestic violence. Nevertheless, other surveys revealed that the reality was more complicated.

When general surveys were undertaken, domestic violence tended to be obscured. For example, in the large national survey of single homeless people undertaken in 1991 (Anderson et al, 1993), interviewing was limited to hostels, bed and breakfast hotels, day centres and soup runs – and not refuges or friends and family. Unsurprisingly, they interviewed mainly men. Most women interviewed were living in hostels and bed and breakfast hotels (23% of the sample); half of these were black. Only 5% reported that domestic violence was the main reason for leaving their last permanent address, a remarkably low figure given previous findings.

This survey found that single women living in hostels and hotels because they were homeless were becoming younger. Fifty per cent of the women were under 24 years of age (see also Dibblin, 1991, which shows that this was an issue which was being raised by pressure groups). A third of the women had been living with a parent or parents before becoming homeless. Over 8% had left because of conflict with parent(s)/step-parent(s) that included physical and or sexual assaults. Most women in hostels and bed and breakfast hotels were looking for permanent homes, although they thought they were a low priority with the council and would have to wait a long time. There was no discussion of whether or not local authorities considered their 'vulnerability' under the homeless legislation. This may have improved some women's chances of being offered a council home.

More specific research illustrated other changes. In their survey conducted in 1985, Welsh Women's Aid (1986) found that 21 out of 37 Welsh authorities automatically considered a single woman to be 'vulnerable' if she was homeless because of domestic violence, but 14 required evidence such as letters from doctors or social workers. (Two authorities commented that their response depended on the circumstances.) This split response was replicated in another survey undertaken with the 35 London boroughs. Fifteen boroughs said they would accept a single woman as 'vulnerable' – the others remained more cautious (London Research Centre Housing Group, 1987, cited in Thompson, 1988). Bull's telephone survey of 52 authorities in 1989 suggested that half of them automatically accepted a single women as 'vulnerable' if she had left a violent man. This was also found by Niner (1989). More detailed case studies reinforced this variable picture. Malos et al (1993) found that their case study London borough and the rural authorities did not accept single women as 'vulnerable' and in priority need under the Act's provisions. Bull (1993) found that only two of her six case studies routinely accepted single women. The others varied in response.

The key to local authorities' approaches appeared to be the way they interpreted women's 'vulnerability'. As Bull found in relation to women with dependent children, lack of pressure on the housing stock from waiting-list applicants was not the explanation for some authorities' more sympathetic interpretation of the legislation. They might have genuinely reconsidered their allocation priorities for single women, perhaps following local pressure from Women's Aid or the Campaign for the Homeless and Rootless (CHAR). Alternatively, they might have seen this as an opportunity to use hard-to-let family property or of taking up their housing association bedsit/one-bedroom nominations (Gilbert, 1986). Whatever the reasons, a more sympathetic response to single women represented a change, but it was far from widespread. Some local authorities still expected proof of violence or of 'vulnerability'. This might be difficult to provide. These distinctions continued into the 1990s. A 1994 survey of local authority practice for the DoE found that 74% of local authorities usually considered single women who had experienced domestic violence to be 'vulnerable' under the legislation, while the comparable figure for men in these circumstances was 64% (Mullins and Niner, 1996).

Many homeless single women did not know that they could obtain priority for housing because of 'vulnerability' (Thomas and Niner, 1989). Others were put off applying because they expected a poor response. Some women had already been interviewed unsympathetically by local authority staff. Rao (1990) identified this in her study of black women's experiences of public housing. They had met with 'rude' local authority staff and gave this as the reason for not pursuing council housing as an option.

Housing association responses to homelessness and domestic violence

Housing associations were generally very small organisations in the 1960s. Some grew in size and influence in the 1970s when they played an important part in the renewal of inner cities. Unfortunately, little research is available on association allocation practices during this time. Greve et al's (1971) small-scale survey of housing associations in London in the late 1960s revealed that most associations were

> neither equipped nor inclined to select in favour of the most severe or desperate cases of housing need, for example, large, low income or unsupported families with a history of rent arrears, anti-social behaviour or unstable domestic arrangements. (Greve et al, 1971, p 237)

Throughout the 1970s, the part played by associations in rehousing women with dependent children who had left domestic violence was small (Binney et al, 1981). They might be important in particular areas. Local associations might be able to rehouse women where the local authority was unsympathetic (Homer et al, 1984). In a study in London of women living in hostels, only a few were rehoused by associations. Others had refused housing offers because the properties were in a poor state of repair or had limited storage space or were located in unsafe areas (Austerberry and Watson, 1983). Still more women had found associations' waiting lists closed at this time.

During the 1980s a number of associations began to develop hostels that were subsequently managed by Women's Aid groups. This was a response to the government's 'hostels initiative' that was designed to provide funding for smaller scale hostel accommodation for homeless people. The amount of 'move on' accommodation (that is, permanent housing) provided by associations to hostel residents later became an issue. Malos et al (1993) and Charles with Jones (1993) reported that few women were rehoused from refuges by the associations that had developed them. It is still not clear exactly why this happened.

Two policy developments were initiated by the Housing Corporation in the late 1980s to improve the rate at which associations rehoused homeless households. The first was improved nominations arrangements to associations. The Housing Corporation issued Circular 48/49, entitled 'Access to housing association homes' together with their *Performance Expectations* (Housing Corporation, 1989), which were the guidelines the Corporation used for monitoring associations' performance. The circular emphasised the importance of establishing and maintaining good nomination arrangements. At least 50% of lettings were to be made to nominated households. A joint statement on nominations arrangements was published by the National Federation of Housing Associations (NFHA) in association with the Association of Metropolitan Authorities (AMA) and Association of District Councils (ADC) (NFHA, 1989). This was also intended to help improve nominations practice. A good practice guide entitled *Tackling homelessness* was produced by the NFHA (Randall, 1989), which included detailed guidance for associations in relation to nominations, the waiting list and internal transfers.

Criticism continued, however, with the Housing Corporation coming under renewed pressure in 1991 from a critical Public Accounts Committee and the National Audit Office (1990). There were still concerns that associations were rehousing few homeless households. The Housing Corporation's head office subsequently devised national targets for its development programme starting in 1991/92 as its second policy response. Half of all lettings in new association rented estates funded by the Corporation were to be targeted towards the homeless. Of these, a minimum of 60% had to be let to statutory homeless households. Each Housing Corporation region then established their own regional targets to enable the national figures to be reached.

Nominations and homelessness

Given growing criticism, research was undertaken on the nominations' performance of 138 associations in London between 1987 and 1988 (Levison and Robertson, 1989). It was discovered that 45% of housing association 'true voids' (that is, net lettings after deducting transfers, decants and mobility lettings) had been let to people nominated by a local authority. Only 34% of those were to statutory homeless households. There was wide variation between associations and larger associations performed better. Nine per cent of lettings in small associations were filled by nominated households while the equivalent figure in large associations was 15%. There were also considerable differences between London boroughs. Three boroughs failed to nominate any households, while in four boroughs 60% of their nominations were statutory homeless households.

There were other practical difficulties in improving the nomination performance of associations. There were genuine mismatches between the size of property that some associations managed and the particular housing requirements of the majority of statutory homeless households. A lack of ethnic monitoring of the system by both sides was also evident in a majority of boroughs. This made it impossible to determine whether racial discrimination was occurring in the nominations process (CRE, 1989a) despite the priority given to the issue following the Commission for Racial Equality's formal investigation of the nomination system used by Liverpool City Council (CRE, 1989b). It had found discrimination in all of the possible routes to being nominated at that time (including being recognised as statutory homeless).

Surprisingly, insufficient monitoring was found again in a later study of associations' race equality policies and practices (CRE, 1993).

Research on nominations then moved to consider areas predominantly outside of London in Bolton, Bromley, Camden, Derby, Exeter and Leeds (Parker et al, 1992). In this study, local authority staff reported little difficulty in ensuring that households were nominated and rehoused on newly-built housing estates in the period 1990/91. They had more difficulty getting nominations for association re-lets, even though these made up most association vacancies. It was not clear why authorities found it easier to nominate to new estates. New schemes may have been easier to deal with administratively or the property being built might have been more suited to local authorities' need for family housing.

Twenty per cent of nominees in this research were single people, 40% were families with children and 33% were elderly people. Association staff reported that local authorities sometimes had difficulty providing nominations to sheltered housing, bedsit property and to certain unpopular areas. Local authorities commented that housing associations were not as popular as they had been in the past because association rents were too expensive. The researchers remarked that "this is in marked contrast to a few years ago when it was frequently said that nominations were highly sought after and reserved for tenants of good standing" (Parker, et al,1992, p 49).

The local authorities did little or nothing to monitor the numbers of nominated households being rehoused possibly because the shortfall in numbers at that time was not great. Associations were no different about monitoring.

Housing associations were asked whether or not they monitored the characteristics of nominees in any way to ensure that local authorities were being fair over who they nominated. None did so, though a few expressed the view that they felt that more homeless people and more people from ethnic minorities could have been included (Parker et al, 1992, p 51).

Responding to homelessness

Research by Withers and Randolph (1994) into housing associations and homelessness provided a national picture of association activity. Two postal surveys of associations and local authorities were undertaken in 1993 in the 100 'homelessness stress areas' that they identified. These were supplemented by interviews with local authority housing department staff and housing association staff in ten local authorities. Statistical data were obtained from two sources: 'Continuous Recording' (CORE) – the system for monitoring associations' lettings across the country – and Housing Investment Programme (HIP) bids – prepared by local authorities for government approval.

Withers and Randolph found that some local authorities were facing severe pressure: the number of statutory homeless households exceeded the expected number of vacancies in the local authority stock. Although this was more common in the London boroughs, it was also widespread in non-metropolitan and rural districts. Surprisingly, they found that relatively few metropolitan districts outside of London were in this situation. Associations had increased the rate at which they rehoused homeless applicants in the period 1990-93, in some instances many times over. Most authorities were satisfied with the way the nominations process worked in their area and the role of housing associations. Their greatest concern was the level of association rents and the inappropriate size of some housing which associations offered (Withers and Randolph, 1994, p 73). They were also unhappy that some housing associations made more than one offer to homeless people who had been nominated. Over 90% of the local authorities in their study made only one offer of accommodation to homeless households.

From the associations' point of view, local authority nominations did not always appear to be in more urgent 'need' than their other waiting list applicants. Surprisingly, over half (46 out of 85) said that homeless households would not necessarily get priority over other applications (Withers and Randolph, 1994, p 101). Existing association tenants who needed to transfer urgently because they were fleeing domestic/racial violence were claimed to be the most urgent priority. Withers and Randolph concluded:

> While there is undoubted scope to improve the level of homeless nominations overall, it seems that both the nature of housing association stock, the geography of homelessness and local authority policy clearly set basic limits to maximising the full potential of the nominations system for alleviating homelessness. (Withers and Randolph, 1994, p 30)

Domestic violence and homelessness

In the early 1990s two studies were undertaken on housing and domestic violence. In the first (Malos et al,1993), 13 of the 52 women were rehoused by housing associations. They were either not in 'priority need' or they had a weak 'local connection' under the legislation. Association housing was favourably compared with the local authority but there was widespread concern about the level of association rents. In the second, a study of Welsh local authority and housing association practice (Charles with Jones, 1993), 40 women were rehoused by associations. The local authority had nominated 10. Women's Aid had nominated three, and 27 were rehoused as direct waiting-list applicants. The difference between the numbers of women rehoused by local authorities and housing associations was explained in terms of the relative size of their housing stocks and the fact that associations did not have a statutory duty to rehouse homeless households. Associations that had developed refuge provision did not necessarily rehouse more women into permanent homes than other associations. Having said that, although the figures were low, housing associations housed more women than the local authority in some areas (Charles with

Jones, 1993, pp 55-6). They had effectively taken on a statutory rather than a complementary role.

Changing local authorities' statutory obligations

By the mid–1990s it was not stretching reality too far to suggest that there was a spectrum of local authority responses towards homeless women who had left domestic violence. At one end of the spectrum, women were treated as individuals with rights, who knew whether or not their former 'home' situation was safe. They were rehoused straightforwardly, and in some senses they were treated as 'deserving'. Local authorities that only helped women because they were mothers of dependent children or were 'vulnerable' took the middle ground. They were rehoused if they remained homeless having followed any local authority advice to pursue civil remedies. In other words, they were tested to make sure that they were 'genuine'. Finally, the most restrictive local authorities treated women as supplicants and 'undeserving' mothers and wives. Far more emphasis was placed on sending them back 'home' to pursue civil action against their violent partner, whether or not it was safe to do so.

Although finding a home with a local authority or housing association was clearly not an easy matter in 1995, a woman was more likely to be successful than she might have been in the 1960s or early 1970s. However, this changed completely once the Conservative government enacted the 1996 Housing Act. This presented the prospect of undermining *any possibility* of women being rehoused by a local authority or nominated to a housing association when they were homeless because of domestic violence.

The 1996 Housing Act

There has been very little research into the effects of the 1996 Housing Act on homeless women who have left violent men (but see Cloke et al, 2000). This legislation was structured to separate the assessment of homeless people from that of waiting list applicants. Homeless people could only join the housing register if their circumstances fitted the priorities determined by the government (see Chapter One). Mullins and Niner (1998) claimed that the Act clearly contained two competing views about the nature of access to social housing. On the one hand, there were rights contained within it – but these were only available to citizens of a certain status and in certain circumstances (Part VII). On the other hand, the Act was structured to severely control access to housing. It was 'rationing' at its worst, designed to exclude from permanent housing those with no full citizenship rights (at the time of application) and those who were homeless (Part VI). Any gains which women had made in relation to their access to permanent housing seemed to be lost with this Act. Certainly, this is the interpretation followed by Morley and Pascall (1996; Pascall and Morley, 1996). However, in practice the 1996 Housing Act became another example of policy makers' lack of appreciation of their own limited influence (Lipsky, 1980).

Mullins and Niner (1998) found that local authorities had generally followed the elements of the legislation which were unavoidable. Surprisingly, they had been far more positive than the government intended in deciding whether or not homeless people had any 'suitable' private sector housing alternatives available to them and in determining their priority on the new housing register. The authors believed this was partly because local authorities were concerned about the potential cost of simply providing temporary rather than permanent housing. Many were also determined to respond to housing need as they saw it, and continued to see homeless people as being in severe housing need. A national postal survey of local authority practice in relation to allocations, transfers and homelessness also concluded that there was little evidence that the 1996 Housing Act had undermined the housing priority of homeless applicants although it was "administratively cumbersome" for local authorities to implement (Pawson et al, 2001, p 15).

Having said that, the situation still appeared to be patchy across England and Wales. Humphreys and Thiara (2002) found that 115 women in their survey (most with children) had applied to the local authority's housing department, but of those only 42% had been accepted as statutory homeless. Twenty per cent had been refused while 18% had problems proving that domestic violence had occurred. The national survey of local authorities (Pawson et al, 2001) discovered that 68% "always or usually" accepted single people who had experienced domestic violence as 'vulnerable'. Authorities in London were the least sympathetic while those in the North of England were likely to be the most sympathetic. Comparable work in Scotland revealed that authorities there were the most likely of all to accept single people in these circumstances (Scott et al, 2000).

Given the difficulties which women faced with some local authorities, would they fare any better with housing associations? The remainder of this book illustrates what happened to women applying to associations which worked within the boundaries of one local authority.

Notes

[1] Richards (1981), citing a 1950 joint memorandum of the local authority associations which was endorsed by the CHAC (1955) and by the Ministry of Health (Circular 4/59).

[2] See Greve et al (1971, pp 126-9) for further discussion.

[3] See Gayford (1975, 1976). Dobash and Dobash (1992, pp 25-35) set Gayford's analysis in context.

[4] Erin Pizzey was one founder member of Chiswick Women's Refuge, one of the earliest refuges. She was good at attracting the attention of the media and became a very well known figure, especially after her first book was published (1974). Unfortunately,

differences emerged between herself and feminist campaigners about the causes of domestic violence and these emerged in consultation with the government of the day (see Dobash and Dobash, 1992, for a more detailed account).

THREE

The local authority, homelessness and the 'enabling' role

Introduction

The local authority in this study owned and managed 70,000 properties at the time of the research. It had 19,000 households on its housing register (or waiting list), and in 1997 let 10,600 properties. The local authority had accepted just over 2,000 households as statutory homeless over the previous year. Over 70% of these were households headed by women (most being lone parents or vulnerable single women), and 14% of these were black or Asian.

From the early 1990s, increasing numbers of women had approached the local authority for help with emergency housing, including women who were homeless because of domestic violence. In the period 1990/91, 295 women were accepted as homeless for this reason, representing 14% of the total accepted as homeless in that year. The figures steadily increased so that in 1996/97, the year before the present study was undertaken, 630 women (30% of the total) had been found to be statutory homeless because they were in priority need, having become homeless because of domestic violence. There was little variation in these figures up to the end of the decade. The housing Research Manager in this local authority believed that the numbers were "almost certainly an undercount" because of the difficulties of maintaining accuracy across neighbourhood offices, central homeless teams and directly-run hostels.

This chapter concentrates on the local authority's role in helping women who were homeless because of domestic violence. It provides the background to the rest of the study.

The first part of the chapter looks at the overarching framework within which women's requests for help were considered, examining the way in which the local authority responded to changes in its statutory responsibilities towards the homeless following the 1996 Housing Act. The way in which a domestic violence policy was constructed and agreed in the housing department is described here, revealing its ambiguous status in practice.

The second part looks at the homeless service in more detail, especially its organisation and decision making. The impact of various organisational pressures on decision making are then described. Three different influences on decision making are reviewed: the new legislation, the domestic violence policy, and the influence of councillors.

The final part of this chapter reviews the nature of the authority's 'enabling' (or 'strategic') role in relation to housing associations and their responses to homeless women. Two aspects of this are considered: nominations and inter-agency working. The effectiveness of the nominations system is explored here from different organisational perspectives. The effectiveness of inter-agency working is examined through the perspectives of local authority staff. (The views of association staff are considered in the chapters that follow.)

Homeless decision making

The authority's response to the 1996 Housing Act (Parts VI and VII)

The 1996 Housing Act was intended to made it more difficult for any homeless person to be rehoused by local authorities into permanent accommodation (Arden and Hunter, 1997). It created a legislative barrier between assessment of a household as statutory homeless (Part VII) and the provision of permanent accommodation for them from the council (Part VI). Some homeless applicants were excluded from any practical help under Part VII of the new legislation. These were 'persons from abroad' (as defined in the Act) and asylum seekers. They were eligible for 'advice and information'. Other applicants might be eligible because they were 'homeless', in 'priority need', not 'intentionally homeless' and had a 'local connection', but also only be entitled to 'advice and assistance' if the authority decided that there was suitable housing in the private sector available to them (s 197, 1, 2). If no accommodation was available, the authority itself could provide temporary accommodation (for up to two years).

These provisions were very reminiscent of the arrangements which had been in place before the 1977 Housing (Homeless Persons) Act, although entitlement, such as it was, was now more strongly bounded than it had been in the past with exclusions and restrictions based on immigration status and nationality.

Homeless applicants who were considered to be in 'priority need' and not 'intentionally homeless' within the legislation were now 'qualifying persons' for the housing register. However, the government's regulations listing preference groups for the housing register had omitted 'homelessness'. Local authorities would have to fit homeless applicants into other preference groups: in effect, homelessness became invisible.

The prospect of changing the waiting list to become the housing register, with priorities determined by a Conservative Secretary of State, was not well received in this Labour local authority. The Housing Committee (as it then was) had already rejected change in 1995. It preferred to keep the 20-year-old system that they were used to, since it enabled councillors to exercise influence. The Principal Officer commented that changing waiting list priorities was a "very, very contentious issue.... Local members would need to be reassured that the needs of their constituents were being met quite fairly – or how they see as quite fairly" (Principal Officer).

The Housing Committee was statutorily obliged to agree changes but decided to keep practical effects to a minimum. This deliberate incrementalism ensured that the authority's long-established group scheme priorities were actually retained, although they were now disguised (Lindblom, 1959, 1979).

The authority used a group scheme to determine waiting-list priorities for council housing. There were four main groups (A to D), each with sub-categories of housing need. Applicants were slotted into a category depending on their main reason for rehousing. Any applicant assessed as statutory homeless continued to be given 'A' priority after the 1996 Housing Act, but they were awarded this because they were living in temporary or insecure accommodation (to reflect the new regulations) rather than because they were statutory homeless. A number of other minor changes were also made to fit other preference groups into the pre-existent group scheme.

The domestic violence policy

The housing department's domestic violence policy was agreed in 1993. It contained a number of important features to help women who were homeless because of domestic violence. First, it expected staff to use a broad working definition of domestic violence when assessing homeless women. The definition included physical, sexual, psychological and economic violence, such as withholding money. Second, staff were not to request nor to consider corroborative 'proof' of violence from women approaching the department for help. Staff were expected to terminate joint tenancies (where they existed) in cases where women had been forced to leave their council home because of a violent partner. The policy included guidance about dealing with rent arrears: staff had to consider arrears as a separate issue from the homeless assessment. Finally, the general importance of other agencies' work in this field was re-emphasised.

The policy had been written by the local authority's Women's Officer. She remarked that she had been helped in this work by a group of "significant women" in the authority. A number of consultation meetings with voluntary sector organisations had considered the final draft. The Regional Officer from the National Federation of Housing Associations (NFHA) attended one such meeting and commented on the proposals. Refuge staff were consulted separately. Generally, comments were supportive and changes were minimal. Staff in the housing department were not consulted as this was not usual practice in this authority.

The Women's Officer felt that it had been difficult to obtain agreement for the policy since some senior staff thought it was controversial and they were reluctant to present it to the relevant committee for approval. They insisted on changes before putting it on the agenda of the Tenancy Sub-Committee for consideration. No financial commitments were attached to the proposed policy. Nor were specific recommendations for housing associations included (for example, expecting them to comply with 'best practice'). The Women's Officer believed that these would have made it even harder to obtain committee approval.

The policy was discussed and agreed by the Tenancy Sub-Committee and then endorsed by a subsequent Housing Committee meeting without discussion. Following this, the Director issued a circular to all managers informing them of the new policy. A copy of the policy was sent to each neighbourhood office and to the central homeless teams for their attention. The policy was kept for reference in each workplace's 'Allocations and lettings procedures' manual. In many ways, for most housing management staff, the domestic violence policy appeared 'out of the blue' since they had not been consulted about it. The review of progress with its implementation was also low key. No arrangements were put in place to actively monitor whether or not the policy guidelines were followed. Monitoring was essentially passive and negative: voluntary organisations were asked to forward any complaints from women; these would then be investigated and action taken if necessary.

By 1996 the Women's Officer had received reports of three main 'bad practice issues' associated with the policy's implementation. Some neighbourhood office staff expected homeless women to provide proof of violence. They would only consider women to be homeless when physical violence had occurred and applications would not be considered from homeless women who had rent arrears.

In a number of ways, this was not surprising. No mandatory training programme had ever been organised. It had been left to managers to decide priorities for staff training and few chose domestic violence training. More generally, the nature of the housing department had changed since the early 1990s. The housing management service was now contracted out and the department was run on new public management lines (Pollitt, 1990; Hood, 1991). It was by no means certain that staff would now comply with centrally originated, equal opportunities-type initiatives, since managerialism was predominantly concerned with financial performance and response times for various measurable services (Clarke and Newman, 1997). The work involved in assessing 'housing need' or undertaking homeless 'investigations' was marginal. Staff would probably take shortcuts with this work as a result of different and more urgent priorities.

The Women's Officer decided to deal with these 'bad practice issues' in two ways. First, she used the committee system to renew interest in the policy among councillors (many of whom would not have been aware of the policy). A positive report on progress was presented to the Housing Committee although the report also identified ways in which staff performance could be improved. Following discussion, an Assistant Director was instructed to issue a formal memorandum to staff reminding them of the policy and the information and training available. Three areas of practice were identified in the memorandum as giving great cause for concern. Staff now knew that any subsequent variations from the policy would be vigorously pursued. In this way, sanctions for breaching the policy had become more transparent.

The second way in which the Women's Officer dealt with the identified 'bad practice' was through disciplinary procedure. A voluntary organisation that had recently complained about the treatment a woman had received from a neighbourhood office was encouraged to make a formal complaint. The department's internal disciplinary procedure was then used to take action against the staff concerned. This action was taken to ensure that staff understood that the memorandum was not "mere words" (Women's Officer). Two members of staff were reprimanded.

> "Although it wasn't particularly made public knowledge about who had been reprimanded, word on the street soon got round and basically it just sent out a very clear message. You needn't think, stuck out there, wherever you are, that you are a law unto yourself. *One* – you shouldn't be doing it and *two* – be sure if you do, there's a whole network of people, *women*, who will make sure that you're found out. So get your act together, mate." (Women's Officer)

Following this action, no further reports of 'bad practice' had been received, although the Women's Officer had no way of checking decision making in practice. Lipsky's (1980) view of the behaviour of frontline staff comes to mind:

> Managers are interested in achieving results consistent with agency objectives. Street level bureaucrats are interested in work consistent with their own preferences and only those agency policies so salient as to be backed up by significant sanctions. (Lipsky, 1980, p 19)

Doubts remained that the sanctions available were neither strong nor effective, especially in relation to the work of neighbourhood office staff. Staff there might continue to respond in ways contrary to the policy because they had different priorities and a limited understanding of the issue. This became clearer in interviews with neighbourhood office managers that are referred to in the following section of this chapter.

The organisation of the homeless service

This local authority provided examples of centrally run specialist and decentralised generalist services for homeless people. The service to households with children was mainly provided by staff in the neighbourhood offices with a small centrally based advisory team to assist them if necessary. The service for single people was centrally based and provided by specialist staff.

This raised three initial questions for the research. First, why were services organised like this? Second, what were the effects of splitting the specialist staff from the generalist staff, especially in relation to responding to the complicated needs of women who were homeless because of domestic violence? Third, what kind of service could generalist staff in neighbourhood offices provide to women in these circumstances?

The local authority's homeless families service had been decentralised in 1991. At the time, the public reason for this was that generic management staff in neighbourhood offices could provide a more accessible service to families. Privately, staff who had been working in the service at the time felt that the decentralisation had been implemented because senior councillors wanted to try to silence the continuing complaints from staff about poor local authority hostel standards and wanted to be able to exert more influence locally over allocations to homeless people. There had been considerable political difficulties during this time with certain senior councillors who did not want homeless people to be rehoused in their constituencies because they were not seen as local (Contract Manager).

A number of researchers had reported similar problems for homeless women leaving violent partners in different local authorities (Homer et al, 1984; Welsh Women's Aid, 1986; Charles with Jones, 1993; Charles, 1994). Three senior staff who had worked in the homeless service when it had been completely centralised believed that councillors had not understood the nature of the service provided by them and the need for staff to have specialist knowledge of the legislation and case law. Indeed, few other local authorities had decentralised services in this way because they recognised the need for staff with specialised knowledge (Niner, 1989).

> "They viewed the decision-making process and how you helped homeless people as so simple. You could do it in between sorting out a few arrears cases and what have you. Completely beggared belief, did that view, to me." (Contract Manager)

The service for single homeless people had been established in the late 1980s to oversee the closure of a very large local authority hostel, and had expanded to encompass work with other hostel providers. There had never been a suggestion that this service should be decentralised since most of its work was with voluntary sector hostel providers.

The central homeless teams

A small residual specialist team for homeless families was centrally based. The team operated in a 'bureau-professional' way and had a number of functions (Clarke and Newman, 1997). It handled 'cases' when a neighbourhood office referred them (because they might be short-staffed or there might be a conflict of interest especially in relation to arrears or antisocial behaviour). The staff also worked with families who applied directly to them for help (although this was on a very reduced scale compared to pre-1991 practice). Staff also worked with women in the hostels for homeless families. A specific member of staff undertook all the 'investigations' of women living in refuges and women's hostels. The frontline staff prepared the reports on applicants while the Principal Officer formally decided their homeless status.

The Principal Officer recalled that his team had dealt with about 700 'investigations' in the previous year (1996/97). About one third of these had been women who had been homeless because of domestic violence. It was clear that he felt that the specialist team provided a service to women that the generalist neighbourhood offices could not match.

> "We've got years of experience here. We've got connections with good solicitors. We're aware of all the other agencies involved around women and violence so if somebody comes to us then we don't just deal with the situation as it stands and rehouse. We look at all the support mechanisms that are needed, which other people the woman should see, what solicitors are appropriate for her and so on." (Principal Officer, Families Team)

The service for single homeless people was organised differently. The centrally based team for single people undertook all the formal investigations relating to single homeless people who applied for help. The Principal Officers believed that the quality of 'investigations' and decision making was better in a specialist team than in the generalist neighbourhood offices. Principal Officers formally decided the homeless status of single applicants.

Centrally based Principal Officers in both teams saw applicants who wanted to be formally referred to another local authority (or be accepted by the present one having come from elsewhere) through the referral mechanisms agreed by local authorities (s 198). Most were women leaving violence. At the time of the research, more were leaving the area rather than coming to it. They also liaised with Social Services in relation to women who could formally receive no practical help under the Act because of their immigration status.

The service to homeless families appeared to have been seriously weakened and marginalised politically by decentralisation. The service to single people was different: it remained a specialist one with a good reputation.[1] Even though there was recognition in the department that some specialisation was necessary, there had been no centrally organised comprehensive training programme for any staff in the central teams or neighbourhood offices since decentralisation. The Principal Officers arranged their own ad hoc briefing and training for their staff on the implications of the 1996 Housing Act for their work; the neighbourhood offices had received none. Unsurprisingly, the view of the specialist staff was that, with a few exceptions, the service provided by the neighbourhood offices was often limited and poor.

The neighbourhood offices

The neighbourhood offices were staffed by a Manager, Assistant Manager, Estate Management Officers and Customer Service Officers. Three adjacent neighbourhood offices were usually grouped together to make a contract area. Some contract areas were distinctly different from others in terms of the housing they managed and the pressures on the housing management service.

The contract area in this research included three inner-city neighbourhood offices. Together they managed about 5,000 properties, including multi-storey blocks of flats. Housing associations in each of their areas had developed a number of new consortium schemes. The Contract Manager and two neighbourhood office Managers were interviewed. A third neighbourhood office Manager in an adjacent contract area was also interviewed because a very large consortium estate had recently been built and let in her area.

Each year across the city the neighbourhood offices dealt with about 1,300 priority homeless families. A third of these were women who were homeless because of domestic violence. Individual offices dealt with very varied numbers of women in such circumstances. The three offices in this study were designated as high-pressure offices for family accommodation, since demand for housing outstripped suitable supply for high priority applicants (including homeless families). The staff in each neighbourhood office helped four or five women a month who were escaping domestic violence.

Compulsory competitive tendering had forced the local authority to contract out the housing management service and manage it along new public management lines (Pollitt, 1990; Clarke and Newman, 1997). Neighbourhood office staff were primarily responsible for managing council homes, and their priorities were arrears control, voids management and repairs. They had a range of performance targets to meet in relation to these. The Contract Manager believed that because of these priorities the homeless service provided by the neighbourhood offices was simply "an appendage".

The circumstances of homeless families were 'investigated' initially by the Estate Management Officers. They wrote a report and recommended a decision about the applicant's homeless status. Each Contract Manager made the final decision about an applicant's homeless priority. Estate Management Officers often had to do this work when under considerable pressure from their Managers to complete different work in order to achieve *other* targets.

> "They haven't got the time to go out and do the homeless investigation fully anyway because we're screaming at them because the repairs are behind, because we're overspending on this budget, because the arrears are going up....."
> (Contract Manager)

The three Managers interviewed for the present study felt that *their* staff did a good job but that generally the service to homeless people provided by neighbourhood offices in other contract areas was patchy. They identified a number of reasons why women who had fled domestic violence might receive different responses from different neighbourhood offices. Often staff did not have enough time to deal with homeless 'cases' that could be time-consuming and sometimes traumatic (especially when domestic violence was involved). The three Managers also felt that it was hard for staff to build up sufficient experience and knowledge in dealing with domestic violence because only a small number of women in this situation were seen every month. To add to the difficulties, staff turnover below Assistant Manager level was a continuous problem in each of the offices. These jobs were difficult and not well paid.

All neighbourhood office staff had received homelessness training in 1991 when the homeless families service was decentralised, but there had been no other comprehensive training on homelessness in the department since then. New staff in neighbourhood offices had to rely on brief induction training, manuals, and other more experienced colleagues to help them to give advice and to complete homeless investigations. Only one neighbourhood office had received domestic violence awareness training because it was in a pilot area designated to improve working practices on domestic violence within its boundaries (discussed later in this chapter).

Deciding women's homeless priority

There were two formal and one informal set of influences on decision making in relation to women applicants who were homeless because of domestic violence. The 1996 Housing Act and the authority's domestic violence policy were the formal influences. They co-existed in an uneasy alliance, which started to unravel in the decentralised services that worked to a range of different priorities. The informal influence was exerted by the very variable impact of councillors' influence over neighbourhood office managers' decisions in relation to allocations.

The impact of the 1996 Housing Act (Part VII)

Surprisingly, the new legislation seemed to have had little impact on what staff in this local authority did when assessing an application from a homeless woman. Contrary to fears that very few homeless people would be helped, this local authority had found a way to virtually maintain the status quo. The way in which the authority's waiting list had been changed incrementally to include the new housing register requirements enabled them to continue with their pre-existing approach almost intact.

Generally, when a woman was homeless because of violence and had dependent children, she would be regarded as in priority need. If she had no dependent children, she was assessed as potentially vulnerable so that she might obtain priority-need status. This distinction between women based on whether or not they were caring for children has been used by some feminists as an example of the welfare state only considering women important in policy terms as mothers rather than women (Binney et al, 1981; Malos et al, 1993). In this authority, however, the distinction did not hold in practice as both were given statutory homeless priority without much difficulty.

The Principal Officers in both central homeless teams and the Contract Manager in this study rarely excluded women from help on the grounds that there was 'suitable' available accommodation for the applicant in the private sector (s 193). They also rarely used the 'intentionality' sections of the legislation in relation to women leaving domestic violence (s 191.1). The 'local connection' provisions (whereby a woman might be referred to another authority) were used when women themselves wanted to move to another area (s 200.4). One Principal Officer remarked that the authority had good working relationships with surrounding authorities, so there was rarely any difficulty with this.

The only grey areas reported by senior staff in relation to the interpretation of the homeless legislation related to single women. There was unease about deciding 'vulnerability'. Some women seemed to be continuously mobile (in turn, doing the hostel circuit, sleeping on friends' floors and sleeping rough). Sometimes there was doubt about whether 'vulnerability' could exist some time after a woman had experienced violence from a partner or partners, or whether some women found it difficult to cope for reasons other than having experienced violence. Some homeless women applicants were so vulnerable that the Principal Officers had doubts about whether self-contained accommodation was appropriate, but there were no permanent alternatives. This was in line with the findings of a number of surveys of single homeless people (for example, Drake et al, 1981).

The effect of the domestic violence policy on decision making

The domestic violence policy was intended to ensure a uniform and sympathetic response to homeless women who had left violent men. The authors of the policy had drawn from a body of knowledge about domestic violence built up by feminist writers (Dobash and Dobash, 1979; Kelly, 1988; Kirkwood, 1993). The policy defined domestic violence widely, far more widely than most authorities had done (Evans and Duncan, 1988; Malos et al, 1993). The definition which staff were expected to work with included physical, sexual and psychological violence, damage to belongings and economic violence such as withholding money. Its guideline about proof was based on an awareness of the difficulties which women might experience in providing corroborative evidence and a recognition that they might be embarrassed and/or feel shame or fear in speaking to strangers about what had happened (Pahl, 1985; Mama, 1989).

Unfortunately, it did not appear to have been drawn up with much awareness of the homeless legislation and how housing management and homeless staff actually worked. This was probably due to the lack of consultation with housing management staff before the policy was agreed. One Manager bluntly remarked that the policy had "been written by someone who hasn't worked in a housing office" (Housing Manager). More diplomatically, the Contract Manager felt that it had been helpful since it had raised the profile of the issue, but "the policy itself is a wee bit too simplistic or its been interpreted in a simplistic way" (Contract Manager).

All the senior staff interviewed felt that the policy objective of obtaining a sympathetic response for women had only been achieved in part. Their reasons for thinking this varied. For some, they included the relative status of the policy compared to the legislation and the *Code of Guidance*. Others were more concerned about the importance of being able to use their judgement or discretion or were concerned about the competing pressures of other priorities on Estate Management Officers who completed the 'investigations' in neighbourhood offices. The lack of staff training on the homeless legislation and case law was also a concern.

The domestic violence policy appeared to have an ambiguous status for the staff who made the formal decision about whether an applicant was statutory homeless (that is, the Principal Officers and the Contract Manager). The legislation and *Code of Guidance* were the primary source of guidance for them. Consequently, they had to interpret the policy selectively. The main reason for this was that the authority's discretion in making decisions under the 1996 Housing Act (Part VII) could not legally be fettered by the blanket approach represented by the policy.

One Principal Officer gave an example of how they assessed single men (and occasionally women) who had been violent towards a woman. A man might become homeless if his former partner terminated their joint tenancy following his violence. The domestic violence policy advised staff not to "offer rehousing support to the alleged perpetrator once the joint tenancy was ended" (agreed by a meeting of the Tenancy Sub-Committee, February 1993). This Principal Officer pointed out that the man might be vulnerable (as defined by the legislation) through being alcoholic or mentally ill. If he was, the assessment would be made and he would be rehoused *despite* the domestic violence policy. The domestic violence policy prohibited staff from asking for proof of violence. If women gave them evidence (in the form of letters, copies of exclusion orders and so on) they were supposed to thank the woman, read the document(s) but not take it/them into account in making a decision. On the face of it, this placed the authority at the more sympathetic end of the spectrum of approaches towards women and the family that were tentatively set out in Chapter Two. However, it emerged in interviews that the Principal Officers and Contract Manager *did* use the documentary evidence given to them by women, *despite* the domestic violence policy (although they made it clear that their staff did not ask women for 'proof'). They actually preferred these situations to those where there was no external documentation: using it in decision making complied with the legislation, made it easier to make a decision and was a safeguard for them against women who 'invented' violence to obtain priority. The Contract Manager identified a further problem for staff in not considering corroborative evidence:

> "There's an acceptance among our client group that if you go along and say that your boyfriend's knocking you about a bit, they'll give you priority ... which we will. And that's counterproductive in some ways.... It tends to clog up the system so that when the genuine one comes along we're at risk of not spotting it because there's a degree of cynicism creeps in ... 'Oh here we go with another one' and that's a problem, I fear. The other thing that worries

me about it is that because we get too familiar with it … sometimes we don't respond adequately. I think the policy has contributed to that in some ways…. We don't filter the risk factor." (Contract Manager)

The Contract Manager felt that this was most likely to happen when women were given priority because of the *risk* of violence occurring. He referred to the *Code of Guidance* which recommended that local authorities consider applications sympathetically when they were made by women who were being threatened with violence, *where it was likely that the threats would be carried out* (DoE, DH and WO, 1996, s 13.9). The authority's domestic violence policy did not make this distinction: staff were not expected to assess whether or not violence was likely to occur.

Although Housing Managers were not responsible for deciding an applicant's homeless priority, they *could* sometimes control the quality and location of council housing offered to women. Occasionally, poor offers were made to reflect exactly what the Manager thought of the woman (or her family). The Contract Manager remarked that he sometimes received 'investigation reports' where there was no evidence of violence except what the woman had told the Estate Management Officer. In these situations, he would agree that she was statutory homeless but

> "I might also say to the Manager 'Make an offer that you might expect will be turned down and let's see if that gives us any more information'. In that sense, you've complied with the legislation rather than argue about access to it, which can go on and on for ever." (Contract Manager)

More generally, women might be advised by staff to consider areas where vacancies were more likely: usually poorer areas. Having said that, one Manager recounted how she had been able to offer a particularly good quality home in a much sought-after area to a professional woman who was trying to escape from her violent partner. Housing Managers' control over housing offers was reinforced by women applicants' lack of choice. There was a 'one offer only' policy: women lost their priority if they turned down what a Manager regarded as a reasonable offer. Guidelines about housing offers had not been included in the domestic violence policy and the quality and/or appropriateness of housing offers was not monitored separately.

The three neighbourhood office Managers felt that the policy ensured a consistent approach in their offices, and yet their views about its practicality differed. One considered it to be part of 'customer care' but a second Manager felt that it created difficulties because it conflicted with broader housing management responsibilities. For example, she questioned whether someone with rent arrears or who was known in the office for antisocial behaviour should be transferred because of (supposed) violence when other applicants were expected to resolve these problems before being transferred. She was "very cynical" about women who wanted to move to an area which she believed was too near their ex-partner or about women who were prepared to wait a long time for better quality housing than they had lived in before. More fundamentally (and less helpfully), she doubted the resolve of any woman to live apart from their violent ex-partner for any length of time: "I do wish women would learn, but women are women. We never do, do we?".

These attitudes were grounded in housing management concerns – a determination to prevent possible abuse of the housing register priorities and concern about the impact of women having to move again in terms of wasted staff time and voids. The policy did not tackle these issues.

The differences of view about the value of the local authority's domestic violence policy when applied to practical housing management illustrate Lipsky's (1980) point about the danger of assuming that policy implementation in any organisation will be uniform and non-contentious. He also made the point that street-level bureaucrats *themselves* make public policy in the sense that the ways in which *they* respond to their work becomes the working policy of the organisation. Viewed in this way, this local authority seemed to have two policies. The formal policy was represented by the domestic violence policy. Principal Officers in the specialist central homeless teams probably kept closer to this policy because they appreciated its spirit: they did not have such a diverse range of demands on their time and did not manage property. Having said that, they could not implement it uniformly. The second informal or unofficial domestic violence policy was represented by what neighbourhood office staff actually did. They used some parts of the policy but ignored or amended others so that they could manage the homelessness work more easily alongside the other work that they had to do.

Staff worked within a management tradition that valued the use of judgement or discretion especially in relation to allocations. They held views about the role of housing management, the nature of domestic violence and the trustworthiness of women when faced with a long wait for alternative housing. Staff were also subject to strongly competing pressures on their time and looked for shortcuts (like proof) to decide what had happened. In assessing women applicants, judgement might be used to decide who was 'deserving' or who was telling the truth – based on the availability or otherwise of proof, the presence or otherwise of physical violence, and the absence or otherwise of other management problems. Making judgements about applicants or tenants' personal circumstances was rooted in the housing visitor tradition. It was common practice on housing visits or when considering applications to draw social distinctions between different types of applicant to help managers decide the type and location of property considered appropriate for them (Tucker, 1966; Daniel, 1968; Gray, 1976; Simpson, 1981; Henderson and Karn, 1987). In the local offices, these attitudes might find a physical expression in the nature and location of properties that were offered to women. It was unlikely that these practices would change without effective training/guidance, the monitoring of all aspects of the domestic violence policy and clear consistent sanctions. None of these was in place.

Working with local councillors

One of the difficulties with managerialism is that it has not understood the political role of local councillors. Their influence has rarely been acknowledged nor their role understood in relation to council staff, local constituents and council services (Pollitt, 1990, p 120). Recent research has shown that, while positive achievements have been made with partnership working of various kinds, there are strong doubts about whether these are continuing to undermine the key democratic role of local government (Wilkinson and Craig, 2002). This is particularly the case for the 'back-bench' non-executive councillors who have struggled to find a role following the reorganisation of many local authorities' representative functions from a committee to a cabinet structure following the 2000 Local Government Act. It was clear in this study that the role of councillors was changing but that they continued to be important on a day-to-day basis to staff working in decentralised council offices.

In research elsewhere, councillors had often intervened in relation to allocations to women who had left violent men (Charles with Jones, 1993; Malos et al, 1993). It was not surprising to discover in the present study that there had been a difficult history of councillor involvement in issues relating to homelessness in the city. Senior staff were aware that they might be compulsorily moved to different offices (or worse still, be sacked) were relationships between themselves and local councillors to become too strained. Some relationships were easier to manage than others: one Manager found her councillors "very, very difficult" especially when they decided to support a constituent whom she felt had "no case". Another Manager presented a different view: he said that two out of the three councillors in his area were very supportive. Furthermore, he felt that they respected his position.

> "You've got to be aware that they've got a standing in the community as well and you've got to – I won't say let them 'win' – but let them be seen to be doing their stuff. And it's not difficult because the stuff they usually bring to us are cases which we should be picking up anyway." (Housing Manager)

The third Manager had a more variable experience. One very experienced local councillor worked well with the staff in the office; two others were more difficult. They had been elected two years previously and neither understood the system (Manager). One councillor expected the neighbourhood office staff to follow his instructions and regularly made promises to constituents at his advice surgeries without consulting the office. The Manager felt that such situations had to be handled carefully. It was important to avoid the councillor losing face with his own community (in this instance, the local Pakistani community) but at the same time staff could not necessarily do what he wanted. The Contract Manager saw this more strategically than the Managers.

"It's the influences that are on ward members to do things.... As far as the Labour group in that ward is concerned, I'm aware of power struggles going on – factions within the Asian community which are trying to exercise authority. We can see ward members leaping one way or another in relation to what's going on beneath them." (Contract Manager)

The approach of councillors towards staff varied across the city. The Contract Manager felt that some of the differences were simply the result of councillors' different personalities:

"[There are] the personality issues which are there. If you drift across the city, the further you go east, the hotter it becomes because it's more personality driven. It's about individuals and it's about just shouting at people." (Contract Manager)

Sometimes councillors exerted considerable influence to ensure that they got what they wanted. There were political advantages to them in ensuring that their existing constituents received priority in relation to housing services since they were 'local'. Certain councillors did not want homeless 'outsiders' to be rehoused in their constituencies.[2] One Manager identified a different problem: male councillors might ally with certain male community leaders and might be unsympathetic to women from their communities leaving violent partners. Rai and Thiara (1997, p 70) had identified this problem in their research on black women's use of refuge provision.

"You can see all these various influences moving. So nothing that members do surprises me. It's a question of trying to work out why?" (Contract Manager)

It had become clear that, despite targets, performance indicators and managerialism, councillors continued to be very influential in the council setting. Did this influence extend to housing associations?

The 'enabling' authority and housing associations

Bramley (1993) believed that for 'enabling' to be effective, there had to be a broad consensus about objectives and trust between the parties concerned. Kennedy et al (2001) built on that, and also emphasised the need for committed staff, good working relationships and communication, adequate time, senior political support and flexibility of approach at a practical, operational level. In the absence of that, enabling or inter-agency working was unlikely to flourish. This was especially the case when professional boundaries acted as barriers and/or there was a lack of understanding about different organisations' duties and limitations.

Local authority senior staff had different opinions about local associations' performance in relation to nominations and inter-agency working. Different perspectives emerged depending on whether staff worked in the central homeless teams or in one of the neighbourhood offices.

Nominations: the central homeless team view

The centrally based Principal Officers were critical of associations' nomination practices and housing advice. Their experience was such that it was clear that "enabling" was difficult. They felt that association staff gave insufficient advice to homeless applicants especially to their own tenants who might have housing difficulties. On many occasions, they had been expected to help association tenants when the association itself had done nothing. The association then expected their tenants (or former tenants) to be nominated back to them.

> "We have a statutory duty towards women who are becoming homeless. Housing associations don't have that statutory duty. So I think it is often … too easy to refer women to us. It's also obvious that housing associations do not even consider how they are going to assist that woman by a tenant transfer, by contacting other housing associations…. It just seems … not too easy but it seems – well, it is easier for the housing association to refer them to us. We do a homeless investigation and for some unknown reason housing associations will ask for a nomination back for their own association tenants. A statutory homeless nomination!" (Principal Officer, Families Team)

The Principal Officers of both central teams felt strongly that this was a waste of time. Staff had to complete 'investigations' that were unnecessary. They believed that associations could simply have transferred women tenants in most instances they had seen. The NFHA 'good practice' guide *Women and violence at home* had recommended this route for women who were association tenants (Davis, 1993). The guide had been circulated to Principal Officers internally by an Assistant Director in 1995 so they were knowledgeable about it and referred to it in the research interviews without prompting. Every time an association tenant applied to the central homeless team for help, a Principal Officer formally wrote to the association landlord to ask why the association itself could not help. Unfortunately, the usual response from the association was that the tenant had requested a high-demand area, there were no appropriate vacancies and/or the association waiting list was too long (Principal Officers).

The Principal Officers thought that associations were now housing fewer homeless people than in the past. Few associations now rang them directly with vacancies (Tulip HA, the local black association, being the sole exception). A few years previously, when they had targets to achieve, associations had contacted them regularly.

Nominations: the neighbourhood office view

The neighbourhood office Managers had slightly different experiences in relation to nominations to associations and their views were more critical. One Manager had recently nominated over 100 households for a newly-built consortium estate. She was pleased that council tenants and applicants had got good housing and resigned to the serious voids problem this had created for her own office. The other two Managers had completely different problems. One could not remember many of his nominations being rehoused into new consortium schemes in his area. He thought that the local authority had generally "been taken for a ride" in relation to nominations to consortium schemes. The rent levels were prohibitive for many working families and he felt that he had no influence over who was rehoused, nominations or otherwise. Like the Principal Officers in the central teams, his staff had encountered association tenants who had simply been sent to his office for help and a nomination. He took a dim view of the practice.

The other had a different problem. He remarked that association staff referred *any* applicant to his office to obtain a nomination, whatever their circumstances: people with low-priority circumstances as well as high-priority circumstances were sent. Somewhat caustically, he remarked "I would have thought it was good practice to find out an applicant's housing need first".

Applicants had been told that they could not join the associations' waiting lists without a nomination. This created work for his staff: formally interviewing people who would not obtain a high enough priority to be nominated. He felt that there was no point in associations sending low-priority applicants, unless it was to make it appear that the local authority (rather than the association) was refusing the applicant access to the association's waiting list. Bluebell HA, Foxglove HA and Tulip HA were named in relation to this practice although Tulip HA was the worst, in his opinion (see Chapter Six for another view). He had also come across situations where low-priority applicants had been rehoused by associations while high-priority applicants had not.

The Contract Manager confirmed the tendency of associations to simply refer applicants and tenants to the local authority to deal with their problems and nominate them back to the association (see Chapter Five). Applicants could be nominated only when they wanted to be considered by an association and they fell into Group A or B on the housing register. But he felt uncomfortable sometimes because

> "quite often a housing association will send people to us to get priority because it looks good on their record and I feel that sometimes we're being used by housing associations.... They're unwilling to try and resolve things for themselves ... I think that messes the person around unnecessarily. Quite often they can help.... The larger ones *certainly* can but they choose not to – because they think that it's better to have a nomination from us.... They'll force somebody to jump through all the hoops here." (Contract Manager)

Inter-agency working and domestic violence

Guidance from the government (Home Office and Welsh Office, 1995; Home Office, 2000) emphasised the need for different agencies to work together to provide services to women who lived with or had left violent men. In this authority, a project had been established to improve organisations' responses in relation to domestic violence and a good practice inter-agency pilot area had been designated in 1992 to run for five years. The aim of the work was to encourage good inter-agency working relationships in that area. Quarterly domestic violence forum meetings and domestic violence awareness training was organised for staff in voluntary and statutory organisations located there. One of the neighbourhood offices and the offices of the three case study associations were located in the pilot area.

Two of the neighbourhood office Managers had strong views about the associations that worked in their areas. One thought that relationships between the associations and the local authority had deteriorated since the 1988 Housing Act. His office was the one located in the pilot area. He thought that associations operated commercially, whereas the authority's culture was different and genuinely more concerned about 'customer care' and responding to housing need. He was very annoyed that a sector which had all the development funding and whose staff typically managed 300 homes expected the local authority to do all the work (including homeless investigations) when his staff each managed 700 homes. The second Manager found it "depressing" that the local authority and housing associations were supposed to be working in partnership when they appeared to him to "be working entirely to their own agendas". The third Manager had no idea what her local associations were doing. She explained that this was because her job had become increasingly stressful and demanding and she had no time for networking.

The local authority Project Worker for the pilot area appeared to be unaware of the strained working relationships between the local authority and local associations. She sent information to organisations in the area through the post every three months. This was predominantly to advertise domestic violence forum meetings. Somewhat sardonically, she commented: "We send it out but we do not know whose bin it goes into". She said that she had prioritised work with staff in the local authority's neighbourhood office rather than the local associations because she believed that they were likely to see more women but it did not seem that this had been a successful strategy.

> "I've had endless meetings with Housing Managers and they look nice and say nice and then do nothing. That's the pattern." (Project Worker)

There was, however, a critical view of the project from the local authority itself at a senior level. The Contract Manager felt that the project had made little impact on the housing staff working in the three offices in his contract area. He felt that they were "already there" as far as domestic violence was concerned because of the domestic violence policy. He believed that the project was largely "plaiting fog" and making too much of what it had achieved. The two Managers in the pilot area spoke more positively about the project's influence, although nobody had time to attend forum meetings. One had attended domestic violence training years before with his staff but there had been no other comprehensive training quite like this. The Women's Officer from the local authority and the Regional Officer from the NFHA had addressed a forum meeting in 1993 to publicise domestic violence policy development. That had been the only forum meeting in five years devoted to housing and no development work had been undertaken with associations. Local authority staff on an individual basis had not attended the forum meetings or domestic violence 'awareness' training in great numbers over that period. Housing association staff had been even scarcer at meetings and training (Project Worker and minutes of forum meetings). In fact, no inter-agency work was done in relation to housing services in the period up to 2000.

More generally, the Contract Manager believed that the working relationship between the authority and the associations in the area was

> "a passive one. It's good because it's not bad.... In terms of role, there's a huge amount we could do together. Really make a difference by pooling information sometimes and by sharing work sometimes but politically there isn't a will to make that happen." (Contract Manager)

This was clearly not enabling in the sense of the local authority influencing associations' management practices nor inter-agency working in relation to domestic violence. Local authority staff had critical views about associations' nomination practices and advice giving. Too often, the Managers saw their staff dealing with people whom associations had referred but not helped. This ensured that associations could be more competitive by reducing the time which association staff spent on interviewing and giving advice to applicants and tenants. This cost was being transferred to the local authority. It appeared to local authority staff that associations were only interested in obtaining nominated applicants. Consequently, it was no surprise that local authority staff believed that inter-agency working did not exist. Rather, they felt that the working relationships with associations' housing management staff were distant and strained. That did not mean that contact was not maintained with like-minded individuals in associations but, as the Contract Manager pointed out, that was "personal networking not inter-agency working".

Conclusion

The local authority in this study played a major role in relation to helping women who were homeless because of violence at home. It had responded to the 1996 Housing Act in ways that helped women, although arguably the incrementalism had also occurred to protect the status quo for councillors.

This local authority's domestic violence policy was also important for raising the profile of the issue although its impact had been more limited than its creators had hoped for. This was because homeless staff had a statutory obligation to make individual decisions under the legislation. These may or may not have fallen within the policy's parameters. Additionally, the policy's status had been undermined because of the effects of managerialism and competition, the use of staff discretion and a lack of staff training. Having said that, the local authority remained very important to women. Could its influence extend to associations through enabling?

Unfortunately, there appeared to be little hope of that. The working relationships between housing staff in the local authority and staff in associations in this study appeared to be distant and somewhat strained rather than constructive. Women might receive a high priority for rehousing with the local authority and be nominated. The question raised by neighbourhood office staff was whether or not they would be rehoused by associations? Associations no longer had externally monitored targets to achieve for rehousing statutory homeless households, and in two out of the three associations in this study their interest had declined accordingly. Page's report (1993) had generated doubt in many associations about the wisdom of rehousing homeless people on new estates. He argued that concentrating vulnerable households created difficult, if not impossible, management problems for associations. A more cynical view was that many associations had never been keen to house homeless people: they regarded them as possibly undeserving or unsuitable tenants.

The impact of competition between the local authority and housing associations was also becoming evident to local authority staff in a number of ways. This affected the possibility of any inter-agency working. In the neighbourhood offices, homeless investigations were a statutory responsibility but not always a priority. Staff had more urgent demands on their time: rent collection, arrears, voids and repairs. Association staff worked under broadly similar pressures but could transfer at least some of their workload (responding to homeless people and giving advice) to their counterparts in the local authority. This kind of behaviour did not make for good working relationships between local authority and housing association staff, let alone inter-agency working.

The next three chapters take up some of these issues and explore them in more depth with housing association staff. Chapter Four looks in broad terms at the changing, privatised world of the case study associations and examines how housing management services were being transformed, not necessarily to the benefit of homeless women who needed to be rehoused.

Notes

[1] See Drake et al (1981) for recommendations that single homeless people needed a specialist service.

[2] Charles with Jones (1993; Charles, 1994) discusses the same problem in the Welsh context.

FOUR

The housing associations – growing into a new role

Introduction

The 1988 Housing Act introduced new funding arrangements for the house-building programmes of associations, reduced security of tenure for new association assured tenants, and removed the requirement to set 'fair rents' on new tenancies. Associations could now use private as well as public funding to provide more social rented housing. The Act had effectively privatised housing associations. The 1989 Local Government and Housing Act followed. This changed local authority funding, reducing even further their power to build. Given these developments, the local authority in this study decided to work with five associations in a consortium to undertake a large building programme up until the mid-1990s. A number of 'beneficiary' associations also worked on specific sites. This was politically more acceptable in this Labour authority than the alternative of a large number of individual associations freely competing for development opportunities, although it was not quite the pure 'quasi-market' envisaged by Le Grand and Bartlett (1993).

Nearly 2,000 new rented homes in a wide variety of locations were built. Most were for families as this was the preference of the local authority (see Watson, 1986, for a broader discussion of this tendency). Although the associations owned the properties, the local authority retained 75% nomination rights to the lettings made by the associations for the next 20 years. A new hostel for homeless women was also built on the same basis. In 1997/98 a total of 2,041 association lettings (relets and new lets) were made across the city. The lettings made by the three associations in this study represented about one third of that total lettings figure (716 out of a total of 2,041). The total number of households nominated and rehoused by associations across the city in the same year was 723. The three case study associations housed about a half of the total of nominated applicants who were rehoused (361 out of a total of 723).

As far as homeless applicants who were rehoused were concerned, out of a total of 723 nominations made to associations across the city, 179 were statutory homeless and 93 were non-statutory homeless applicants. Homeless people made up 37% of all the nominations rehoused by associations in that year. In the case study associations, Tulip HA rehoused by far the most homeless people at 58% of its total lettings (109 out of 189). Bluebell HA trailed behind at 19% (64 out of 353). National figures only were available for Foxglove HA but there was no reason to think that the local picture would be much different. Its figures were 20% (946 out of 4796). The situation of Tulip HA, the smallest association in the study and the one committed to rehousing black and Asian people, was astonishing.

Each of the associations in this study had grown to varying degrees since the 1988 Housing Act. Two had restructured mainly due to the perceived need to become more financially efficient. Housing management services had also changed in response to these pressures. The impact of shifting 'organisational regimes' (Clarke and Newman, 1997) and the growing influence of managerialism were becoming much more evident within association housing management (Walker, 1998, 2000). New ways of working did not completely replace older practices or attitudes: they both appeared to exist in an uneasy relationship at different levels of each association.

This chapter uses information from interviews with senior staff in the associations, an interview with the Vice-Chair of one association, the annual reports of associations, as well as policy documents to provide a dynamic account of the changing management service which women might receive from the three case study associations.

The chapter is divided into a number of discrete but interrelated sections that provide an overview of associations' changing role and work. The first section describes the associations in brief, giving a broad overview of the ways they responded to privatisation. This is followed by an analysis of their changing housing management services, including their relationships with other organisations. The relationship with local councillors is then examined, since they became more interested in associations as they started to provide more new rented housing.

Another influence on housing management services was whether or not associations had domestic violence policies to help staff decision making. This issue is then discussed. Finally, the relationship with the local authority is described in relation to its help to homeless women and the significance of local authority nominations for association rehousing. In conclusion, the nature of the service provided to women and whether it was appropriate for associations to refer to women as 'customers' with 'choices' is discussed.

The case study associations

1. Bluebell HA – the local association

Bluebell HA had been a small, predominantly inner-city association in 1987. In ten years, it increased the rented accommodation it owned from 450 to 1,700 properties. Staffing had increased over this period from 12 to 60. The chief executive believed that the association's continuing independence had been assured by the growth made possible by the consortium. The association had built between 200 to 300 homes each year and a hostel for women over the consortium's five year life. It had moved away from its inner-city focus:

outer-city sites had been developed more recently to contribute to the association's financial viability. Over 10 years, the proportion of property it owned in the inner-city had decreased from 60% to 25%.

Bluebell HA was the only association not to have recently reorganised. Its chief executive believed that reorganisation would be more disruptive than beneficial. He had a very strong task-oriented focus: he enjoyed "getting things done" and described himself as having a "detailed" understanding of most of the association's work as well as a "controlling" approach. He thought that it took a strong manager to contradict him. Although he identified a need to move to a "more collegiate style" with his senior managers, he was "not prepared to sacrifice service standards in any moves in that direction". He also thought that the organisation had moved forward up until then through the contributions of "talented individuals".

The Chief Executive firmly believed that private-sector methods could be used to build and manage social housing. But recent changes to working practices in Bluebell HA did not appear to sit easily with older approaches and attitudes. More housing was coming into management in the next year but no new staff would be recruited to deal with the increased workload – Housing Officers' patch sizes would be increased instead. In this way, unit costs could be reduced, making the association more competitive. Performance-related pay had been agreed for senior staff and was then being considered for everyone. The new approach was 'more work with less resources' – a well known managerialist phrase (see Hood, 1991). This accorded with a developing 'competitive regime' (Clarke and Newman, 1997).

The new approach had not been accepted without challenge by other staff. The Chief Executive referred to "tensions" with housing management staff about declining service standards in the face of relentless increases in work. He thought that many of those staff wanted the growth and increased work to stop, but *he* believed that the association "has to grow to survive". These differences of opinion about the direction in which Bluebell HA's services were developing reflected competing attitudes and practices (Clarke and Newman, 1997, pp 62-3), though it was clear that frontline staff had little influence over the direction and pace of change.

2. Foxglove HA – the multi-regional association

Foxglove HA was a multi-regional association that had owned and managed about 1,000 properties in this local authority in 1987. The association owned about 30,000 properties across the country. Staff in the area office in this study worked with five local authorities including the one in this study. The association had grown slowly over five years, developing between 400 and 500 rented homes and a small number of hostels including a women's hostel. Since it was not locally based, it had not been given preferential treatment for development opportunities by the local authority.

Staffing levels in the area office had remained static over this time although the association had recently reorganised. The reasons for the restructuring were wide-ranging. It wanted to increase its competitiveness against local associations, improve working relationships with local authorities, improve its service to 'customers' and increase "accountability to the local community" (Area Director). Most of the staff who now worked in the area office were doing new jobs and were focused on working within the framework of an Area Plan which linked to the association's corporate objectives. Decision making and budget *holding* (previously quite tightly controlled from the head office) were partly decentralised to the area offices. The head office retained control over policy development, budget *setting* and strategic control and monitoring. The reorganisation followed the 'new public management' model (Pollitt, 1990).

Several staff remarked that Foxglove HA's reorganisation had severely undermined staff morale. It had taken too long (over two years) and had involved too many difficult group discussions. The association had previously been a very stable bureaucratic organisation. The Team Leader was not alone in commenting that it had now lost its "family feel". He thought that the area office staff were no longer prepared to "go that extra mile now", such as working extra hours to ensure that work was completed on time. This was ironic since they now had more direct responsibility for decisions and their implementation.

3. Tulip HA – the black association

Tulip HA had registered as an association in the 1980s to rehouse black and Asian people who were homeless or living in poor housing conditions. It had been given a "great opportunity" for growth through its involvement in the consortium (Chief Executive). About 500 of the association's 700 homes had been built in this way and the number of staff had increased from one to 17 over ten years. Nevertheless, the association had little choice over where it could build since it had been a 'beneficiary' rather than a full member of the consortium. The Vice-Chair believed that Tulip HA had been given the worst sites to develop. Some had been in predominantly white areas that had a history of racial attacks. A number of black applicants had refused to consider property built there. The association had restructured in 1996 to make it

> fit for an increasingly competitive future but also to achieve a more customer-focused housing service with quality and performance as the key components.
> (Tulip HA, Annual Report, 1996)

The reorganisation had been undertaken to deal with concerns about the association's financial viability. It had led to the departure of most of the pre-1996 staff. All the current staff were new, with the exception of the Chief Executive. This was viewed positively by the Vice-Chair and the Chief Executive, although they both remarked that the recruitment process had been "a difficult time". Some posts had been hard to fill and work had "piled up" (Vice-Chair).

Some staff later complained about this outstanding work. They had been obliged to deal with muddles that should have been handled by their predecessors.

The association's Board was trying to create a "changed ethos" and different working priorities in the association (Vice-Chair). This was similar to the 'competitive regime' outlined by Clarke and Newman (1997). The association's most important priority now was financial: staff had to ensure that rent was paid and that arrears were dealt with promptly. Arrears had been unacceptably high two years before. The Board believed that tenants' views about what might happen if they built up arrears *had* to change because it affected the association's financial viability (Vice-Chair).

> "The emphasis *had* to be on getting the records straight, getting the money in and issuing notices to quit, if necessary." (Vice-Chair, Tulip HA)

As a consequence, the association's links with the local community had been put under considerable strain. This was a major concern given that it was a relatively recently established black association.

The changing housing management service

Senior management were working to create new 'competitive regimes' in all the case study associations (Newman and Clarke, 1997). There was now an overt emphasis within each of the associations on financial 'performance' with a focus on maximising rental income and minimising the costs of staff and overheads in the housing management service. This was accompanied by a lack of priority for more intangible processes like the provision of advice and/ or 'support' to applicants and tenants (Pollitt, 1990; Hood, 1991; Clarke and Newman, 1997). All of the recent changes in the three associations were commensurate with this.

There was a consensus among long-serving senior staff in the three associations that the housing management service had deteriorated generally. The nature of jobs had recently changed a great deal in all the associations. For example, in Bluebell HA, the professional autonomy of housing management staff had declined. Even though some Housing Officers might try to continue to offer a service tailored to the individual, lack of time and knowledge reduced the possibilities of continuing this alternative, older approach. A similar process was evident in Foxglove HA. It had previously been much more bureaucratised than Bluebell HA, but had recently adopted what might be called the neo-Taylorist version of housing management (after Pollitt, 1990). Housing Services Officers now had little discretion and were closely monitored using computerised management systems in relation to arrears and voids-control work. Tulip HA's Senior Managers were also changing Housing Officers' priorities so that far more time was now spent dealing with rent arrears and undertaking court work.

Applicants' or tenants' queries were dealt with at the lowest level possible in the organisation (Customer Service teams in Foxglove HA and Tulip HA) or had to be squeezed into Housing Officer time. Their priorities were arrears and voids work (Bluebell HA). In all of the associations, arrears and voids were part of the "core business" of the organisation (Clarke and Newman, 1997, pp 78-9) while advice and support for general needs tenants were not.

Although senior staff expected that the amount of time taken to interview applicants would reduce, the reality was different. This was an area of work where older practices and values might persist (though for different reasons) in Bluebell HA and Tulip HA. Part of the job satisfaction of staff in Bluebell HA derived from positively helping an applicant in a difficult situation. This was evident from the amount of time that some duty-officer staff took when interviewing people in Bluebell HA. Tulip HA staff also spent more time with applicants. This was largely due to the fact that many of their tenants and applicants could not read or write English, nor was English their first language; rather, everything had to be explained orally. The situation in Foxglove HA was different. Customer Services Officers were expected to simply concentrate on telling applicants in English what the association itself could offer.

Having said that, the *direction* in which these services were developing emphasised ways of working (including using standard procedures) that minimised the time that had to be spent with each applicant. This was another aspect of the increasing dominance of managerialist ideas, especially in relation to 'efficiency' and the commonplace maxim to 'do more with less resources'. This was the source of local authority staff criticism of the practices they saw in their day-to-day work: of associations doing less and less to help people even though some were in very difficult circumstances. How would these pressures affect the services available to homeless women applicants who had left violent men?

1. Bluebell HA – the local association

Bluebell HA's housing management service had changed over the previous ten years. Staff who had been in post before or around 1988 could remember being able to provide a very personally tailored service for tenants and applicants. Housing officer jobs had been generic then, dealing with all aspects of housing management. Managers said that longstanding tenants still expected the same service and complained when they did not get it (Director of Housing and Housing Manager). The Director of Housing described how incremental changes to the Housing Officer job over the years had reduced its scope: some tasks were eroded away and specialist staff took over others. This had produced a situation

> "which leaves the Housing Officers with probably the dregs – the least desirable elements of the post. So they've got arrears, they've got voids, anti-social behaviour...." (Director of Housing, Bluebell HA)

Housing Officer formal priorities had changed to arrears control, voids and dealing with 'anti-social behaviour'. They met with the Housing Manager every six weeks to review "the things that can be measured" and "kept under control"; that is, mainly arrears and voids (Housing Manager). This more intense monitoring by the Manager had only recently been introduced and had not been well received by frontline staff. The Director of Housing thought that Housing Officers resented the changes, believing that senior management were only pursuing improvements to the arrears and voids performance to obtain financial bonuses for themselves. The more intangible aspects of management, such as getting to know tenants or building good working relationships with other organisations in the field, had reduced in importance (Walker, 1998, 2000). Interviewing had to be done as quickly as possible given the pressure of other work.

> "Dealing with applicants is far more geared to 'Do we have a vacancy? Can we let it?' than 'Here's someone who needs housing. How can we provide the best form of advice?'" (Chief Executive, Bluebell HA)

The Director of Housing regretted these changes.

> "I've understood the [association] as ... a very supportive environment and there have been quite significant changes over the last couple of years – in terms of a more business-like environment, pressure to perform and different management styles being seen in the organisation.... Suddenly it all seems to be changing – from being a very 'touchy-feely-supporty' kind of environment to suddenly the whip's being cracked. That's produced difficulties, I think, for all the Managers in some way or another." (Director of Housing, Bluebell HA)

It was also proving difficult for senior staff to maintain good communication between staff about what was needed and why. There were other pressures on their time. The pay issue was a particularly good example. Frontline staff were becoming reluctant to contribute in staff meetings. They may have been reacting to the changes: showing interest might lead to a request to do more. Frontline staff or new staff were encouraged to consult colleagues when they were unsure about anything. Managers recognised that they might receive different responses depending on who they asked. Limited training and a lack of staff guidelines on a range of issues meant that staff were probably not making consistent decisions about the same issue each time it arose (Manager).

Senior staff in Bluebell HA were positive about rehousing homeless people. The association had set its own targets in the first half of the 1990s for rehousing homeless households, which had been higher than those expected by the Housing Corporation and had been exceeded. Ironically, relatively new tenants now had more complex problems than tenants had experienced in the past but staff now had no time to help them (Director of Housing).

2. Foxglove HA – the multi-regional association

Foxglove HA had undergone "a role change" in the late 1980s and started to house more people living in poverty than previously or, as the Team Leader put it, "more problem families and the homeless". Even though new tenants might need more help, there was far less contact with them than in the past. The housing management service had changed. The Team Leader felt that there was

> "[a] very great difference between what senior Managers *think* they're doing and what *is* actually happening.... I know that this image we have about how close we are to tenants and how responsive we are to their demands – it's not there. We were achieving a great deal more when we were doing door-to-door rent collection because you were *there*. And you *saw* people and you were *aware* of conflicts within families and difficulties that people had. And you saw improvements that people were making in their standards and you saw standards that were deteriorating. Because you were there regularly, you could follow things up.... You could operate on two levels with people. You had an official line but also an unofficial, supportive-if-necessary kind of behaviour. And that's gone. We spend a lot of time *within* organisations talking about customer service but I'm *not* convinced that it's there." (Team Leader, Foxglove HA)

The Team Leader thought that the job of the Housing Services Officer was more difficult than it had been in the past. Their current priorities were dealing with rent arrears, voids, waiting-list visits and nuisance neighbour disputes. Progress was recorded in considerable detail and monitored through the computerised housing management system. This provided a good example of Pollitt's (1990) view that the early stages of 'new public management' unleashes a new form of Taylorism[1] via new technology.

Until a few years before, Foxglove HA could have been described as "liberally minded" (Area Director). It had rarely evicted tenants for arrears or 'anti-social behaviour'. Now there was a tougher approach to arrears and anti-social behaviour, including speedy eviction. The association's reorganisation, Corporate Plan and Area Plans had reinforced this culture change. Changing dominant attitudes within the association meant that other work had not been pursued. The Team Leader referred to inter-agency working as "window dressing".

> "There's not a year goes by without some other new initiative ... that calls upon more time being spent and *they can't do it*.... It's sad but true. However we want to dress it up ... the amount of practical assistance we give to people, the amount of useful advice we give, I think it is very limited." (Team Leader, Foxglove HA)

Nevertheless, the Area Director expressed interest in developing links with local organisations concerned with domestic violence because establishing a more local presence fitted into the Area Plan's objectives. He delegated a member of staff in the area office to investigate further.

3. Tulip HA – the black association

Apart from the Chief Executive in Tulip HA, no member of staff could reflect back to a time when the housing management service had been differently organised with different priorities. Most of the new staff were black and "very young" (Vice-Chair), but the association expected staff to "learn on the job". In the 18 months since their recruitment, no housing training had been provided. The Housing Manager said that there was no budget for any such training.

Attempts to change the 'ethos' and work priorities of the housing management staff had particular repercussions in Tulip HA. There had been a significant increase in evictions for arrears and in property abandonment. This had affected Tulip HA's reputation with some community leaders and local councillors. The Vice-Chair could remember when the association was first established. She spoke with regret:

> "It's become much more of a business. The pressures on the organisation have changed it immensely. It's lost its community base." (Vice-Chair, Tulip HA)

The Housing Manager remarked that the priorities for Housing Officers were controlling arrears and dealing with voids. Occasionally they dealt with other issues such as racial harassment (Tulip HA's reputation as a black association hinged on dealing with this effectively). The Housing Manager remarked that Tulip HA's culture was intended to be "open" and "customer focused", although Housing Officers might not agree. They had to be very task-focused since they had large and difficult workloads. Currently they met every two to three weeks with the Senior Housing Officer to review their progress on arrears and voids.

Tulip HA rehoused large numbers of homeless households and the association's staff maintained good working relationships with Bluebell HA's women's hostel, the black women's refuge and the local authority's central homeless teams. Those organisations spoke highly of Tulip HA as the only association that continued in this commitment. Nevertheless, the relationship between the association and some council neighbourhood offices was not the same (see Chapter Three). It had also run into disputes with councillors over actions taken against individuals with rent arrears and had experienced significant problems with councillors promising new properties to constituents. This created considerable anxiety for some of the housing management staff directly involved.

The relationship with councillors

In the local authority studied here, there was a history of at least some councillors strongly intervening in the council housing management service on behalf of constituents. It was expected that they would do the same with housing associations since they had the same representative role to play. (See Cole and Furbey, 1994, pp 120-8, for a detailed account of councillor intervention in council housing.) It was clear however, that demands which might have been complied with by neighbourhood office Managers were not necessarily treated in the same way by their association equivalents. Rather, the nature of association accountability was different. Housing association staff were ultimately accountable to their unelected Boards/Management Committees and the Housing Corporation rather than locally elected councillors. This 'dispersal of power' from local authorities to housing associations was one formal example of a 'democratic deficit' (Stewart, 1993). Whether there was a *significant* diminution in the practical individual constituency role of councillors was a moot point. Certainly, they did not appear to be slow in coming forward on general issues or in support of particular constituents.

The extent of consortium house building had led councillors to pay greater attention to associations' work. The new housing should have been in great demand. Development staff had expected the new estates to have regenerative effects on the surrounding poor council housing, but this did not always happen. Few local council tenants were transferred to them and a small number of estates in Bluebell HA and Foxglove HA were vandalised and became virtually impossible to let. In some instances, local residents did not regard these estates as part of their local community, and so made no effort to protect them from vandals. In others, the new houses had been built on the outskirts of the city and were not overseen or protected by anyone. Senior staff in all of the associations thought that there were particular housing estates where women who had already had experience of violence would be ill-advised to live: they would not survive there long. Lone parents (Asian, black or white) with black or Asian children would be likely to be racially harassed in some areas. In others, any single women or lone parents would be vulnerable were they to be considered by the existing local residents as 'outsiders'.

This was a different, more complicated picture of difficulties which associations might face with new housing estates than those which had been described by Page (1993) or Cole et al (1996). This picture also raised awkward questions about the somewhat rosy nature of the 'communities' which associations were now expected to create (see also Griffiths et al, 1996; DETR and DSS, 2000).

This was not the main concern of councillors, however. Senior staff reported that they had complained about high rents, the lack of priority for local council tenants, the condition of the stock when it was vandalised or left empty and the rehousing of 'outsiders' into their areas. A small number of schemes had generated the most critical comments: usually the 'low demand' consortium housing which had been vandalised and left empty. The associations in this study had experienced differing degrees of councillor intervention.

The Area Director of Foxglove HA reported apparently minor difficulties. Councillors in one area had been critical of one of the association's consortium schemes because of vandalism and empty properties; but he provided little information on this. The Chief Executive of Bluebell HA had experienced more difficulties: some councillors had been annoyed about the level of rents charged for the new homes. They were higher than the equivalent local authority rents and even families in paid work could not afford them. They were also unhappy about Bluebell HA's new tenants. They knew that it would be years before the local authority could refurbish particular council estates and had mistakenly thought that the new houses would be available for local council tenants/their constituents. (No meetings had ever been arranged to discuss how these new properties would be let.) Unfortunately, most local council tenants had low priority on the local authority's housing register because they were not in serious housing need. They could not be nominated to Bluebell HA because of this, whether or not local councillors were supporting them. (See Chapter Three for the neighbourhood Housing Managers' views about nominations and rehousing.)

Tulip HA seemed to have experienced the most difficulty with councillors. The Vice-Chair felt that councillors had often been unsupportive of the association's work. One had refused to intervene to support Tulip HA in relation to a disputed site in an area of the city where they had wanted to build homes. The local authority earmarked the site for the association but a local Muslim group also wanted it, to build a community centre. The Vice-Chair remarked that the local white councillor chose to "sit on the fence" rather than intervene in the ensuing public row between two black organisations.

The Chief Executive of Tulip HA felt that, where councillors are involved, "the biggest cause of friction is over who gets housed". He believed that local Pakistani elders had learnt how to use the political system to their advantage and engage the support of the two local Pakistani councillors (see Chapter Four for similar remarks from the Contract Manager). This had produced considerable difficulties for staff when councillors promised Tulip HA houses to their constituents (Chief Executive and Senior Housing Officer). Of the three housing associations, Tulip HA was closest to the local black and Asian communities. This had its advantages, but it also led to difficult contradictions when the local councillors tried to exercise undue influence.

Tulip HA's Chief Executive believed that local authority nominations were "a complete and utter shambles" because of councillor influence over neighbourhood office Managers across the city. He believed that some Managers would give an applicant a high-priority nomination when a councillor was supporting them – regardless of whether or not they merited it. He emphasised that Tulip HA staff assessed applicants independently, sometimes giving a much lower priority to high-priority council nominees. Consequently, they would not be rehoused and instead lingered on the waiting list. This led to difficulties for the association as neighbourhood office Managers and councillors expected high-priority nominations to be rehoused quickly.

It is worth noting that Foxglove HA, on occasion, did exactly the same thing. However, they included an explanation when the nominations were returned to the neighbourhood office, especially in relation to homeless women who had left violent men. They had not faced the same difficulties as Tulip HA.

Women might find it difficult to get help from some councillors. This was not surprising given research to date (Charles with Jones, 1993; Malos et al, 1993), but it raised a wider question about political representation. Why was it that councillors failed to pursue the issue of women's safety in their concerns about some of the consortium housing estates that had been built by these associations? It was surprising that this appeared never to have been raised, given that the authority had a domestic violence policy and homeless women were being nominated to associations. Councillors seemed to be focused on the concerns of established residents and local groups. Possibly the nature of local politics was such that some councillors had to seriously consider where their political support would come from in the next local election. Davies pointed out some time ago that

> It is of the essence of intra-ward politics to be able to claim credit for everything and to permit no rivals for public esteem. (Davies, 1972, quoted in Malpass and Murie, 1987, p 218)

Rehousing homeless women (and the associated issue of domestic violence) were potentially controversial issues. Women who had left violent men were stigmatised by the general public, especially within particular communities. Councillors might not be willing to support women publicly, fearing the antagonism of established interests.

Domestic violence policies and 'good practice'

The local authority's domestic violence policy had deliberately made little reference to the work of housing associations. This was a lost opportunity in terms of local authority 'enabling' since it might have encouraged associations' own policy and practice development. It would also have 'raised the profile' of safety issues generally in consortium housing schemes. The NFHA had published a 'good practice' guide *Women and violence at home* (Davis, 1993) but the Housing Corporation had not been in a position to include reference to it in the 'Performance Expectations' at that time. Developing domestic violence policies within associations remained a discretionary activity.

Reasons other than rational ones precipitated policy development (or attempted policy development) in the three case study associations: political opportunity, personal interest and managerial panic. None of the associations had started to develop a formal policy because of the numbers of women they were rehousing in these circumstances. None of the senior staff in any of the associations knew about the local authority's policy on domestic violence and surprisingly few had heard about the NFHA's 'good practice' guide. The senior staff were not aware of the increasing numbers of women who were being rehoused by the local authority because of domestic violence and were unaware that many might be nominated to consortium housing estates as priority homeless applicants.

I. Bluebell HA – a policy in construction

In theory, any member of Bluebell HA's staff could write its policy documents. The Chief Executive believed that there was always the opportunity for "a talented individual" to contribute in this way. There was no tradition of establishing working groups or teams to undertake various aspects of the process. Indeed, the Chief Executive HA had written most of the policies in Bluebell. Occasionally, other senior staff had written them too. Draft policy documents usually had to be considered in staff meetings (sometimes several times) before being considered by the relevant Management Sub-Committee.

The way this meritocracy worked in Bluebell HA was illustrated by what happened to the 'proto' domestic violence policy. A Housing Officer had started work on drafting a policy in 1996 on her own initiative. Although personally interested in the issue, she had not done this sort of work before and the process proved more time-consuming than she had anticipated. She presented a draft to a staff meeting, received a number of comments that had to be followed up and then ran into difficulties. Although she tried to complete the policy, the draft was eventually abandoned because of other work pressures. This was not surprising as she had to fit this around her main Housing Officer work.

Her task had not been made any easier by only having partial information. She knew about the local authority's policy but did not know that the NFHA had produced a 'good practice' guide (Davis, 1993). Ironically, the Chief Executive knew about the NFHA guide but did not know that any work had been undertaken to create a policy in Bluebell HA! Clearly, information had not been passed to him by senior staff in housing management (possibly because the policy had not been completed). This was another example of poor communication in the association to which senior staff themselves had contributed.

The reality of relying on individual efforts (without giving individuals formal organisational backing or power) was evident in the fate of the draft domestic violence policy. Senior staff knew that abandonment was a common fate of draft policies unless a Committee had specifically requested a piece of work. Nevertheless, they were not prepared to take on the task of writing the domestic violence policy once the initial work faltered. In practical terms, researching and writing formal policy documents required an individual staff member to have time, knowledge, persistence and power. The reality was that most staff in Bluebell HA (including senior staff) had too many other, more immediate, demands on their time to voluntarily take on researching and writing unsolicited policy documents.

2. Foxglove HA – a formal policy

Foxglove HA had a formal harassment policy that had been agreed in 1992, and which included dealing with domestic violence. There were two themes that emerged in considering the way policy had been developed. The first was the way in which domestic violence was incorporated into the harassment policy. This was an example of an issue initially being perceived as marginal but through bureaucratic manoeuvring becoming mainstream and acceptable within the association's waiting list priorities. Second, the experience of Foxglove HA also showed how waiting-list priorities could change, given changing circumstances. In this instance, the association's operating environment and changing organisational priorities strongly influenced definitions of 'housing need'. It later proved difficult to defend the status of 'harassment' including domestic violence in the longer term.

The first work on devising a harassment policy had been started in 1990 when Foxglove HA came under external pressure from the Housing Corporation to change its waiting list priorities (Business Support Manager, Head Office). The Corporation wanted associations to rehouse more homeless people (see Chapter One). A review team was established to come up with a solution. This was a rational approach to the possibly contentious issue of reconciling existing waiting-list priorities with new ones. A Business Support Manager at the Head Office recalled that there was some feeling at the time that new priorities were being forced onto the association by the Housing Corporation, which had a wider political agenda. The association was now expected to prioritise homelessness although it had never done so before. It developed a formal policy and procedures in relation to harassment, as part of its response to homelessness.

The association's Equal Opportunities Advisor at its head office had been part of the review team. She explained that she had helped to ensure that domestic violence was linked to a broad definition of harassment because she knew that senior staff wanted "an equal opportunities slant" in the new waiting-list priorities. 'Harassment' generally had more provenance at that time than 'domestic violence', partly because associations were monitored by the Housing Corporation on their policy and practice in relation to dealing with racial harassment. Had domestic violence been proposed as a separate 'housing need' category, the review group would not have given it the same priority. In this way, external political pressure created an opportunity in which domestic violence could be accepted as a priority for rehousing. But it only had contingent status, and this later became a problem (discussed in Chapter Five).

A copy of the harassment policy (and associated procedures) was kept in the procedure manuals for lettings and estate management in each area office. As far as domestic violence was concerned, its key features were that 'a supportive and positive approach' and a 'victim-centred approach' should be offered to each woman applicant. Applicants were to be offered an interviewer of the same sex and ethnic origin where possible. 'Evidence' was not required to award priority. In addition, a 'harassment pack' was made available for staff use.

Just as in the local authority, it became clear after a short time that there were problems with the policy. By 1995 Head Office realised that some area offices were having difficulties. The main problem was that the housing application form asked applicants to tick a box showing their main reason for rehousing. Many ticked the 'harassment' box (possibly because it attracted very high points). This meant that the lettings staff (as they were then) prioritised the application for a Housing Officer visit. When applicants were visited at home to discuss their circumstances, it became clear to Housing Services Officers that many were experiencing simple neighbour disputes – not racial or other harassment. This had created bad feeling between the letting staff and Housing Services Officers. The Housing Services Officers officers thought these visits were unnecessary and a waste of their time.

In this bureaucratically run association, there was a need for consistency and the minimum of disruption to procedures. Rather than alter the boxes to be ticked (with more information for applicants), however, the process was changed. Staff were instructed to ask applicants who ticked the 'harassment' box to provide further details on a new separate sheet ('the harassment assessment form'). In effect, women who had left domestic violence were now being asked to write about it in detail for the approval of the lettings staff.[2] The application was to be held in 'pending' until the second form was completed and returned. The housing application would then be awarded the appropriate points (on a provisional basis) and join the waiting list for visits by Housing Services Officers. It is worth pointing out that women leaving violent men had not generated this problem. Rather, domestic violence had been caught up in the confusion between neighbour disputes and racial harassment.

Foxglove HA's Equal Opportunities Advisor justified this change of procedure: Foxglove HA had to be satisfied about the women's circumstances (to be fair to other applicants) and had to be convinced that a move would resolve the problem (internal memorandum, June 1995). This represented the re-establishment of the bureaucratic needs of the association (consistency through 'proof' or evidence) and professional judgement (staff deciding whether a woman would benefit from rehousing) in preference to the acceptance of the legitimacy of the woman's understanding of her situation. This new approach created difficulties for some women who had no 'proof' but an urgent need for rehousing. It also contradicted the NFHA 'good practice' advice.

The Equal Opportunities Advisor thought that, in the near future, women would be asked for evidence of domestic violence. She acknowledged that some women did not like writing these details down, but believed it was "unrealistic" to expect staff to personally interview each woman to obtain a detailed statement. The trend in the association was to move to a more telephone-based service.

> "The issue is time…. If something is not practical it is not going to be used at all. Women may visit an office personally if *you're* lucky. Staff may have a few minutes if *she's* lucky. The emphasis now is on getting information on the telephone or through an application form. So staff need guidance on how to ask the right questions and get the right information from applicants. They need to know what to ask applicants to supply." (Equal Opportunities Advisor, Foxglove HA)

There would be more emphasis on turnover (that is, getting answers quickly) than on process, or, as Clarke and Newman put it:

> Where need was once the product of the intersection of bureaucratic categorisation and professional judgement, it is now increasingly articulated with and *disciplined by* a managerial calculus of resources and priorities. (Clarke and Newman, 1997, p 76)

Women have found personal interviews difficult especially when they have been conducted insensitively (Binney et al, 1981; Mama, 1989; Malos et al, 1993). It was likely that standard questions on the telephone from an unknown member of staff or standard questions on a housing application form would act as another deterrent to women applying for housing. This was an example of the management needs of the association dominating considerations of sensitivity or propriety. It might also become another example of an association effectively transferring costs elsewhere. Women might abandon their application to Foxglove HA and instead apply to landlords with a more 'human' approach. This was a practice that was identified in Chapter Three, where local authority views of association practice were considered in detail.

3. Tulip HA – no policy yet

The situation in Tulip HA in relation to policy development was different again. All of the existing policies in the association were being reviewed. Where the senior management team identified a 'gap', new policies would be written. The Housing Manager planned a greater emphasis on "customer care" than in the past.

Work on writing a domestic violence policy was planned but the timetable seemed to be largely arbitrary and a reactive response to a specific complaint that had been received from the local authority. The Vice-Chair thought that it was likely that the Board would be receptive to a domestic violence policy although most of the Board members were black men. She felt that they understood race issues but did not understand domestic violence. However "as liberal men they might be guilt-tripped into accepting a domestic violence policy". The Vice-Chair believed that the Housing Services Committee would be harder to convince because they tended to get too "bogged down" in detail. Attendance at meetings had also been poor over the previous year: a number had been inquorate. None of this suggested speedy progress, and it seemed likely that, once local authority attention moved away, other more urgent issues would come to the fore.

Producing a domestic violence policy would have helped staff since it would have established guidelines for what was expected. As it was, they responded in ways they felt to be appropriate. They had all received domestic violence 'awareness' training (from a member of the Board), but it had not been housing-specific. Staff had no idea how to relate the content of the training to their own jobs. This meant that they would continue to find this work stressful and complicated, and decisions about housing applications would not necessarily be made coherently or consistently (see Chapters Five and Six).

The relationship with the local authority

When a woman who was homeless (or about to become homeless) approached the case study associations, she would have received different responses from staff because of the different pressures they worked under. Local authority staff had complained that association staff did very little in terms of giving advice and help to people, and although this seemed to be the case the reasons became clearer: senior staff expected frontline staff to reduce the amount of time they took in interviewing applicants and tenants. One result of this was that most staff told women to go to the local authority for help; they did not refer people to any other organisations for help or advice. They were not familiar with most of them. The pressure to reach nomination targets also strongly influenced this tendency. Again, the local authority staff had remarked on this but did not appreciate the pressure that some association staff were under to reach targets, especially with the new consortium estates.

There was a very strong emphasis in Bluebell HA and Tulip HA on insisting that all their applicants got a nomination from the local authority. For example, Bluebell HA included a covering letter with their housing application which told applicants that a nomination was "essential" if they were to have any chance of being rehoused. In reality, this was not strictly true: a woman with children needed a nomination more than a single woman because the demand for family housing was higher than that for housing for single people. However, a different picture was presented by Foxglove HA. In its literature to applicants, the association mentioned nominations from the local authority as a route to its housing, but did not emphasise it. The Area Director commented that the association "struggled" to reach its nominations targets each year. This was reflective of very weak links between the association and the local authority's staff generally.

The relationship with the local authority revealed another aspect of housing management: there was minimal understanding among association frontline staff about how the homeless legislation worked. There was even a lack of knowledge about who actually dealt with homelessness in the local authority. The staff in Bluebell HA sent women to the central homeless teams. They did this because they thought that women would get a better service there than in the neighbourhood offices. The staff in Tulip HA and Customer Services Officers in Foxglove HA told women to go to the central teams because they mistakenly thought that the homeless service was centralised. They did not know that the local neighbourhood offices provided a service to homeless families. This clearly indicated the poor level of knowledge and training in relation to homelessness in these two associations. No staff formally referred a woman – or checked to make sure that she had arrived as had been recommended as good practice (Davis, 1993).

Women's dependent position and lack of choice were reinforced in these arrangements. Even as tenants of the association, or if wanting to apply to an association rather than the local authority, they were obliged to approach the local authority to obtain the required nomination. This was especially the case where they had dependent children: because of the demand for particular areas and the infrequency with which vacancies occurred within them. It was clear that the local authority's Contract Manager was accurate about associations making women "jump through hoops" to obtain a nomination rather than helping them directly (see Chapter Three). Attention to individual applicants' needs and liaison with other organisations was also suffering because of competing stronger priorities for Housing Officers' time. The local authority was being expected to take on these responsibilities. This was possible because unlike

> [private] companies vying for consumer loyalty, customers of one [social housing] service will also be customers of another; and that, especially for stretched services, far from seeking to *retain* customers, they may wish – and plan – to pass them on. (Harrow and Shaw, 1992, p 120)

Conclusion

Rehousing more homeless people coincided with that period in the history of housing associations when they were becoming very competitive and concerned about costs and risks. This permeated the housing management service in a myriad of ways – service organisation, the nature of housing management jobs, the time spent with applicants and tenants, and relationships with other housing organisations including the local authority. In Bluebell and Tulip HAs, staff were positive about their association's strategy of rehousing more homeless people. This was not the case in Foxglove HA, however, where only political expediency had led to homelessness being prioritised in the waiting list. The position of frontline staff in all the associations paralleled that of the Estate Management Officers in the local authority neighbourhood offices. They all had other priorities which senior management regarded as more important because of the overwhelming pressure to be efficient, reduce costs and maximise income.

It was clear that frontline staff in the associations actually spent most of their time dealing with what may be called the overt social control elements of housing management. Apart from making their jobs particularly unattractive, they were also less likely to want to deal with any complex problems which new tenants might bring with them. The housing managers reacted personally in different ways to these changes. In Bluebell and Tulip HAs, they were concerned about this trend, while the Team Leader in Foxglove HA was not. He was happy with the increased control he had over staff workloads that the new computerised management system in the association now gave him. It also meant that Housing Services Officers in Foxglove HA had even clearer 'cut-off' points than their equivalents in the other two associations.

'Customer care' terminology was commonplace in the interviews with housing management staff – even in Bluebell HA where the Chief Executive was dismissive about the ideology's value. The obvious question that might be asked in relation to this was whether 'customer care' actually masked deteriorating services for applicants and tenants? It did not appear that homeless women who had left domestic violence *would* be treated like 'customers' with a 'choice' – it was not clear *what* it meant in a housing management context. It seemed more likely that women were being treated as 'supplicants' (Lambert et al, 1978). This issue will be explored in more detail in the next three chapters.

Notes

[1] Taylorism was a form of factory work organisation commonplace in the early part of the 20th century. Processes were mechanised and human (worker) involvement routinised and timed in such detail that there was little difference between humans and machines in the quest for greater 'efficiency' and profit.

[2] Subsequently, the lettings staff were made redundant in the re-organisation of Foxglove HA. Their jobs were absorbed by the new Customer Services Officers (that is, non-specialists).

FIVE

Applying for association housing

Introduction

All of the housing associations in this study had offices in one particular area of
the city where the city's large African Caribbean and Pakistani communities, as
well as many other minority ethnic communities, could be found. The offices
had been there for a long time: Foxglove HA over 15 years; Bluebell and Tulip
HAs over 10 years each. Having a local office had been regarded as important
from the 1970s onwards. Associations could provide services in an easily
accessible way: the assumption was that many applicants and tenants would call
into the office personally (NFHA, 1987; Housing Corporation, 1989). There
had also been an expectation from the early 1980s onwards that the ethnic
origin of staff would reflect that of the areas in which associations worked.
This would show a willingness to provide an appropriate and fair service (NFHA,
1982, 1983; Housing Corporation, 1989). How associations provided an
accessible and appropriate service in this multi-ethnic location was a key theme
in the analysis of the process of applying for housing. The findings here illustrate
the complexities involved. They provide evidence of the need for some
associations to seriously review their race equality strategies (an especially
pertinent issue following the 2002 Race Relations Amendment Act).

In general terms, 'customer care' was emphasised rather than fairness or diversity
in service provision. In Foxglove and Tulip HAs, 'customer care' had been
introduced ostensibly to usher in a more responsive approach to 'customers'
(that is, applicants and tenants). The 'customer care' ideology had not yet officially
penetrated Bluebell HA. The Chief Executive believed it had little to offer the
association because services to applicants and tenants were already of a high
standard (and this had been confirmed in a recent tenant survey).

Potter (1987) identified a number of elements that provided the 'structural
underpinning' of this consumerist approach including 'access', 'choice' and
'information'. The implications of these will be examined in detail in this
chapter.

The first part of this chapter looks at the nature of the services provided to
people when they approached the association. It evaluates the service provided
by customer services and Duty Officer teams to applicants and tenants. The
reception service in each association was observed on two separate occasions,
each for three hours, on days that were known to be busy. A number of themes
were identified from these observations that had particular relevance for homeless
women who had left violence.

The second and main part of this chapter considers the initial stage of the housing application process. There were two sources of data for this:

- information given to applicants and the application form itself;
- interviews with particular staff about their work in this setting (Bluebell HA: Housing Officers and the waiting-list staff; Foxglove HA: Customer Services Team Leader; Tulip HA: Housing Officers and the Housing Services Administrator).

How helpful could staff be?

Reception services: enquiries and applications

1. Bluebell HA – The receptionist and the Duty Officer system

In Bluebell HA the Duty Officer system dealt with the majority of enquiries from applicants and tenants. The rota for the Duty Officer job included the Housing Officers and Housing Assistants. Staff included black, Asian and white men and women. Two of the men could speak Urdu and Punjabi; everyone else was limited to English. All were very experienced staff and a number were professionally qualified. Some had previously worked in the local authority's homeless unit (when it had been centralised).

The receptionist welcomed all personal callers and answered all incoming phone calls. In a busy period, every hour she answered about 40 incoming telephone calls and saw nine or ten applicants and tenants who called into the office. Contractors, staff from other associations, and Committee members also called in, so the actual number of visitors was higher than this. A recent tenant survey had shown that 75% of those responding (who represented 61% of the association's tenants) had contacted the association by telephone only in the previous year. Most personal visitors lived locally and the majority of callers were black or Asian people. The receptionist worked to the association's rule that nobody had to wait more than 10 minutes to see a Duty Officer. When a person appeared upset or unhappy, she called the 'back-up' Duty Officer to come and see them as quickly as possible. (Some Housing Officers were easier to persuade to do this than others in this situation. It all depended on their workload.)

Most personal callers were black and Asian women, often accompanied by their children. Most could speak English, especially if they were younger men or women. Older Asian women relied on other relatives or their own children to translate or send messages. Edwards (1995) remarked that women's reliance on other family members to translate might prove problematic if they had to find help to leave a violent husband (see Chapter Seven for further discussion of this point). Staff had access to an interpreting service if they needed it.

Any applicant or tenant who needed help was referred to the Duty Officer: to make rent payments, to report a repair, to talk about a housing application or to complain about a neighbour. (Housing Officers were expected to deal with queries from their own tenants when they were in the office.) All personal callers were interviewed in private in one of three interview rooms. Most interviews seemed to last between 15 and 20 minutes (though rent payments were dealt with in a few minutes). In one period, the Duty Officer moved from one interview to the next without a break over a period of two hours. In the tenant survey, 88% of those who had called in over the previous year remarked how friendly the reception service was in the association.

2. Foxglove HA – Customer services teams

Foxglove HA's area office provided a different example of organising reception services. The association had established new customer services teams in its area offices. They all wore distinctive and smart uniforms. The four Customer Services Officers were expected to provide a service to all applicants, tenants and members of the public. They did this via the seven telephone lines, or personally when people called in. They dealt with housing applications or arrears (up to a certain level), ordered day-to-day repairs, and answered any other queries that arose. (Tenants paid their rent at a post office or through their bank.) They could pass complicated queries to Housing Services Officers but were under great pressure to handle everything themselves.

At any one time, two Customer Services Officers worked at the public counter that faced into the reception area. There was a perspex screen between staff and all visitors. Two seats were pulled up to the counter on the public's side (separated by a narrow perspex divider) so that conversations could be held sitting down. The screen had been installed five months previously after two minor incidents. There was a security camera trained on to the counter area that could be viewed on monitors upstairs. This was the only association that had such visible security/protection measures in place.

Each of the Customer Services Officers was white. This was reflective of the staffing of the housing management service based in this area office (where all staff were white except a temporary Asian Housing Services Officer). This was unexceptional historically. Nobody in the office spoke any other language but English. A translating service contracted by the association nationally was available by telephone, when required.

The customer services team had been operational for nine months. The four officers dealt with on average 40 incoming or outgoing telephone calls per hour. Most telephone calls were concerned with repairs. Others included applications, rent account queries or calls for particular members of staff. Application enquiries were straightforward requests for information about where Foxglove HA had property, the likelihood of vacancies occurring, visit arrangements to view particular areas or properties, or details of a new housing scheme. Each call was dealt with quickly.

Incoming telephone calls (taken via a headset) usually took precedence over personal callers. The Customer Services Officers automatically spoke to the telephone caller in the middle of conversations they were having with personal visitors to the office. Personal callers had to wait, with no explanation or apology. On average, five tenants/applicants called into the office each hour. Most were white women with a small number of African Caribbean women. No Asian men or women visited the office. Contractors and other staff also called in. Staff spent longer with personal visitors than enquirers by telephone.

Most people who visited the area office came at different times during the day; it would have been impossible to maintain confidentiality otherwise. Several people lowered their voices when speaking through the screen. None were offered a private interview. The one interviewing room adjacent to the front door was not used in either of the two observation periods.

3. Tulip HA – Customer Services Officers and Duty Officers

Two Customer Services Officers worked on the reception counter of Tulip HA. One concentrated on requests for repairs while the other dealt with application queries. They took rent payments across the counter. Both were Asian women: one spoke English and Punjabi, while the other spoke English, Urdu, Punjabi and Batwari. The Customer Services Officer dealing with applications was helped by the Housing Services Administrator. She worked in an office behind the reception area and helped out when the other staff were very busy, or a more detailed and private interview was required. She spoke English, Urdu and Punjabi.

A Duty Officer system was in place, staffed by the Housing Officers on a rota basis. At that time, the Housing Officers were a black woman, an Asian man (who spoke Urdu and Gujarati) and a white woman. One was professionally qualified. The Duty Officer dealt with complicated enquiries including those from tenants of the other Housing Officers if they were not in the office. The duty officer system was not always available. Some staff did not keep their allotted rota time free of external appointments.

The Customer Services Officers dealt with about 25 incoming or outgoing telephone calls each hour. About one third were repairs queries and nearly as many again were for specific staff. Only four were about housing applications. The Officer who dealt mainly with applications said this was an unusually low number of application enquiries. Six applicants and tenants called in each hour. Most were black. Only three were unaccompanied women: the immediate area around the office had a reputation for mugging and women may have been reluctant to call in by themselves. Personal visitors usually called in about housing applications and offers or to report repairs. Application enquiries took the most time. The Customer Services Officers answered enquiries across the reception counter. They pointed out that they could not provide private interviews (even though the Housing Manager wanted them to) because they had to answer the telephones, speak to personal callers and help each other provide the service in the reception. Private interviews were available with the

Housing Services Administrator or Duty Officer using the three interviewing rooms.

Reception services: discussion of issues

The way the staff were organised

Foxglove and Tulip HAs had recently reorganised their reception services, partly for financial reasons and partly as a response to increasing telephone enquiries. Although the same trend was evident in Bluebell HA, this association had yet to consider restructuring the reception service (although the staff dealt with far more enquiries in person and by telephone than the other two associations).

The way in which the reception service was provided in the three associations in this study affected the working relationships that were possible between staff, applicants and tenants. This was particularly important in considering what kind of service homeless women might receive. For example, the Duty Officer systems in Bluebell HA and Tulip HA were staffed with Housing Officers. Their aim was to provide a knowledgeable service to tenants or applicants who called in or telephoned. This system complemented the patch system of housing management and it presumed that there was a body of knowledge and experience which staff needed in order to manage people and property appropriately. Duty Officer staff provided private interviews without question. Interviews of this kind took time, but women with complicated problems at least might feel that they were being listened to and perhaps helped.

Customer services staff in Foxglove and Tulip HAs were actually reception staff with extra responsibilities – usually minor repairs ordering and the first stage of the application process. They had no experience or knowledge of managing social housing. It was clear that providing customer services staff instead of Housing Officers to respond to callers was cheaper and thus entirely in keeping with senior management concerns to reduce overheads and/or control costs (especially staffing costs). To make it possible for customer services staff to provide the service, the expectations of that service had to change. For example, the possibility of private interviews (which might take longer) had to be minimised. The level of advice expected to be given by staff also had to be standardised and reduced in scope (to suit the grade of staff and to save time).

Senior management presumed that customer services staff could deal with most straightforward enquiries so that Housing Officers could chase arrears and so on. In reality, the enquiries which they dealt with in Foxglove and Tulip HAs were sometimes complicated and training had been inadequate or non-existent. They could answer simple enquiries (such as the whereabouts of a particular housing scheme) but could not deal with more complex situations (for example, involving harassment and violence). This problem did not arise in Bluebell HA. Its Duty Officer rota was made up of experienced staff who could respond to applicants and tenants who were in difficulty. Their only problem was whether they had time to do so properly. Unfortunately, the same could not be said with confidence of Tulip HA's Duty Officer service since its staff were mainly young and inexperienced. The issue here was the lack of guidelines for staff and appropriate training and support. Each of these were senior management responsibilities.

Staffing – ethnicity and gender

Since the early 1980s, associations had been urged to become fair employers (NFHA, 1982). This was particularly relevant for the associations in this study because of the location of their offices and their housing stock. There were particular employment issues associated with providing an appropriate service to women who had experienced domestic violence.

Foxglove HA employed white staff. Very few black people had ever worked in its area office. This was surprising given staff turnover and the recent reorganisation. Bluebell HA employed Asian, black and white staff in housing management, the most senior being the Housing Manager who was an Asian man. At the time of the research, no Asian women were employed despite a number of efforts to publicise vacancies widely. Tulip HA, the black association, employed more Asian and black housing management staff than Bluebell HA. The most senior position in housing management was the Housing Manager's post, which was held by an Asian man. The Vice-Chair of the association remarked that it had been essential to recruit Asian and black staff to housing management – not least because it was the most public part of the association's service.

Employing Asian, black and white staff in the reception area opened up the possibility of women having a choice of interviewer to talk to about their difficulties. This had come to be recognised as 'good practice' in interviewing. The NFHA's 'good practice' guide (Davis, 1993) had suggested that associations should offer to 'match' the interviewee and interviewer by gender and ethnic origin in these circumstances. The Code of Guidance had recommended a "same sex interviewer wherever possible" in situations involving domestic violence (DoE, 1996, para 11.4). It might put a woman at ease if she felt that she shared some common ground with her interviewer. There were, of course, a number of caveats to this. For example, 'women' do not have shared perspectives on male violence, though as importantly, the Code also recommended that interviewers should preferably be "trained specifically in dealing with circumstances of this kind" (DoE, 1996, para 11.4). Could the case study associations offer a choice of interviewer to women?

The associations varied in this. Having a formal policy which included offering a choice of interviewer did not necessarily mean that 'street-level' practice reflected it (Blau, 1963; Lipsky, 1980). Foxglove HA had a harassment policy that expected staff to offer ethnically and gender 'matched' interviews. As all the Customer Services Officers in the area office in this study were white women, this could only partially be achieved. Both Bluebell HA and Tulip HA could offer a choice of interviewer, but gender and ethnic 'matching' was more limited in Bluebell HA because there were no Asian women members of staff. Male Asian housing staff might not be acceptable as interviewers. Women might be reluctant to speak to men for fear of criticism, or because of worries about their address being passed to family members, shame and embarrassment (Mama, 1989; Rai and Thiara, 1997). This was not always the case. One Pakistani Muslim woman interviewed for this research had found it acceptable to be interviewed in Punjabi by a male Indian Sikh Housing Officer. She had been accompanied by an English-speaking Hostel Support Worker. There had been some difficulties with *language* differences rather than gender differences but these had been overcome satisfactorily at that time (see Chapter Seven).

The possibility of women having a choice of interviewer was not advertised in any of the associations. Women had to take the initiative and ask (the 'supplicant' role). Staff might also use their own judgement in particular interviews. If a woman was clearly reluctant to speak or was embarrassed or distressed, a male interviewer might suggest a female colleague take his place. Male Housing Officers in all the case study associations mentioned this possibility. However, staff in Bluebell and Tulip HAs also identified issues about good interviewing which went beyond simple 'matching', for example the importance of shared language and culture, the impact of kinship networks on the interview, and the proximity of the 'community' on women's perceptions of safety and privacy.

Languages other than English

Employing multilingual staff who spoke the main community languages (Bengali, Sylheti, Punjabi and Urdu) was particularly important for those whose first language was not English. Tulip HA, the black association, was the best able to respond in this way given the number of languages which staff spoke between them, although no one spoke Bengali or Sylheti. In Bluebell HA, the Housing Manager spoke Urdu and a Housing Officer spoke Urdu and Punjabi (as an Indian Sikh). This was not entirely satisfactory for women who spoke Punjabi and came from Pakistan because words and dialect were different. The woman who had been interviewed in this way said that she could 'just about' understand the Housing Officer (see Chapter Seven). Bluebell HA staff could also ask staff at a local interpreting service to help.

The situation in Foxglove HA was completely different. Foxglove HA staff appeared to be unaware or indifferent to the difficulties in obtaining information and services which people are likely to experience if they do not speak English (Modood et al, 1997). Senior managers referred to the association's telephone interpreting service when asked about language provision, although they thought it had been little used. There was nobody in the office who spoke any of the main community languages in the area. The Customer Services Officer did not think that language differences created any difficulties for people approaching them: if someone did not speak English, the staff could use the telephone service. She recalled that it had been "very, very useful" on the few occasions she had used it for repairs queries. Usually, Asian callers were asked to bring a friend to translate. She recalled that on one occasion an Asian man had asked a passer-by in the street to translate for him. This was recalled as an example of the straightforward way in which these situations were handled.

Few arrangements were in place at this time to make any of the associations more accessible to women who were blind/partially sighted or deaf/partially deaf. Nobody signed and only Foxglove HA had a minicom system in place. However, staff were not familiar with how it worked and it had hardly been used since its installation. Nor had any of the associations provided larger type information for applicants.

It appeared that the largest and most financially secure association in this study was very distant from non-English speakers and the local black and Asian communities. Its policy emphasised accessibility but practice revealed a different picture. This was mainly because its recruitment practice had been such that there were no multilingual and/or black and Asian staff in post. The nature of the reception service provided was not very welcoming to *anyone* because of the emphasis on answering the telephone and the physical environment of the office itself. In particular, however, it lacked warmth to people who did not speak English. By default non-English speakers were effectively being channelled elsewhere, especially to Tulip HA.

Staffing – employing local people

Recruiting Asian and black staff had also been promoted as a way of fostering a greater sense of connection between associations and local Asian and black communities. None of the associations engaged in 'housing plus' initiatives, but some staff (especially black and Asian staff who lived locally and who worked in Bluebell HA and Tulip HA) were actively involved in other local community organisations and activities in their spare time. Tulip HA was anxious to develop these links because its reputation had been undermined by its changing focus to become more 'business-like' (Vice-Chair). Bluebell HA was also anxious about establishing better contacts with local groups and organisations because it wanted to improve access to its housing for Asian applicants (Director of Housing). Foxglove HA was the exception. None of its housing management staff lived locally or were involved in local organisations. Some senior staff were not concerned, although the recently-arrived Area Director was more open to this as the association's Area Plan had emphasised more local involvement.

Links between staff and local community organisations usually had positive effects, but this was not always the case. Staff in Tulip HA raised this issue, possibly because they experienced some of these contradictions first-hand. However mistakenly, women were sometimes reluctant to approach staff who lived locally. They feared the possible negative effects of kinship and friendship networks on the help they might receive. They worried that their private circumstances would become public knowledge or that their social standing would be undermined. For example, one African Caribbean woman was a Housing Officer in Tulip HA. She was a member of one of the large extended families in the area but had been approached only rarely by other African Caribbean women about personal problems due to violence. Local African Caribbean women talked to the Asian Housing Services Administrator who did not live in the immediate area. The most acceptable arrangement for women seemed to be a sympathetic but clear professional distance between the association's staff and local women applicants. Clearly, 'matching' a staff member's gender and ethnic origin with that of the applicant to undertake an interview was more complicated than had originally been conceived in 'best practice'.

Privacy

Given the danger and difficulty that many women faced when making arrangements to leave their home or to find another one, the importance of privacy to discuss their situation could not be over-emphasised. All the case study associations had private interviewing rooms: Bluebell HA and Tulip HA had three each. Foxglove HA had only one, a reflection perhaps that it expected many of its more widely geographically dispersed tenants (and applicants) to telephone rather than visit the area office. Tulip HA was the only association that had rooms that could not be overseen by others. Bluebell HA and Foxglove HA had rooms with clear glass windows and partly-glazed doors. This was to allow more light in and in Bluebell HA allowed the reception staff a clear view of what was happening. Unfortunately, these design features afforded women little privacy: they could be seen even if they could not be heard. A partner or ex-partner (or one of their friends) might see her there so a woman could not be sure of being entirely safe in these office environments.

Bluebell HA was the only association that arranged private interviews automatically. In Tulip HA, people had to ask for a private interview, but it was not unusual and Housing Officers and the Housing Services Administrator usually offered one. Foxglove HA was different: the association's formal harassment policy indicated that people in these circumstances should be interviewed privately. However, private interviews in the area office in this study appeared to be unusual. The Customer Services Officers preferred to conduct 'interviews' with applicants through the perspex screens in the reception area. There was no privacy and it was not safe practice for women. But it went further than that. For example, an elderly African Caribbean woman wanted to move because she was being racially harassed in her council home. She was not offered a private interview and had to give an account of her circumstances in public through the screen. She was interrupted twice while the white Customer Services Officer spoke to a telephone caller via her headset and then started to order minor repairs (tasks which could have been handled by a colleague) before returning to talk to her. At another point in this 'interview', the woman found she could not be heard as another Customer Services Officer slammed her telephone down, swearing and complaining loudly about a heating contractor. All of this was a graphic illustration of a point which an Asian member of staff in Tulip HA had made: many black and Asian women were wary of white agencies because they interpreted the lack of time, consideration and sometimes the body language of white staff as racist.

It was recognised in 'good practice' that some women would not talk much when first interviewed because of fear, shame or embarrassment. They might say more to staff at a subsequent interview if they felt safe and believed that they were not going to be criticised (see Chapter Eight). The Housing Services Administrator in Tulip HA remarked that occasionally African Caribbean women were reluctant to give her information. She only obtained these details from 'support letters' accompanying the housing applications, which usually cited depression and anxiety. Women's reticence may have been because they were embarrassed about the violence or because their situation contradicted stereotypes of 'strong' black women. They might also have been worried about being seen as mentally ill (Bryan et al, 1985).

The need for privacy, safety and flexibility had been identified in the NFHA's 'good practice' guide (Davis, 1993) and in the DETR's guide (1999). The DETR guide emphasised the importance of 'flexibility' in application and assessment procedures to ensure that women were not excluded because of initial reticence. In practice, this was acknowledged in both Bluebell HA and Tulip HA. They had flexible application procedures and sympathetic staff. This was not the case in Foxglove HA, however, where the process and the staff lacked flexibility and sensitivity.

It is worth pointing out that telephoning the offices did not necessarily ensure a useful private conversation. The observation sessions revealed that callers who were housing applicants tended to ask straightforward questions (for example, where the association's property was located). Customer Services Officers in Foxglove HA did not expect or encourage applicants to engage in long conversations on the telephone. Applicants were expected to complete application forms themselves. Customer Services Officers in Tulip HA also did not like dealing with details on the telephone, but for a different reason. They positively encouraged telephone callers to visit the office to obtain detailed help with filling in the application form as many of their enquirers were people who were not literate in English or familiar with applying for housing.

Confidentiality

Associations were expected to have policy and procedures that ensured that personal information given to them was kept confidential. If there were exceptions, these had to be identified and applicants told of them in advance (Housing Corporation, 1989, Performance Expectation G3.3). There were two ways of looking at this obligation from the point of view of women who had left violent partners/ex-partners: could confidential personal information be given out to other people by accident or was it available to others on request?

All of the staff interviewed understood how important confidentiality was to women who had left violent partners/ex-partners but what happened in practice sometimes undermined that. The observation sessions revealed that their working environment sometimes acted against them. The pressure to complete telephone calls quickly meant that insufficient care was sometimes paid to issues of confidentiality (see Davis, 1993 and DETR, 1999, for detailed discussion). For example, one Customer Services Officer in Foxglove HA *first* confirmed to a telephone caller that an application was held and *then* asked to whom she was speaking. The caller could have been an ex-partner trying to locate a woman who had left because of violence. This intense focus on answering telephone calls did not occur in Bluebell HA (where the receptionist handled incoming calls as a 'sign-posting' service). It also was not noticeable in Tulip HA, although Customer Services Officers there might be vulnerable to this pressure because their jobs were similar to those in Foxglove HA.

A slightly different situation emerged in the interviews with Bluebell HA staff. Housing management staff understood the need for confidentiality but questioned whether there were any limits to it. In this association, applicants and tenants' confidential details might be passed on in some circumstances for particular organisations. The Director of Housing dealt with requests for information on an ad hoc basis. There *was* a formal written policy in Bluebell HA which said that the personal details of applicants and tenants would be confidential to the association. As it happened, none of the staff who were interviewed were familiar with the written policy. One member of staff who had worked in the association for many years was asked about the confidentiality policy:

> "Yes, there is a confidentiality policy. It's probably kept in somebody's drawer, in a file. Again, it's one of those procedural things which we have, which nobody knows about."

This was another example of a formal policy not being consistently implemented in practice, but the reasons for the difference between formal policy and practice were different here. In Foxglove HA, as in the local authority, formal policies were sometimes not implemented by frontline staff because of different management priorities and a lack of training in relation to domestic violence. The confidentiality policy in Bluebell HA had been written before other organisations (like the police and utilities) had started to approach the association for information about the whereabouts of particular tenants. In some instances, the association was legally obliged to help but that was certainly not always the case. Although the Director of Housing decided what to do on a 'case-by-case' basis, the fact that this was done with no explanation to staff undermined their confidence in relation to undertakings to applicants and tenants about confidentiality generally. As in Foxglove HA (and possibly Tulip HA in certain circumstances), where the pressure of constantly answering the telephone might lead to breaches of the policy's code, keeping people's personal details entirely confidential was not completely assured.

Applying for housing

The application form

Women could apply for housing association accommodation in a number of ways. They could go to an association's office personally and fill in a form there. They could send a form by post. They could be nominated by the local authority and subsequently be sent an application form by the association to complete. Each association had a different form and accompanying information. The information varied in content and quality, some being wordy, out of date or inaccurate (Bluebell HA). None of the associations gave applicants information about completing the form if they needed to be rehoused because of domestic violence.

Bluebell HA and Foxglove HA had translated a short message on the forms into different languages which said that help to fill in the forms was available from staff in the local office. Ironically, this would have proved difficult for both associations. In Foxglove HA, the staff only spoke English, while Bluebell HA could only offer interviews in Punjabi and Urdu without having to employ external interpreters.

Curiously, none of Tulip HA's forms or information was written in different languages. Given that it was a black association, this would have been expected. In fact, association policy was that frontline staff should encourage applicants to visit the office to complete the application forms with staff help. This ensured that many applicants who were not literate in their own languages would obtain sufficient help and provide appropriate information without having to make special arrangements. Practically, it was felt that it was not so important that there were translations about help on the forms although it was recognised that they did have symbolic value. Staff spoke most of the community languages and had access to interpreters for Chinese, Bengali and Sylheti.

Given that research has illustrated the difficulties which women have experienced in talking about domestic violence (Dobash and Dobash, 1979; Binney et al, 1981; Pahl, 1985; Malos et al, 1993), it seemed likely that they would be reluctant to write about it in detail. Generally, the forms and accompanying information did not help women. The forms were not clear about what was required. This illustrated an aspect of the relationship between associations as landlords and women as applicants. Women had very limited information about their position, contrary to Potter's (1988) view of the structural underpinning of 'customer care'. They would have to ask about what was needed or make a number of visits to supply information that the association wanted. Their position seemed to be that of 'supplicants' (Lambert et al, 1978) rather than 'customers' or women with rights (as people who were statutory homeless).

Priority on the waiting list

All of the associations gave a very high priority to applications from people who were homeless because of domestic violence, but only Bluebell HA named 'violence in the home' in its waiting-list priorities. In two associations, domestic violence was included in a broader 'housing need' category. In Foxglove HA, this was 'harassment', and applicants also had to be homeless or about to become homeless to obtain this priority. In Tulip HA it was 'violence/harassment/abuse', but this priority was mainly intended to deal with racial harassment and not domestic violence (the latter had simply been added later). The ways in which domestic violence had been incorporated into pre-existing waiting-list priorities was an indication of the marginality of domestic violence compared to racial harassment in some associations. This was perhaps due to the fact that the Housing Corporation only monitored whether associations had racial harassment policies.

Much work has been completed to understand the nature of the violence which women experience (see the discussion in Dobash and Dobash, 1992). A number of definitions have been suggested to capture the range of behaviour that may be considered violent and/or abusive. However, there appeared to be little of this broad understanding in the case study associations. Staff were familiar with the idea of domestic violence involving physical violence (including sexual violence) but were less clear (or convinced about) the impact of psychological intimidation and abuse. For example, in Foxglove HA, in practice (if not in policy) a woman who was being intimidated or threatened would not be regarded as experiencing domestic violence (or it might not be thought of as sufficiently serious). She had to have left physical violence to be accepted on to the waiting list.

There were some circumstances in which none of the associations would accept an application. The main group of people in this situation (ex-tenants or ex-joint tenants) had rent arrears. This was not surprising given the increasing importance of maximising rental income in associations (Ford and Seavers, 1999). Tulip HA would not accept anyone in this situation because they were considered to be too risky, given the association's financial situation and the current level of arrears. Bluebell HA and Foxglove HA (both of which were larger and financially stronger associations) would only accept applicants with arrears in cases where the debt was being repaid regularly (and there was a strong element of negative discretion attached to this in Foxglove HA, as will be seen in Chapter Six). Associations were ignoring the local authority's formal policy, 'good practice' advice (Davis, 1993; DETR, 1999) and the reality of some women's financial difficulties (Pahl, 1980; Binney et al, 1981; Davis, 1993).

The first stage of assessing the housing application

The three case study associations had two main ways of dealing with housing applications. Bluebell and Tulip HAs employed specialist waiting-list staff to ensure that applications were filled in correctly and registered on the waiting list. The generalist customer services staff did this work in Foxglove HA (the lettings team having been disbanded with the reorganisation). It was difficult to determine which was the most effective way of dealing with the waiting list, although from the point of view of women applicants, specialist trained staff gave more advice to applicants than generalist untrained staff.

The associations used two different schemes to assess applications, one based on points and the other on merit. Bluebell HA's merit scheme was strongly influenced by the local authority's own priorities; therefore, it was not entirely reliant on the discretionary judgement of staff. Previous research identified the problematic influence of personal judgement in merit schemes (Niner, 1985). Women would receive the highest priority in the association as long as the local authority accorded them the highest priority.

Foxglove HA and Tulip HA operated points systems to assess priority. They could give an applicant a priority which could be different from the local authority priority (and the local authority's nomination) in certain circumstances. For example, Foxglove HA might reassess and return an application and nomination to the local authority of a woman who had Group A priority because of homelessness due to domestic violence. The association would not accept the priority nomination had the woman made temporary accommodation arrangements that *they* regarded as secure and a 'solution' to homelessness. (This included a shorthold assured tenancy.) Once again, this revealed the degree of independence which associations had in relation to the local authority and the limitation of the authority's 'enabling' role. Surprisingly, staff judgement also emerged as a significant feature in the points schemes. For example, even in an association with a formal policy (Foxglove HA), staff made judgements about women who had experienced domestic violence. These were based on whether or not a woman had been physically assaulted and whether or not an agency could write a 'support letter'. This was because the 'harassment assessment form' stage had introduced this discretionary element into the assessment procedures (see Chapter Four).

The information required

Each association had slightly different requirements of applicants. Women might be forgiven for becoming frustrated at the prospect of what might be required. A completed application form was essential, and a nomination from the local authority was required in Bluebell HA and Tulip HA (although this was not emphasised in Foxglove HA). In addition to this, Foxglove and Tulip HAs each required extra forms to be completed that, in effect, acted as a sieve for housing applicants: only successful completion of this form, determined through staff judgement, would ensure that the full application was registered. This might be helpful for some women (in Tulip HA), but for others it might seem to be a deterrent (which it was in Foxglove HA).

In Tulip HA the Housing Services Administrator completed an 'initial assessment form' with potential applicants. From these details she was able to calculate the likely points total a person would receive were they to complete the full application form. Women who had experienced domestic violence benefited from this because they were alert to the problem and asked appropriate questions, even when the woman had not initially mentioned violence. The opposite approach was evident in Foxglove HA. Applicants who ticked the 'harassment' box in the housing application form were then sent the 'harassment assessment form'. They had to complete and return it with supporting evidence in the form of 'support letters', copies of injunctions/exclusion orders, and so on. If the 'supporting evidence' was insufficient in the view of the Customer Services Officer, the application would be cancelled. The officers remarked that it was through this that they identified which women were 'genuine' and which women were not.

Support letters, supporting evidence or proof

The extent to which associations could act independently of the local authority was illustrated by the requirement that women provide 'proof' or 'support letters' to supplement their housing applications in Foxglove and Tulip HAs. This applied to women who had been nominated by the local authority with Group A priority as well as direct applicants. In both situations, women would only become aware *after* they had applied that they needed to provide extra information about the violence that they had endured.

Although Foxglove HA's harassment policy emphasised that women should be believed and that proof was not necessary, the 'harassment assessment form' required more details and 'supporting evidence'. The Customer Services Team Leader thought that proof was essential.

> "Regardless of what the policy says, what my problem has always been *and still is* with harassment or with domestic violence is proving it. If we were to believe everybody who claimed it and *especially* if somebody had concocted a story and got rehoused, it spreads like wildfire." (Customer Services Team Leader, Foxglove HA)

A woman needed to send in support letters from agencies to show that she was a 'genuine case'. The Customer Services Officers would not accept letters from relatives or friends (which they believed would be biased). The assumption was that, were a woman 'really serious' about leaving, she would have contacted other organisations for help. Once all this documentation had been received, they would calculate the 'provisional' points total and would register the application on the waiting list. The applicant would then be visited in due course by a Housing Services Officer (see Chapter Six). They would finally decide who was 'genuine' or not (as the Customer Services Team Leader remarked). A woman's application would be cancelled if no supporting evidence was sent in or the form was not completed in sufficient detail or she had experienced threats but no physical violence.

In Foxglove HA there appeared to be no checks on the way in which these staff responded to applicants or handled housing applications. There was certainly no check on cancelled applications. It appeared that there was a formal and an informal policy in Foxglove HA. This situation was reminiscent of the local authority. The importance of the formal policy seemed small compared to the actual practice of Customer Services Officers. There appeared to be few sanctions attached to the policy in cases of it being breached, so they simply used their own judgement when they found situations that were difficult or where they did not believe a particular woman applicant.

In Tulip HA, there was disagreement about whether women should provide proof of violence. The Housing Manager said that it was not necessary but, oddly, he was not the person who made the final decision about priority and allocations. The Senior Housing Officer made these decisions. She was keen on proof, although only about a half of the housing management team agreed with her. The issue of proof was unresolved within the association at the time of the research. In practice, the Housing Service Administrator tried to make sure that women forwarded letters from agencies, relatives or friends.

There were a number of reasons why staff in Foxglove HA and Tulip HA were keen to obtain proof or corroboration of the violence which women had experienced. In Foxglove HA, Customer Services Officers' opinions were reinforced by the association's new requirement to ask for supporting evidence. The Customer Services Officer interviewed in Foxglove HA had little sympathy for women in this situation. She believed they created work when they applied for housing which was then wasted when they returned to the violent partner/ ex-partner. She thought that women often did not tell the truth: they simply wanted the highest priority. Her job was to ensure that the association's waiting-list priorities were not abused. In Tulip HA the Senior Housing Officer worked in a very different and difficult environment. She was also keen to protect the waiting-list priority system from abuse, but at the same time she wanted to protect herself from possible criticism of her decisions (internally from more senior staff or externally from councillors). Requiring proof in the form of support letters, injunctions/exclusion orders and so on was her way of ensuring this protection.

The response of Bluebell HA was different: support letters were not generally required. Senior and frontline staff believed that they were unnecessary and inappropriate. Several staff had previously worked in the local authority's formerly centralised homeless service when the policy had been to ask for proof. One senior Manager recalled how deeply embarrassed she had been when, having asked for evidence, one woman had simply stripped to her bra in front of her revealing an upper body covered in bruises, cuts and burns. The

Manager remarked that she was not potentially going to put any woman or member of staff through that kind of experience by requiring evidence or proof. In this association, a woman would only be asked to provide extra corroboration in rare situations where there were very strong doubts about what she had told them. The staff in Bluebell HA erred on the side of the woman because they believed that to do otherwise ran the risk of their being wrong and possibly seriously jeopardising a woman's safety. Staff here also realised the impact such demands had on women and on hard-pressed 'support' agencies. Senior staff in the other two associations did not have that experience or awareness.

Conclusion

Associations were not statutorily responsible for homelessness and did not have to work to the priorities contained within the homeless legislation. Most staff had not received training on domestic violence or, if they had, it was not specific enough to directly apply to their jobs. Very few staff in the case study associations knew about the local authority's domestic violence policy or the NFHA 'good practice' guide. So how could the differences in the initial approach of the case study associations be accounted for?

It might have been anticipated that the most sympathetic association would have been the one which had developed a formal policy in relation to domestic violence. However, this did not turn out to be the case. In the main, the differences seemed to hinge on the personal influence of senior staff (or lack of it) rather than whether there was a formal policy in relation to domestic violence. Senior staff in Bluebell HA were more sympathetic and experienced and 'set the tone' for housing management staff. Some of them had worked in the local authority directly with homeless applicants: they were not suspicious of women's motives. This was not the case in Tulip HA, where there was confusion about the appropriate approach, nor Foxglove HA, where unsympathetic frontline staff worked largely unchecked in ways which undermined the spirit of the formal policy.

Nevertheless, the sympathetic staff were under pressure to work in different ways which would affect the quality of service available to homeless women. Frontline staff in Bluebell HA or Tulip HA were not being given an absolutely clear line on what was acceptable management practice by senior management so older practices and attitudes remained, but it was not clear how long this would continue to be the case. There were now general 'tensions' in Bluebell and Tulip HAs about staff workloads and concerns about the quality of the housing management service. More specifically, these focused on the length of time taken in interviews, the amount of help and advice which could be provided to any applicant, whether there was a need for proof from women (in Tulip HA) and what might be expected of the local authority in relation to advice.

In responding to their new competitive working environment the three case study associations had inadvertently created a range of practices that reinforced the dependency and lack of power of women on the waiting list. For example, women had to apply to the local authority and get nominated. The associations then assessed these applications again. Associations might expect to be given proof. These requirements were also another illustration of the local authority's lack of power and influence in relation to its 'enabling' role. Even when the authority assessed and nominated women's applications, two out of three of the housing associations in this study assessed them again (and might give them a lower priority or return them if they disagreed with the definition of violence or thought they were not homeless).

Foxglove HA and Tulip HA had also established 'customer care' services in their reception areas, but it was clear that the role of 'customer care' was ambiguous. There was, in fact, a possibility that the application of consumerism in the form of 'customer care' practice in housing associations disguised or masked worsening relationships between associations and applicants/tenants (Clarke and Newman, 1997). 'Welfare' organisations such as housing associations were not entirely akin to 'customer oriented' private companies. The ways in which they were expected to respond to 'housing need' meant that ideologies prevalent in the private sector could not be applied without difficulty. Applying for housing as a 'customer' (applicant) was far more complicated in a social welfare setting (like a housing association) than in a purely commercial one (such as an estate agent).

For a homeless woman who had left a violent partner it was not just a case of exercising 'choice' by walking, customer-like, through the office entrance or picking up the telephone (see Clarke, 1998, for a wide discussion of this issue). The transaction was not dependent on how much a woman could pay but her particular personal circumstances and how these were formally and informally assessed by housing management staff. She might be embarrassed or feel ashamed to relate what had happened. She might be afraid of saying too much, because of a concern about her own safety or for fear of the possible reaction of staff (see Fleur's comments in Chapter Seven). It was also very likely that the way staff reacted personally would affect a woman's confidence in giving information about her circumstances. This would be reinforced by information available to her from the association (or not, as the case might be). Had staff the knowledge and the time to discuss the woman's circumstances sensitively, they would be more likely to obtain relevant information for the housing application and be more likely to provide a helpful service to her, and to other women more generally. The difficulty for women lay in the reality that association staff in this study increasingly did not have the training and/or time to do this effectively.

Although women leaving domestic violence would formally receive the highest priority for housing in these associations, it would remain more difficult for anyone in this particular situation (compared to others) to proceed through the application process. Having to deal with insensitive staff, fill in extra forms or get additional proof or supporting evidence from organisations or individuals were all extra and stressful hurdles which women had to get over despite their circumstances. The violence that had precipitated them into homelessness remained as a personal barrier that had to be overcome before they could complete their housing application in a way acceptable to each association. Other women with different housing circumstances did not have to overcome such difficulties in talking about their circumstances or 'proving' them. Black and Asian women who were homeless because of domestic violence might also have difficulties because of institutional racism. This was most obviously apparent for those women who did not speak English, but there might be other difficulties including inappropriate staffing and a lack of knowledge and understanding about the situation in which black and Asian women might find themselves. Only Tulip HA, the smallest and most financially insecure association in this study, was able to provide a service for women in these circumstances.

SIX

Assessing applications and allocating property

Introduction

The three case study associations varied in the numbers of properties they had available to let and the numbers that were allocated to homeless people, including women who had left a violent partner/ex-partner. As far as women's applications were concerned, a broad range of influences affected whether they obtained sufficient priority to be rehoused. These are explored in this chapter.

The local Bluebell HA handled twice as many lettings (353) as the multi-regional Foxglove HA (174) in the year when the interviews for this study took place. Surprisingly, the smallest association in the study, Tulip HA, also handled more lettings over that year (189) than Foxglove HA in this particular local authority area. (It was possible to directly compare all three associations in relation to this since the local authority supplied information about Foxglove HA's performance from CORE statistics it obtained on a local authority-wide basis.) However, the staffing complement to deal with this work was similar in the three associations. Practically, this meant that staff in Bluebell HA had far more assessment and allocations work than the staff in the other two associations.

Tulip HA, the small black association, was the only association which rehoused homeless applicants in significant numbers. It exceeded both Bluebell HA and Foxglove HA *numerically* (109 compared to Bluebell HA's 64) and in the *proportion* of its total lettings which were made to homeless applicants (58% compared to Bluebell HA's 19% and Foxglove HA's 20%).

More women leaving domestic violence were rehoused by Tulip HA than the other two associations numerically (31 compared to Bluebell HA's 14) and proportionately (16.4%, 3% and 3.8% of the total applicants rehoused within each association, respectively). (Tulip HA's figure represented an increase from 1996/97 when the equivalent figure was 21, or 11%.) Whether or not women were statutory homeless and had or had not been nominated was impossible to say from the data available.

There were significant differences in the ethnic origin of applicants rehoused by the two local case study associations. Just looking at the information that was available on those new tenants who were black, white or of 'mixed' ethnic origin, 59% of Tulip HA's new tenants were black (113 out of 189); another 11% were of 'mixed' ethnic origin (22 out of 189); and 22% were white (43 out of 189). Bluebell HA rehoused 15% of applicants whose ethnic origins were black, and 3% of 'mixed' ethnic origin (13 out of 353); 74% were white (263 out of 353). There were no local statistics available for multi-regional Foxglove HA.

It was not possible to monitor the quality and age of the property into which women moved, since the associations did not have these data. This would have been one way of monitoring to ensure that black and white households were being allocated a similar range of property. It would also have revealed whether homeless women leaving domestic violence were being allocated good quality, new consortium housing in reasonable numbers, compared to other needs groups. This detailed analysis of ethnic monitoring data had been recommended to associations as a way of preventing inadvertent racial discrimination (CRE, 1993). It might also have provided a detailed illustration of the 'racialisation of space' described by Smith (1989, 1993).

The first part of this chapter looks at how staff in each association assessed applications that were registered on the waiting list and the various influences that came to bear on this decision making. There were three distinct aspects of assessment:

- face-to-face interviews;
- evaluating support letters and other supporting evidence from agencies or individuals who knew the applicant;
- undertaking the 'landlord check' into the applicant's housing history.

The second part of this chapter builds on the first, and considers how allocation decisions were made in the three associations. The process of allocating property was organised differently in each, but the judgements which staff made about women's applications when domestic violence was involved were broadly similar. Allocation decisions involved more than a straightforward comparison of the 'housing need' of different applicants to judge which was the most urgent. Staff made decisions about their suitability for particular properties rather than their urgency to be rehoused. They made judgements about different types of household, the relative importance of domestic violence (compared to other circumstances) and considered specific management issues which might be associated with particular applications.

The assessment process

The main purpose of the assessment process in all of the associations was to enable a decision to be made about whether or not to give a woman the highest priority for rehousing because she was homeless because of domestic violence. Assessment reports were written usually by Housing Officers or Housing Services Officers. Other staff might also help, but the main influence on the time they could spend on each application appeared to be the sheer volume of work they had to complete.

In Foxglove and Tulip HAs, more senior staff were involved in the final decision about an applicant's assessment and priority for rehousing. Foxglove HA's Team Leader and Tulip HA's Senior Housing Officer had strong views about women and domestic violence. In contrast, the Housing Manager in Bluebell HA became involved only when the staff had difficulty with assessing an application, and this rarely happened. The informal culture around this issue which had been established by senior staff who had worked with homeless women in the local authority 'set the tone' for the different way in which women applicants were considered in this association.

Although the purpose was the same, the ways in which the staff in the three associations undertook the assessment of applications differed quite noticeably. Two different sets of attitudes and related practices underlay these differences. The first related to attitudes towards women who had left domestic violence. Could women be trusted to tell the truth about the violence and their particular housing circumstances? The extent to which staff understood the dynamics of violence in personal relationships was clearly important in shaping how staff viewed particular situations. The second related to different views about what housing management staff should find out about applicants and how far it was appropriate to use this information to 'manage' (that is, restrict) access to housing. There were three discrete parts to assessment in Foxglove HA and Tulip HA, but two in Bluebell HA.

The face-to-face interview

Why interview?

The Housing Services Officers in Foxglove HA and staff in Tulip HA described the aim of the assessment interview as "verification". Foxglove HA staff had to ensure that the area office worked within the association's letting policy priorities. The Housing Officers and Senior Housing Officer in Tulip HA interviewed applicants because the association had to be seen as independent from the local authority. They felt that this was important since Tulip HA was a black association with different priorities from other social housing landlords. These views contrasted with Bluebell HA. Although Housing Officers tried to interview all applicants, they were under considerable pressure to meet nomination targets. Nominated applicants often simply had a 'pre-tenancy interview' where their circumstances and housing requirements were confirmed immediately before being offered a vacancy. Sometimes staff did not interview nominees at all because they had no time: the local authority's priority was accepted without question. This was not surprising given the number of vacancies they had to fill at this time.

Attitudes and training on domestic violence

Some staff had completed various domestic violence 'awareness' courses (Foxglove and Tulip HAs) although the training seemed to have had little impact on day-to-day practice since it had not been specific to housing work. A structural explanation based on the abuse of power in relationships had been used as an explanatory model in much of the training. This explanation for violence seemed to have had little impact on staff even in Foxglove HA, where its formal policy was based on this model. In practice, staff had many views and a number of explanations for domestic violence. The most usual was that men were physically stronger than women. Many staff linked different explanations together: men might be violent because as children they had witnessed their father's violence towards their mother. It might be a phenomenon that was more common in certain 'social groups' and more acceptable in those 'groups' as a consequence. Certain cultures were more violent than others: within them, violence from men was regarded as 'accepted and respected'. Discovering this muddle in thinking about domestic violence went some way to understanding why staff assessed women's applications in the ways they did (Hunter and Nixon, 2001, in their analysis of evictions, point out the same problem).

Experience gained 'on the job' and the advice of other colleagues were important sources of knowledge about what to do for all the association staff involved in assessing applications. Foxglove HA staff also had information in a procedure manual. However, Housing Services Officers only used this when more experienced colleagues were unavailable.

The majority of applicants who had applied for housing because of domestic violence in the three associations were women. A handful of men had applied for this reason: some were gay men with violent male partners while others were men with violent women partners. The experienced staff who had interviewed male applicants in Bluebell HA pointed out that, because their situation contradicted the usual picture, men were less likely to be believed than women. They would probably get little sympathy from most staff whichever association they approached.

'Genuine' and 'non-genuine cases'

The Housing Services Officers and the Team Leader in Foxglove HA were concerned to separate the 'genuine' from the 'non-genuine' applicant. This had affected the way in which the formal assessment system worked in practice and it was clear why this distinction had emerged. It obtained its legitimacy from the 'harassment assessment form' which could only be completed by providing details of the domestic violence and external supporting evidence in the form of support letters from agencies, injunctions/exclusion orders, and so on. The Team Leader's strong views about domestic violence also reinforced these distinctions.

In Tulip HA, some of the Housing Officers and the Senior Housing Officer also felt that it was important to only rehouse 'genuine cases'. The association was relatively small and any controversy about allocations (for example, mistakenly rehousing someone who had not experienced violence) would have a disproportionate impact on its reputation.

Staff in Bluebell HA did not distinguish between 'genuine' and 'non-genuine' applicants. The general view was that abuse of the system was rare and it was not worth trying to identify it because of the considerable risks to the woman were staff to make a mistake.

One long-serving Bluebell HA staff member assessed women who had been nominated by simply writing as a report: 'Domestic violence – assessed by the council'. She said that many women were "relieved" that they did not have to describe their circumstances again. Housing Officers in Bluebell HA were pragmatic about the possibility of women abusing the system through inventing violence. An experienced Housing Officer who had previously worked in the local authority's centralised homeless service remarked:

> "I don't think you can have any doubts. I've seen too many cases, especially girls, in here. I mean, fine, you may be rehousing someone who may not be experiencing domestic violence but for every one there's twenty that have. It's better doing that than asking people [for proof]." (Housing Officer, Bluebell HA)

Detailed accounts of the violence

Staff in all of the associations recognised the need for women to be given sufficient time to talk about the violence which had occurred. It was likely that interviewing in Bluebell HA was less intrusive than that in the other two associations since they were not trying to identify 'genuine' from 'non-genuine' applicants. If a woman applied directly, staff would take details that would form the basis of an assessment report. She would then be advised to approach the local authority for help (and a nomination), and when the nomination arrived (which it usually did) the two would be linked together. The application would then be considered for vacancies. (It might be considered before were an appropriate vacancy to occur.) In some cases where a woman had already been nominated, they simply accepted the local authority's priority and did not take details at all.

The approach in Foxglove and Tulip HAs was different. The formal policy on domestic violence in Foxglove HA clearly stated that "evidence of abuse" was not necessary for the association "to act". In reality, the introduction of the 'harassment assessment form' created a new expectation that applicants should provide supporting evidence. Those who could not were now regarded as "doubtful" (Housing Services Officer, Foxglove HA). Staff were still expected 'to believe' women because of the formal policy but at the same time Housing

Services Officers felt that they had to identify those who were 'genuine' to prevent property being allocated to people whose needs were not as serious as others. Consequently, they did not necessarily believe everything they were told.

> "What occurs to me straight away when you talk about judgement is the fact that – you can't get away from the fact – that there are women out there who know that it can be a quick route to being rehoused by claiming it. But again, our policy does state that women should be believed and that's the bottom line. But we know in reality we can't house everybody and we can't transfer everybody. So although women should be believed, because of the difficulties involved in rehousing, you've got to go into it in more detail and try and get some hard and fast proof if you can. Some more information. Something that is the proof that this is a genuine case. I'm not talking about bruises and so on but perhaps doctor's information, information from the police or solicitors or whatever. Those would be the main ones." (Housing Services Officer, Foxglove HA)

Staff in Tulip HA generally had the same approach. They took as much detail as they could about the violence. Some staff were sympathetic, others were not. One male Housing Officer thought that he had to get enough detail to decide who was right and who was wrong in the situation. A female Housing Officer was most concerned to avoid the possibility of giving priority to women who falsely claimed they had violent partners or ex-partners. She recalled a recent experience of this and used it as a justification for being tougher on every other woman in similar circumstances. Other housing staff were more sympathetic so there were different possible responses which the Senior Housing Officer (and the Housing Manager if there was disagreement) had to consider.

The role of the local authority and nominations

Housing Officers and Housing Services Officers and lettings staff in the three associations did not liaise or network with the local authority (nor any other relevant organisations) to find the best solution for the woman applicant. They usually only contacted other organisations when they were following up information provided in support letters, undertaking the 'landlord check' to find out more about an applicant's current circumstances and past housing history, or trying to obtain a nominated applicant quickly to fill a vacancy (see Chapter Three).

As far as their working relationship with the local authority was concerned, association staff simply sent the applicant to the authority for a nomination and advice. This saved them time. The impression which staff gave was that it was not their job to know about the services available, advise an applicant in detail, or sort out bureaucratic muddles which occasionally occurred between the association and the local authority over nominations. Very few staff in any of the case study associations knew about the inter-agency work of the domestic violence project in the area in which their offices were located.

All of the staff in all of the associations said that they would advise any woman to go to the central homeless teams for help if she was homeless because of domestic violence. There was a clear preference for the central teams over the neighbourhood offices, although for different reasons. Staff in Bluebell HA thought that a woman would get a better service there. Staff in Foxglove and Tulip HAs did not know that the neighbourhood offices provided a service to homeless families. All the staff would advise women who were council tenants and who were still living with their violent partners to talk to their local neighbourhood office manager (the mistaken presumption being that they were not homeless).

The predominant view was that the service provided by the authority's neighbourhood offices was generally poor. Applicants' complaints about the local authority, the condition of some council property offered to waiting-list applicants, and the difficulty that Housing Officers and Housing Services Officers experienced when asking particular neighbourhood offices for high priority nominations, all contributed to this view. There was little personal contact between association staff and local authority staff in the neighbourhood offices or the central homeless teams (the exception being Tulip HA where association staff regularly contacted the local authority's centrally based homeless staff). Association staff had no idea of the poor impression their own practice had been making on local authority staff (see Chapter Three).

The role of support letters or supporting evidence

Getting support letters and supporting evidence

In Foxglove HA the need to complete the 'harassment assessment form' legitimated the requirement to provide supporting evidence even though this undermined the association's original formal policy. The Team Leader felt that giving the highest priority to a woman because of domestic violence had to be 'justified', and support letters and other supporting evidence were one way of doing this. Both Housing Services Officers confirmed that support letters were "definitely important", although they were not always taken at face value. One remarked that she was aware

> "of the fact that some women are very good at getting support. They're very vocal and they're all too happy to go everywhere to get supporting letters because they know the system.... It's a minefield." (Housing Services Officer, Foxglove HA)

In Tulip HA the Senior Housing Officer expected women to provide support letters despite the Housing Manager's view that they were unnecessary. She was particularly concerned that waiting-list priorities were not undermined because 'harassment' (which included domestic violence) was given the highest priority. She felt that she needed to be able to justify each applicant's position on the waiting list and allocations to more senior staff and Board members within the association, as well as to 'the community' and to the local authority, if necessary. She was aware that the impact of external pressure on Tulip HA was much greater than in a larger association because of its much smaller size, relative dependence on local authority goodwill for development opportunities, and relative closeness to various 'community' networks. Nevertheless, the Senior Housing Officer and the Housing Officers in Tulip HA were selective in their use of support letters. They did not regard letters from friends or relatives as useful. One Housing Officer also dismissed solicitors' letters as she thought that solicitors merely wrote what their clients "told them to write".

The staff in Foxglove and Tulip HAs thought that being able to produce support letters from agencies also showed that a woman was "making an effort" to resolve her situation. This was regarded positively. The converse of this was that women who did not want or need other agencies' help or who had only asked other family members or friends for help were regarded less sympathetically. They had no "proof" and were clearly "not trying". Indeed, in both associations they might not be given sufficient priority to be rehoused because of this.

In this situation, women who were living in hostels were probably in a better position than women living with friends or family or still living with a violent partner. Support staff in the women's hostel which was owned and directly managed by Bluebell HA had a reputation for consistently "nagging" (as one male Housing Officer in Tulip HA put it) until their residents were rehoused. They sent support letters to other associations and the local authority to help women with their applications. The black women's refuge pursued the same strategy. Bluebell HA staff recalled support letters from Women's Aid, but generally Women's Aid had a much lower profile with the associations in this study. Foxglove HA and Tulip HA staff felt that they had no contact with them. Relatively few women applied to associations from the Women's Aid refuge at that time because of worries about rent levels (Deputy Manager, Women's Aid). They also had a different approach to helping women residents (supporting them rather than advocating on their behalf).

In Bluebell HA support letters and supporting evidence were not needed. Women were trusted. Several staff members remarked that this reflected 'the ethos' of the association. This was confirmed later by one woman: she could have produced numerous letters and copies of injunctions from over 20 years of living with her violent ex-husband but had never been asked for them.

The 'landlord check'

Would women applicants make good tenants?

Each association required information about where applicants had lived before. These details had to be included on the application form. Bluebell HA staff did not check these for anything other than rent arrears. Foxglove HA and Tulip HA staff went much further. Previous landlords were contacted to find out if there had been any problems from their point of view. The aim was to ensure that only people who were likely to be 'good tenants' were rehoused. Applicants who were considered to be 'poor tenants' were likely to be excluded at this stage. As the Team Leader in Foxglove HA remarked, "Past behaviour is a good predictor of future behaviour".

Enquiries were made about a number of issues. These included the applicant's rent payment record with previous landlords (and the payment record with utilities or the council tax, in some circumstances). How the applicant had treated accommodation in the past (its physical condition; whether it had been abandoned) was also important. How the present home was cared for and past and present relationships with neighbours were investigated. Finally, the 'honesty' of applicants in relation to their past and present circumstances was a consideration. Foxglove HA staff routinely called these 'conduct of tenancy' investigations (Housing Services Officer), although the Team Leader also referred to this as "taking up references". Tulip HA staff thought similarly: that they were "taking up references" (Senior Housing Officer). Undertaking these enquiries and giving them a significance in the assessment of applications might not be helpful to women applicants who had left their previous home because of violence. They might be held responsible for situations that had been beyond their control.

Rent arrears

Rent arrears from previous tenancies were the most usual situation that might cause problems. Arrears were not unusual among applicants: most were poor and reliant on housing benefit to pay the rent. This meant that payment was not always straightforward, especially when household circumstances changed. This aside, there were two circumstances which particularly affected women who had lived with and left violent partners. First, a woman might be regarded as responsible for arrears built up after she had left her former home if she had been a joint tenant. Second, a woman who left home because of violence might have been liable for two rents (for her former home and for a hostel place) until the local authority reached a decision on her homeless status under the legislation. It was not likely that she would have had enough money to pay both rents so arrears would have built up on the former home.

Each of the associations was more concerned about the arrears rather than the reasons for the arrears. Disputes over who should be liable (in the case of joint tenancies) were not their concern.[1] Bluebell and Foxglove HAs' official positions were that they would accept applicants with arrears so long as they were paying them off. Tulip HA would not, the view of the Board being that they would not rehouse 'poor risks' given the financial circumstances of the association and the fact that rent arrears had become unacceptably high in recent years. This rule applied across the board even in the most difficult circumstances. One council tenant who applied to Tulip HA had to pay off £100 rent arrears before she was offered a vacancy. She needed to move because a male neighbour had sexually abused her young daughter. In Foxglove HA, arrears could be looked at more or less benignly. In some circumstances, they could be used to exclude applicants regarded as undesirable for other reasons. For example, one family had applied because they were being victimised by neighbours. However, the Housing Services Officer suspected that the behaviour of the family might be the problem. The Team Leader suggested that she look for arrears that would enable the application to be cancelled.

Housekeeping and decorating standards

In Foxglove HA and Tulip HA, housekeeping and decoration were taken into account in assessing applicants. Staff in Foxglove HA were expected to try to obtain this information from any previous landlords if women had left home because of domestic violence. The Team Leader explained that care was exercised in handling this information.

> "I'm looking at it in terms of the applicant's ability and willingness to care for the property that they're in and I don't necessarily agree that *because the way of life between the partners is of a poor standard that necessarily means the house is kept to a poor standard.* I don't think they go hand in hand at all." (Team Leader, Foxglove HA, emphasis added)

An applicant who had been registered on the waiting list and given a high priority might find their application was cancelled following a home visit to assess their circumstances. These decisions could be appealed and considered by the local Area Committee. One application had been made because the mother and her daughter were being physically and sexually assaulted by a male friend of the mother's son. The 'friend' visited the house when he pleased and had become a very dominant force in the household. Despite this, following a home visit and report by the Housing Services Officer, the Team Leader decided that the application should be cancelled because of poor housekeeping and decoration. In considering the applicant's appeal, the Area Committee had not accepted this and had asked the association's Tenant Support Officer to visit and report. She commented:

> "I just know that it was this tangled web of this one person coming at any time of the day or night, getting into the house, abusing the daughter – saying

what he wanted to her, touching her where he wanted – also to the mother. When I visited, she had scratches down both sides of her neck where somebody had got her by the neck – bruises on her leg. That had happened that Sunday before I went. But the report was very much geared to the state of the property.... I found it really judgemental and I was thinking, 'For God's sake!'" (Tenant Support Officer, Foxglove HA)

The Area Committee considered the Tenant Support Officer's report and reinstated the application with the proviso that the mother agree to accept the help of the Officer with 'her' housekeeping once she was rehoused. (Ironically, the Officer remarked that this would probably not happen: in several years' work with the association she had never been asked to provide support of any kind to women who had been rehoused because of domestic violence.)

Staff in Tulip HA also routinely collected information about housekeeping and decoration when they undertook assessment visits. Comments such as 'neat and tidy' and 'reasonable' were observed on visit reports, and these comments were sometimes considered in allocation meetings. Many women who applied to Tulip HA were living in a hostel or temporary accommodation and views on housekeeping/decoration were not important in these circumstances. They were more likely to be significant when a woman was living in their own home (as a tenant or owner-occupier) or where information emerged during the 'landlord check'.

Property abandonment

The Housing Services Officers and Housing Officers in Foxglove and Tulip HAs regarded property abandonment very critically, whatever the circumstance. It created management problems, especially rent loss and possible vandalism. A woman would not be viewed positively if she had a history of frequent moves and tenancy abandonment. One Housing Services Officer in Foxglove HA remarked:

"The only other consideration would be what sort of tenant we believe they would be. To be harsh, you're looking at management in the future. When I do an application visit, if I see over the last three years that somebody has had six or seven addresses and they've fled violence from every single one, I would be thinking about that seriously, really."

Researcher: "In terms of cancelling...?"

Housing Services Officer, Foxglove HA: "Yes ... because it could be a potential management problem and you can't always do something about it."

Distance from an ex-partner

All staff expressed concern about women who wanted to be rehoused in an area that they felt was too close to a violent ex-partner. They questioned how determined a woman was in trying to escape the violence. In most instances, staff would discuss this with the woman. In instances where there were strong reasons to justify the area requested (for example, important family ties) then the priority of the application would be confirmed. If they were not satisfied, the woman's application might be cancelled. Staff were concerned about the woman's safety and wanted to ensure that she could settle permanently into a new home.

Being joined by the violent man after rehousing

Staff in Foxglove and Tulip HAs were likely to take a very dim view of women who had been rehoused before and who had subsequently been joined by their violent ex-partner.

> "In many cases, the length of time between the woman signing up for a property and the man being present in the home is 24 hours. It's as quick as that. So it makes one very distrusting – often to the detriment of the genuine." (Team Leader, Foxglove HA)

This had also occurred in Tulip HA. The underlying suspicion left by such examples influenced attitudes towards all women. Staff seemed to be unable to draw a distinction between the occasional instance of collusion to obtain rehousing and the vast majority of applications from women who had no intention of reuniting with their ex-partners. They also seemed to lack understanding of the danger women might be in should their ex-partner find them (see Iris's account in Chapter Seven).

Honesty

Finally, there was the difficult issue of the relationship between the woman applicant and the association as landlord. This involved staff making moral judgements and potentially holding the woman responsible for matters that were outside of her control. For example, were a Housing Services Officer or Housing Officer in Foxglove HA or Tulip HA to discover that there were discrepancies between what they had been told by the woman applicant and what they had discovered through their own enquiries, it was possible that the application would be cancelled. Staff believed that the issue here was honesty. One example will suffice.

A Housing Services Officer in Foxglove HA cited a recent application from a woman who had abandoned her former home following threats from her former violent partner. When staff had checked her housing history they found that she had held a secure tenancy with another association which she had not included in her application details. The association concerned had no record of violence at that tenancy although she had terminated it without notice. Even though the woman was statutory homeless and had been nominated by the local authority, the application was cancelled because she had "misled" Foxglove HA.

As it happened, the woman concerned was living temporarily in the hostel managed by Bluebell HA. The Hostel Support Worker decided to investigate further because the woman was insistent that she had told her former landlord that she had to move because her violent ex-partner had found her. After a number of telephone calls, the Support Worker finally managed to speak to the woman's former Housing Officer who confirmed what she had said. The woman was rehoused by another association.

Why should staff be so bothered about details in the past? There are a number of possible reasons for staff concern. They might suspect women of being dishonest – this was commonplace in Foxglove HA and to a certain extent in Tulip HA. They might be concerned that their authority was being undermined and believe that action was necessary to re-establish it. They might want to ensure that housing was only allocated to applicants in the most need of housing (or who were 'deserving.') Finally, an element of individual personal antipathy was evident in relation to a small number of assessments in Foxglove and Tulip HAs. These feelings might also affect the outcome of assessment decisions in these associations.

Organising allocations

Who makes allocation decisions?

Senior staff were involved in the allocation decision making in Foxglove HA and Tulip HA, but not in Bluebell HA. The restraining influence of the Team Leader (Foxglove HA) and the Senior Housing Officer (Tulip HA) in relation to applications from women has already been noted, and it became clear that this influence extended to allocations. At least one other member of staff was involved – usually the Housing Officer or Housing Services Officer who directly managed the property which was vacant (although this was not always possible because of other commitments). An alternative way of organising allocation decision making was provided by Bluebell HA. The Housing Manager there was not so involved in allocations: they were made by the Housing Officers and waiting-list staff who met and then reported their decisions to him for final approval. Although the personnel might differ, there were some similarities between the associations in the judgements used in allocating property.

Local knowledge

Local knowledge was incorporated into the allocation process through the opinions of the Housing Officers and Housing Services Officers who managed the property concerned. They used information about neighbours and the surrounding estate or neighbourhood to make judgements about the most appropriate type of household for the vacancy or vacancies that occurred.

Important as such information was, it was also often inconsistent and incomplete. In interviews with women who were association tenants, several instances emerged where they had been endangered because housing management staff had not exercised sufficient care in thinking about the wider implications of specific allocations (see Chapter Seven). In Foxglove HA a woman tenant had been discovered by her violent ex-partner because *his* mother was rehoused by the association into the house opposite her own home. There was a similar situation in Tulip HA where a woman had been housed next door to a family from the same area of the city. The woman discovered that her children knew her new neighbour's children. She now felt it was only a matter of time before her ex-partner found her, either through the children or through the neighbour's gossip (her family had 'stood out', as she put it, where she had lived before because they were a black family in a predominantly white estate).

The numbers of applications considered

There were different ways of selecting applications to consider for vacancies in each association, and the numbers of applications considered also varied. This had practical implications for women who had left violence because they were more likely to be in urgent need of rehousing and less likely to be able to wait a long time before being rehoused.

In Foxglove HA the Team Leader and appropriate Housing Services Officer only considered a maximum of four assessed applications for each vacancy. These were the two longest-held, highest priority nominations and the two longest-held, highest priority direct applications. The association's rule was to consider applications by 'date order'. Although this could be varied (as 'an exceptional letting'), this was rarely done. Staff did not check the other highest priority applications to see whether or not anyone was actually in more urgent need, so women who might have recently applied would have to wait however urgent their circumstances (see Chapter Seven for Iris's experiences). In Bluebell and Tulip HAs, staff considered *all* the highest priority applications and could identify the most urgent applications. In theory, *if* a woman's circumstances were particularly urgent, she could be allocated property before another household with the same priority even if they had been waiting longer.

Staff in Bluebell HA and Tulip HA could increase or decrease the number of applications they considered for a vacancy. Usually, this was done to increase the number of nominated applicants they considered. This would be to the advantage of homeless women with dependent children who were most likely to be nominated. Staff could also increase the number considered to reach race equality lettings targets, if necessary. This benefited homeless black and Asian women, although Tulip HA rarely had to do this as it met its targets. Bluebell HA sometimes had difficulty with particular areas. Foxglove HA had only one target that applied to all of the housing it managed from the area office (in five different local authority areas). It was quite low but the office rarely reached it (Area Director). This was not surprising given the lack of flexibility in allocation practice that became apparent.

Staff might reduce the numbers of applicants they had to consider by excluding particular applications or groups of applications from consideration. An applicant might have wanted a particular type of house. They might have too few or too many children for a particular house or estate. There also appeared to be a growing tendency to consider setting aside applications from some lone parents, partly because of child density on particular estates (so two-parent families were preferred), and partly because some lone parents were considered too 'vulnerable' to live in certain areas.

In all the associations, transfer applicants seemed to fare badly compared to direct applicants or people who had been nominated. In Foxglove HA various staff remarked that transfer applicants were often "forgotten" when property was allocated. The overwhelming emphasis was on rehousing people in 'date order' (either as nominations or direct waiting-list applicants). In Tulip HA transfer applicants were not usually regarded as being as urgent as external applicants (even though they might have the same points total). Their applications also might suffer because of internal decisions taken for purely housing management reasons. For example, transfer applications could be 'frozen' before long holiday periods to reduce the voids for which the association was responsible. Few transfer applicants were rehoused in Bluebell HA because the association wanted to increase its chances of meeting its nomination targets especially on consortium estates. This contrasted with the view about association transfers found in other research (Withers and Randolph, 1994).

The process of allocating property

The process of allocating property involved *comparing and contrasting* applications to finally 'whittle down' the numbers so that ultimately only one and a reserve were left. It was more or less complicated depending on the number of applications considered and the particular vacancies that had to be filled. The process in all of the associations involved judgements about applicants and their circumstances as well as knowledge of the property or properties and the areas in which they were located.

Staff judged applicants in three ways in the allocation meetings that were observed in the case study associations. They had views about particular kinds of household, attitudes towards domestic violence and particular concerns about how the applicant or their neighbours might be managed. The ways in which staff responded were often complex and contradictory. The allocation meetings took noticeably different amounts of time. Bluebell HA and Tulip HA meetings were by far the longest because staff were considering all relevant applications. For example, the allocation meeting observed in Bluebell HA took 40 minutes to allocate one property. In theory, staff in Bluebell HA and Tulip HA could consider applications in some depth. In practice, ways of dealing with too many applications had to be found. These were based on the practice already noted of setting aside particular households or applicants with particular circumstances for some vacancies. Foxglove HA's allocation meetings were always short. Staff only considered a maximum of four applicants. Often these were considered singly, as home visits were completed. The problem with this approach was that urgent applications might be missed as they waited to get to the front of the time-ordered queue. Even given the smaller numbers, staff still made judgements about applications in order to make a decision.

In each of the associations the understanding which staff had of applicants was partial at best. To make decisions, they looked at the 'facts' in the assessment report and on the application form, and used the local knowledge from Housing Officers and Housing Services Officers. They also judged, made assumptions, and relied on stereotypes of applicants to help them reach a decision. This combination of different types of information and personal judgement affected applications from women who had become homeless because of domestic violence in particular ways. The flexibility inherent in these meetings might sometimes work in their favour, but it became clear from the meetings observed in this study that it could also work to their detriment.

Bluebell HA's allocation meeting

Bluebell HA staff met to decide who should be allocated a three-bedroom house on an estate. There were six 'high priority' nominated applications to consider. The vacancy was unusual. The former tenant had been transferred away from the area. She had been physically assaulted by her neighbour and her neighbour's new partner. Ironically, the neighbour had been rehoused into that property to escape domestic violence. Her *new* partner had recently been released from prison where he had been serving a sentence for assault.

The Housing Officer who managed the estate was anxious to rehouse a family with young children into the property because he thought there were too many older children on the estate. The waiting-list staff allocating the property felt that an additional consideration was *the composition* of the family unit. They were determined *not* to rehouse a lone parent into the property since they felt that a woman by herself would be particularly vulnerable in this situation. They wanted to avoid any violence in the future between the neighbours. Ironically, one way of doing this might have been to take action against the violent neighbours, but the association had taken no action against them because there were no witnesses.

The first stage of the meeting was used to reduce the number of applications that had to be considered. Surprisingly, the view that a lone parent should not be rehoused into the property did not initially affect the way in which the staff reduced the numbers. Two applications were from lone parents but they were not excluded at this point. The staff were also not concerned about the ages of the applicants' children. No applicant with older children was excluded (even given the Housing Officer's request for a family with younger children). Following detailed discussion, four applications were set aside.

The staff used different reasons to set applications aside. First, a lone parent applicant who had the support of her local councillor was excluded because her circumstances were not regarded as sufficiently serious. She wanted to move nearer to her seriously ill mother because she was caring for her daily. (She was not excluded because she was a lone parent.) One member of staff commented that the councillor could hardly complain about it: they had recently rehoused another applicant the councillor had been supporting. A couple with children who had priority because their home was due to be demolished by the local authority were excluded next because it was felt that they should be the responsibility of the local authority. Two more applicants were then set aside because they were thought to be inappropriate for this vacancy: they were too vulnerable. The first application was from another couple with children. The family was homeless and living in a hostel. The husband was seriously mentally ill: he had attempted to kill himself and his son. The second was from another couple with children. The woman had been assaulted by a neighbour, and her children were now being victimised. Offering them this vacancy would not be an improvement.

The choice that now had to be made was between two applications. One was from a lone parent and her children who were severely overcrowded. They were living in her parent's home following a relationship breakdown. The second application was from a couple and their children who were living in a homeless hostel. They had recently returned to the city, the woman having previously left a violent partner.

Each application was now considered in detail. The lone parent's circumstances were recognised by staff as particularly difficult but eventually they decided to offer the property to the couple living in the hostel. The fact that they were a couple *and* they were living in a hostel seemed to make the difference. They seemed the most suitable and the more urgent. Nevertheless, there were outstanding queries about this application. There was no information about where the woman's violent ex-partner was currently living and no medical verification for an epileptic condition which one of the children had and which had influenced the decision positively. The staff barely referred to the woman's experience of domestic violence but assumed that her new partner would protect her from the new neighbours even though they had no information about this man.

At this point, the application from the lone parent was the reserve until one member of staff recalled that they had decided at the beginning of the meeting not to allocate the property to a lone parent. Consequently, her application was discarded and they then quickly trawled through all the applications that had previously been set aside. They were looking for a couple with children who might be tough enough to live next door to potentially violent neighbours. The staff decided to reconsider the two-parent family who were 'a clearance case'. This family became the reserve.

In this way, the 'ideal type' couple with children predominated over the lone parents in this 'pool' of six applications. The ages of the children were not considered (even though this had been the first concern of the absent Housing Officer). It was clear that the Bluebell HA staff felt that only a couple with a resident man would prevent (or protect against) a possible recurrence of violence.

Foxglove HA's allocation meeting

A slightly different scenario presented itself to Foxglove HA. The allocation of property was dealt with quickly by the Team Leader and the Housing Services Officer. Four applications were considered for each vacancy but not all at the same time. Some applicants needed to be visited to confirm the details of the application and the points total. Others had already been visited and assessed.

One applicant had just been visited in relation to a three-bedroom vacancy. The family had applied because of domestic violence but were recommended for cancellation after the visit because of their standard of housekeeping and decoration. Another application was from a couple and children who were being harassed by neighbours. The Housing Services Officer had visited them at home but was not happy. She raised doubts about them in her discussion with the Team Leader, particularly in relation to their role in the harassment they were claiming. The first concerns she had were about the children whom she thought might be troublesome. She was doubtful too about the man whose name was on the application (who was the father of the youngest child). He did not live with the family but now wanted to be rehoused with them. She queried how stable the adults' relationship might be and the nature of the family. The family had the support of their GP but the Housing Services Officer undermined this by claiming that, in her view, the GP had misused the association's medical form that had been sent to him to complete. He had returned it with 'violence/intimidation' written on it instead of a medical condition. The 'solution' provided by the Team Leader to the dilemma posed by the application was to advise the Housing Services Officer to search for debts which would enable them to justify the cancellation of the application.

The family had been compared against an 'ideal type' nuclear family and had been found wanting. The Housing Services Officer was also not keen to rehouse a family who might be a nuisance or violent towards their neighbours. Foxglove HA's own policy stated that the association would not rehouse applicants who had behaved like this. However, what was surprising was that the Housing Services Officer ignored medical verification of the violence towards the applicant's family and made *no attempt* to investigate their version of events before raising doubts with the Team Leader. It was clear that this was one instance where the formal harassment policy and the informal staff interpretation could move in different directions. This illustrated the extent of informal discretion available to the staff in Foxglove HA in allocating property despite having a points system.

Tulip HA's allocation meeting

Fourteen of the most highly-pointed applications were considered for a vacancy of a three-bedroom property in Tulip HA. Although allocation meetings were usually arranged to include the Senior Housing Officer and Housing Officers, on this occasion only the Senior Housing Officer was present because a staff member had been taken ill at the last moment. As a meeting had already been cancelled before, she decided to allocate alone as vacancies needed to be filled. She had obtained the views of the appropriate Housing Officers before the meeting. These were not local knowledge, but, rather, their opinions about which applicant should be allocated the property. The reasons for the Housing Officers' selection were particular to the applicant and property. They did not extend to comments about the neighbours or the area.

The Senior Housing Officer started by looking for applications that she could set aside. Six of the 14 applications were internal transfer requests, and these were excluded. Eight applications remained and this was reduced to six as two did not want to be considered for this housing scheme. One was being offered something else and the relevant papers could not be found for another. This meant that four applicants remained to be considered.

Two were lone parents, one with one child and the other with two children. Both had left violent partners and were statutory homeless. The third application was from a single man. His partner and child lived with her parents. They wanted to live together. The fourth application was from a couple who were living in a high-rise council flat. They were visited every day by a nephew who currently lived in a hostel for homeless men. Another young relative visited in the summer holidays. They wanted a bigger home.

The Senior Housing Officer considered the applicants' circumstances, checking their points totals and whether or not they had been nominated. Her main concern, however, was the structure of the household. She wanted a family which would 'fit' the vacant property. It was a three-bedroom house with very small second and third bedrooms. At this stage, the Senior Housing Officer was clear that she should *under-occupy* the house because of its size. However, her more detailed reasoning when looking at the applications moved her in a different direction.

Two applicants were homeless lone parents, one living in a hostel and the other living with friends temporarily. They had the highest points total and the highest priority nomination. Their families would have under-occupied or occupied appropriately the property in question. Neither were selected. The Senior Housing Officer selected the single man whose partner lived elsewhere. She regarded them as 'a split family'. Of relevance here was that both Bluebell HA and Foxglove HA had rejected his application because he was 'adequately housed' in a self-contained, two-bedroom, privately rented flat.

However, the Senior Housing Officer remarked that the Housing Officer had said that he had kept the flat in very good condition. The applicant had not been nominated and had not applied to the local authority. Had he done so, he would have received a low priority (Group D) and could not have been nominated. His partner had not been interviewed, and so her intentions were not clear. Another daughter (from a previous relationship) visited regularly, so could use the second bedroom. The reserve for the vacancy was the couple living in a council flat who wanted more bedrooms. To justify this, the Senior Housing Officer had to consider the regularly visiting relatives as permanent members of the couple's household.

Considerations in allocating property

Attitudes to household types – the influence of the 'ideal' nuclear family

The clearest 'ideal type' which staff used in making allocation decisions was that of the two-parent heterosexual nuclear family. It was regarded positively. The man and the woman were expected to live together to bring up their children. The man was presumed to be protective of the woman. The woman was held to be responsible for the housekeeping, the childcare and the emotional well-being of the family. Other arrangements were seen as less satisfactory and/or potentially problematic. This 'ideal type' or stereotype was used in various ways by staff in making allocation decisions.

In Bluebell HA two nuclear families were given preference in the allocation meeting. For the family that was allocated the property, it was the presence of the man that was important – the presence of a violent neighbour strongly influenced the allocation discussions and final decision. Although lone parents were considered, in the comparing and contrasting of applications for suitability, the outcome had to be that only two-parent nuclear families were selected. In Tulip HA the clear preference for two-parent nuclear families extended to setting aside higher priority lone parents' applications in preference to apparently 'split' families.

Attitudes towards domestic violence

Staff had no explicit views about the women who had applied because of domestic violence but it was clear that they were not viewed straightforwardly. One obvious way this emerged was that other applicants were often offered vacancies in circumstances that were far less serious or urgent than those of homeless women. Why was this? The only explanation had to lie in attitudes towards the violence. It seemed as though staff implicitly regarded the violence as less important than the circumstances of other applicants. This happened whether the other applicants had higher, equal or *lesser* formal priority than the women concerned. They either failed to acknowledge the seriousness of the violence or regarded it as less urgent because it had happened in the past. In

Foxglove HA one application from a woman and her family was recommended for cancellation because of poor housekeeping and decoration even though she was regularly being abused. Similar disregard of the need for urgency in rehousing women who were homeless because of domestic violence was seen in Tulip HA's allocation meeting.

Management concerns and domestic violence

A number of new concerns emerged in the allocation discussions relating to women's applications. There was a general presumption that they were 'vulnerable' and needed 'support' of various kinds. This might preclude their being rehoused in certain areas. It did not mean that they got extra 'support' from the associations (see Chapter Seven). In fact, the Team Leader in Foxglove HA thought that the offer of 'support' would merely increase the stigma which women in this position often felt. In Foxglove HA and Tulip HA suspicions were voiced that some women were using violence as a ploy to gain priority on the waiting list; consequently, there was a degree of antipathy generally towards women in this situation. This was reflected in the amount of checking and evidence-gathering necessary for applications to be accepted. This flowed over into a tendency to doubt whether the new tenancy would be permanent. Would the man move in? Would she abandon it? Would all the work in protecting the property when it was empty have to be repeated after a short period of time? To staff with very heavy workloads, these issues mattered a lot.

More generally, housing management staff would try to ensure that they selected 'a mix' of households when they came to allocate a new estate. They specifically wanted to avoid rehousing too many homeless households and too many lone parents, although there were difficulties with this that they all recognised. There were a number of reasons for the antipathy towards lone parents. Some staff felt that they were, by definition, vulnerable, and 'concentrating' vulnerability in this way was inadvisable because of the potential pressure on public services this created (including pressure on housing management staff). Child density was also identified as important – lone parents meaning fewer adults to control children in public spaces. (These views did not extend to single women who had experienced violence.)

An alternative way of looking at this might have involved an expectation that the association would take action against tenants who were violent and might ensure that there were adequate facilities for children when building new estates.

Nobody thought that it might be helpful to rehouse women who had experienced violence near to one another for mutual support. The impracticality of this was pointed out since applicants or tenants would probably not know why someone else had been rehoused. Certainly, encouraging this was not considered to be the role of housing management staff. Similarly, no staff spent time making sure applicants knew about local organisations or services when offering property and had not considered that this might help women to decide about offers.

Viewing the property and making a decision

Housing Officers and Housing Services Officers did everything they could to avoid having property standing empty for long. They needed to maximise the rental income from it and avoid the possibility of it being vandalised. In many instances, staff fixed steel shutters over doors and windows in empty property (including new property just 'handed over' by the builders) as a protection against vandalism. Their concern about letting times extended to the amount of time which women applicants had to view the property. All of the women who had been accompanied by a Housing Officer or Housing Services Officer to view a property were given the absolute minimum of time to look around. In one instance, five minutes was allowed. In another, the woman timed the Housing Services Officer and found that she and her mother were expected to view a three-bedroom house and make a decision in three minutes (see Chapter Seven). Applicants who viewed property independently had longer although they were also expected to 'sign up' on the same day.

On signing the tenancy agreement, women immediately became liable for the rent (and the association avoided further losses of rental income). Most women then had to wait for a Department of Social Security (DSS) grant for furniture, bedding, a cooker and carpets before they could move in. Associations had been willing in the past to vary the tenancy commencement date (or give rent free weeks) to give women some time to make arrangements, but this was no longer the case. This meant that arrears built up because the local authority would not pay housing benefit to women for two properties. Sometimes, women used part of the grant for furniture to pay off the arrears that had built up.

The women in this research who were rehoused by associations all remarked that they never saw the Housing Officer or Housing Services Officer who managed the property once they had moved in. New tenants were supposed to be visited a few weeks after they had moved into their new homes, but none of the women in this research had been visited. The relationship between themselves and their new landlord was a distant one. Staff acknowledged that this was not conducive to encouraging women to approach the association when they had any problems. This, of course, was particularly hard for women who did not speak English.

Conclusion

It became clear in observing how assessment and allocation decisions were made that the associations in this study worked in ways that were largely independent of the local authority. Although the authority might be regarded as an 'enabler', it actually had no influence over the ways in which these decisions were made. The relationship which Housing Officers and Housing Services Officers and their Managers had with organisations external to themselves (whether city-wide or local) appeared to be very limited. It certainly was nothing like the 'multi-agency cooperation' promoted by the previous and present government as the best way to respond to women who needed help because of domestic violence. It is worth pointing out that the council's neighbourhood managers also found the demands on their time were such that they could spend little time meeting with colleagues in the association or voluntary sectors.

Attitudes towards women who had become homeless because of domestic violence ranged from sympathetic to hostile. The response varied depending on the applicant's circumstances and/or the suspicions that staff might have personally about women inventing violence to gain priority for rehousing. Each association had developed its own approach. This was influenced to varying degrees by the views of its staff, policy development and interpretation, the dominant organisational culture, and the strength of feeling about the relative importance of other management issues.

The views and involvement of senior staff in decision making varied between the three case study associations, as did the issues regarded as important in making a decision about the woman's priority or whether she should be offered a particular property. The senior staff who were less sympathetic could and did influence decisions directly (Foxglove HA and Tulip HA). Bluebell HA's senior staff relied on their informal personal influence and the culture of the organisation. But this might change with staff changes, and neither association was clear enough to give current staff an entirely consistent approach. In the less sympathetic Foxglove HA and Tulip HA, women were not believed without 'proof' or supporting evidence from other organisations. Staff thought that, by approaching agencies, women were 'making an effort', while letters from other family members or friends were not acceptable. This expectation placed unnecessary barriers in front of women – especially black women. Asking for support letters from women had different effects on women depending on their ethnic background and religious beliefs. Black and Asian women might be less likely to seek a divorce or legal protection because of the impact of these on the family's reputation (Mama, 1989). They might be reluctant to approach advice organisations for help. Had organisations not been located within their community, they might be concerned about how they and their families might be considered. Alternatively, if organisations did have connections to the local black or Asian communities, they might worry about maintaining their privacy and safety. (See Rai and Thiara, 1997, for a discussion about help and support provided in black refuges.) Asian women (especially Muslims) might be less likely to approach family and friends, especially when they wanted to leave and live independently because it was not likely that this would be regarded as acceptable (Mama, 1989; Imam, 1994). This had been clear in the accounts of the Muslim women in this study. Nevertheless, those who could provide proof were regarded as 'genuine cases'. Those who could not provide proof were likely to be rejected. Why were women not trusted to tell the truth?

In part, the answer lay in staff misunderstanding about the nature of domestic violence. Many did not understand the potential severity and nature of the violence and were not aware of the difficulties, shame and embarrassment which women felt when having to raise the problem (see Chapter Seven). Consequently, in Foxglove HA and Tulip HA some staff thought nothing of expecting proof. The impact of this misunderstanding extended to the allocation of properties. This must have been the reason for staff being willing to juggle different high-priority applications to find one which, in their view, 'fitted' the vacancy – instead of regarding domestic violence as the most urgent situation. This may also have been the explanation why purely management concerns such as rent arrears could be regarded as more important than rehousing women who had become homeless because of domestic violence. It was also evident in the lack of time and care given to women when making offers of accommodation.

Despite these difficulties, Tulip HA was rehousing far more women who had left domestic violence, many of whom were black or Asian (31 out of 189 lettings made that year, or 16%). Most of them must have been nominated and they would have supplied sufficient proof to satisfy the Senior Housing Officer and other Housing Officers. This rehousing rate was astonishing and clearly raised a number of questions about the assessment and allocation practices in all of the associations. Were homeless applicants being channelled to Tulip HA while the other associations had a broader range of applicants in high priority and could more easily 'pick and choose' who to rehouse? Most of the properties that Tulip HA let that year were new. The association had the same proportion of relets as the other two associations, so the vacancies were not being generated by turnover. Had Tulip HA developed in areas that were particularly popular with Asian and black people, especially women? Were there other reasons for the significant differences in the circumstances of people rehoused by the three associations? Perhaps these related to the attitudes and language skills of frontline staff?

Chapter Seven looks at the experiences of women who were rehoused by the associations in this study to see what their views were about the advice and help that they received in trying to start a new life away from violence.

Note

[1] In Hunter and Nixon's study (2001), women were evicted because of their violent partner's 'antisocial behaviour' or disruptive children. Arrears were used as a ground for possession.

SEVEN

Women's experiences of finding a new home

Introduction

The final part of this study considers the views of women who were tenants of the case study associations. They had been rehoused as they had become homeless because of domestic violence. What did they think about the services they had received from hostels, the council and housing associations? Were they happy in their new homes? How settled did they feel in the areas in which they were now living?

The first part of this chapter considers the nature of the temporary living arrangements that some women made when they left their former homes. It also looks at the position of other women who could not leave like this. Women experienced a number of practical and emotional difficulties in trying to obtain help despite having a high priority for housing. Women's fear of their ex-partners, their desire to maintain ties with their wider family, and their own personal beliefs, values and self-confidence all influenced their actions and choices. Certain routes to help and accommodation (temporary and permanent) were blocked in different ways: because of lack of income, language differences, distance between family members, family size, the age and sex of children, ill health or disability.

The chapter then moves on to consider women's views about the ways in which their housing applications were dealt with by housing staff. The usefulness of trying to keep pressure on staff in relation to their applications and their views about the need of associations for supporting evidence or proof are explored. Their perceptions of the helpfulness (or otherwise) of housing management staff illustrates how assessments of quality have to move beyond simple performance indicators to accurately capture people's feelings about the services which are provided. The range of offers of accommodation which were made to them by the local authority and housing associations, as well as the difficulties they had in dealing with staff who gave them little time, are then considered. Finally, women's attitudes to their new home were considered. Some women were very positive about their new homes but they all feared being found by ex-partners. Women highlighted the lack of help provided by housing management staff once they were rehoused as a potential problem for women in this situation.

The women who participated

Eight women were interviewed. Seven were rehoused by housing associations and one by the local authority. Seven women had left violent partners or ex-partners. One woman had moved to get away from a former male neighbour who had sexually abused her daughter. She had lived in fear of him since this discovery. Further details about the women who were interviewed are included in Table 1. Each of the names and certain personal details have been changed or omitted to prevent identification.

Research over the last 30 years on domestic violence has revealed the wide range of relationships in which violence may occur, the different kinds of violence that can occur, and its short and longer-term effects. This diversity of experience was reflected in this study. The Asian women had been living with husbands (Raihaanah and Zahrah in a nuclear family and Zaahirah in an extended family). The white women had all been living as lone-parent families. Their circumstances varied. Iris and Fleur had been rehoused before because of violence. They had lived safely and independently for many years until their whereabouts had been revealed by chance to their ex-partners. Belle had left her home because she believed it was the only way that she could end her relationship with an extremely possessive and violent partner. Lily's former husband had lived nearby. She had continued to find him too intimidating and frightening. Rose had to move away because she feared a neighbour who had sexually abused her daughter.

Table 1: The women who were interviewed

Name	Former tenure	Former home	Age	Ethnic origin	Number of children
Lily	Owner-occupier	Lone parent	Late 40s	White European	Four: one lived with her
Iris	Housing association tenant	Lone parent	20s	White European	Two
Rose	Local authority tenant	Lone parent	20s	White European	Three
Zahrah	Owner-occupier	Lived with husband	20s	Asian	None
Raihaanah	Owner-occupier	Lived with husband	Late 30s	Asian	Five
Fleur	Housing association tenant	Lone parent	30s	White European	Three
Zaahirah	Owner-occupier	Lived with husband	20s	Asian	Two
Belle	Private tenant	Lone parent	20s	White European	One

The experience of Rose was the most obvious example of a woman moving to protect her children (and herself) but this had been important for the other women in this study. All expressed concern about the potentially damaging effects on their children of witnessing violence. This was not surprising. Early research identified the frequency with which children might see violent attacks against their mother (Dobash and Dobash, 1979, pp 154-56). More recent research (Abrahams, 1994; Mullender and Morley, 1994; Hester et al, 2000) has shown the wide-ranging but variable impact of violence on children (depending on personality, age, gender, ethnicity and the support network of the child). The possible link between domestic violence and child abuse is also becoming more recognised by childcare professionals (Mullender and Morley, 1994; Mullender, 1996, pp 144-50; Local Government Association, 1998). Belle and Iris left because they feared that their young sons would grow up and copy their father's violent behaviour were they to stay. Boys are widely believed to be directly influenced in this way, although such a strong link has not been substantiated by research (see the discussion in Mullender, 1996, pp 40-2).

The need for temporary arrangements

Immediate protection and the need for temporary accommodation are the most important requirements of women when they first leave their violent partners (Dobash and Dobash, 1979; Bull, 1993; Charles with Jones, 1993; Malos et al, 1993). Many women leave their homes suddenly because they fear for their lives and/or the safety of their children (Bull, 1993; Rai and Thiara, 1997). Some have returned after a short period to give their partner another chance, for the sake of the children, or because the prospect of finding a new home looks remote (see BMA, 1998, pp 16-19 for a discussion of these and other reasons). Women have lived in the homes of family or friends, bed and breakfast hotels, hostels and refuges on a temporary basis (Binney et al, 1981; Mama, 1989; Welsh Women's Aid, 1986; Bull, 1993; Malos et al, 1993). Women who have relied on the local authority's assistance to find temporary accommodation have been more likely to be working-class council tenants with few resources at their disposal (Binney et al, 1981; Malos et al, 1993).

The women in this research were no exception to this general picture (see Table 2). Acute fear of their violent partner(s) or ex-partner(s) was a significant influence in their deciding to leave suddenly, usually after being badly assaulted. Not all the women were able to leave like this. Women found immediate temporary safety in a number of ways: moving in with family members, moving into refuges or hostels or a combination of these. Three women moved to a completely different part of the country in order to escape. The possibility of women making alternative arrangements depended on their income, the understanding and resources of other family members and/or the availability of refuge/hostel accommodation.

Table 2: Temporary accommodation used by women in the study

Name	Temporary accommodation			Permanent home
	1	2	3	
Lily*	Son's home			Housing association flat
Iris	Parent's home			Housing association house
Rose	None used			Housing association house
Zahrah	Aunt and uncle's home	Black women's refuge		Council house
Raihaanah	None used: 'stayed put'			Housing association house
Fleur*	Women's Aid refuge	Second stage house		Housing association house
Zaahirah*	Women's hostel	Black women's refuge	Women's hostel	Housing association house
Belle*	Black women's refuge			Housing association house

* Indicates that the woman had to move from different parts of England, Scotland or Wales in order to

Having to 'stay put'

Most of the research into housing and domestic violence has concentrated on the experiences of women who have moved into refuges (Binney et al, 1981; Pahl, 1985; Charles with Jones, 1993; Malos et al, 1993). Not all of the women in this study were in this position. Some decided that their best option was to make arrangements secretly to leave (to avoid becoming quite literally roofless). In this study, women who had 'stayed put' remained in their former homes for various lengths of time while planning to leave. They did this for different reasons and with varying degrees of success, but staying put for all of them was an indication of the constraints they were experiencing rather than the exercise of choice. Some women had no help from their families. Some found that the temporary accommodation for homeless families in the city could not be used. Another woman mistakenly thought her ex-partner would be imprisoned. She expected to be transferred. Others felt that they could cope for a little while longer, knowing that they had applied for another home and it was just a matter of waiting.

Middle-class women have sometimes 'stayed put' because they have wanted to avoid the disruption and difficulties attached to leaving, including possibly losing economic security and social status (Kirkwood, 1993). If they have left, more money and family connections have meant that they might avoid living in hostels and bed and breakfast hotels, and many have never applied to local authorities as homeless because they think they will not be eligible for help. Nevertheless, they may have difficulties should their assets not be realised. Lily, for example, only approached the local authority because of the encouragement of her son. She thought that being relatively comfortably off and an owner-occupier would disqualify her from council housing even though she could not sell her house and was extremely ill.

Alternatively, women might find their birth families and other relatives unhelpful or unavailable. They might hold different views about the importance of maintaining the relationship or a woman might be blamed for the violence. Some women might not be able to afford to travel to rejoin other family members and they might expect little understanding or sympathy from them. Raihaanah had been violently assaulted by her husband for 20 years. She had stayed because, being Muslim, she wanted to keep the family together. She had no other options. She believed that her parents in Pakistan would blame her for his violence and she had no other members of her birth family in this country.

Other women faced difficulties in using hostels because of physical disability and mental ill health. Lily, an older white woman interviewed for this study, was physically ill and mentally close to a breakdown when her eldest son persuaded her to leave her home and move in with his family. She could not have lived in a refuge or hostel because of her very poor health and need for intensive help.

Mama (1989) found that many of the black and Asian women she interviewed had tried to resolve their difficulties themselves or received inadequate help from organisations which forced them back onto their own resources. When Raihaanah finally decided to leave because her husband had become "murderous", she discovered that there was nowhere for her family of six to go without separating her children. Her son was too old at 17 to be accepted within a refuge setting.

Staying with other members of the family

Dobash and Dobash (1979) found that women were most likely to initially approach their own birth family for help if their partner was violent. They had to overcome feelings of shame, reticence and self-blame in order to do this. Parents would first be approached for informal advice. As the violence became worse, women were more likely to approach their parents for temporary accommodation. Interestingly, the women in this study *only* approached family members if they believed that they had a reasonable chance of getting the help they needed.

Dobash and Dobash (1979) found that parents might be ambivalent about their role but this was not apparent in the experience of Iris, Lily and Zahrah in this study. They were offered a temporary alternative home by other members of their family – their mother and father, their adult son from a previous marriage and their aunt and uncle. Zahrah's aunt and uncle unsuccessfully tried to obtain a reconciliation because the success (or otherwise) of the marriage was a matter of the family's reputation. They did not want their niece to move to a refuge because of the effects on her (and her family's) reputation. Iris's parents took their daughter's side. They were practising Catholics and were very critical of her ex-partner and his violent behaviour. They would have contacted the police had he attempted to threaten or attack her when she was living in their home. Lily's son had left home when he was a young teenager partly because of the behaviour of his stepfather. Helping his mother was not a situation of divided loyalty for him.

Moving into someone else's home led to overcrowding, so no arrangements were permanent (although each family was happy to accommodate their daughter/mother/niece until she found somewhere permanent to live). They also helped in other ways, although their reasons for helping varied. The relatives of the white women presumed that they should live independently and actively helped them find a new home. For example, Iris's mother accompanied her on visits to housing offices and to look at housing offers. Zahrah's aunt and uncle based their help on a different premise. They went to Pakistan to discuss the situation with the parents of her husband, but were unsuccessful in reconciling them. Zahrah's husband had no interest in her. He went to live with a white woman he had been seeing before the arranged marriage. These differences of approach were indicative of particular philosophies (Muslim, Christian and liberal individualism) which regard the relationship between the individual and the family differently (see Imam, 1994, pp 188-99 for a discussion of this from a Muslim perspective).

In this study, women had not always approached their parents. They first considered what different family members' views were about marriage and relationships, as well as their likely concern about the family's reputation should the violence become public knowledge. The women in this study felt that their birth family's attitudes to their husband/partner and his violence were not straightforward. They were filtered through views of what was acceptable behaviour for men in personal relationships with women and about the position or status of their daughter in relation to them. The woman might be regarded as part of her own birth family or part of her partner's family, or she might be seen as a person in her own right. Sometimes parents or other relatives had views that were framed by religious beliefs (Muslim or Christian). More usually they had not.

Four women in this study chose not to involve their families in their difficulties: Rose, Raihaanah, Fleur and Zaahirah. Raihaanah, Fleur and Zaahirah did not expect to get a sympathetic hearing, and so did not ask for help (Raihaanah was later proved wrong about this). Rose did not ask because she thought that she did not need any help.

Staying in refuges and hostels

Four women were interviewed in this study who had lived in a Women's Aid refuge, a black women's refuge and a women's hostel. Stays lasted between four and twelve months over a period of seven years during the 1990s.

Women's Aid and black women's refuges have provided safe temporary accommodation to women leaving violence since the 1970s. Refuge staff help women in ways that support women's own decisions. Residents have a room of their own but often share facilities with other residents. They are responsible for keeping the refuge clean. This approach was designed to encourage women's self-confidence so that they might be better able to deal with problems once they moved into their own homes (Dobash and Dobash, 1992). They could use the refuge to decide what they wanted to do next: to return home, apply for housing from the local authority and/or housing associations, or move to another town or city (Bull, 1993; Dobash and Dobash, 1992; Rai and Thiara, 1997). Since facilities were shared, women also had opportunities for meeting other women who had experienced violence (Binney et al, 1981; Dobash and Dobash, 1992; Bull, 1993; Malos et al, 1993; Rai and Thiara, 1997). This might enable them to begin to overcome the anxiety, isolation and/or self-blame that they might have felt in their relationship with their violent ex-partner.

Many women who have lived in refuges have valued them especially because they have provided a safe temporary home (Binney et al, 1981; Charles with Jones, 1993; Malos et al, 1993). Black women living in black women's refuges have generally been very positive about staff members' acknowledgement and validation of language and cultural differences between women residents (Rai and Thiara, 1997). Indeed, the feature of living in refuges which the women in this study valued above everything else was the certainty of their own personal safety and that of their children. Belle also spoke of the mutual support between women:

> "It's hard moving from a hostel into a house because with stress I don't sleep much. I'm up at three in the morning having a fag and pacing around. When you're in the hostel you can go and sit in someone else's room. Someone else is awake.... Like I'd be asleep and one of the girls would knock on my door – 'Come in'. 'I can't sleep'. 'Oh, it's alright. Just sit there'. Next night I can't sleep so I sit on the end of her bed. You're just *there* for each other...." (Belle)

Women in other studies had commented about this (Binney et al, 1981; Bull, 1993; Charles with Jones, 1993; Malos et al, 1993). Nevertheless, it was clear from research that there had been difficulties with some services in refuges. There might also be tensions between black refuges and their relationship with longer-existing white or mixed refuges (Mama, 1989; but see also Dhillon-Kashyap, 1994, for a broader and more positive perspective). Malos et al interviewed two women who refused to use refuges because of the poor reputation which some refuges have (1993, p 60). Rai and Thiara interviewed black women who were put off refuges because they thought that they were only for white women, were overcrowded, or would mean living in very poor conditions (1997, pp 16-17). The extent of sharing within refuges was problematic, with children finding it difficult to get space to do homework quietly and women getting frustrated at having to clean up after others with different standards (Binney et al, 1981; Malos et al, 1993; Rai and Thiara, 1997; Batsleer et al, 2002). The amount of help which women had received during their stay was another issue (Bull, 1993), as was whether women's particular language, cultural and religious needs had been recognised and supported by staff (Mama, 1989). Were any of these criticisms repeated by women in this study?

Unfortunately, all four women were critical of the services and cleanliness in the refuges. It was clear that some women did more than other women residents. The women in this study equated the cleanliness and nature of services in the refuge with others' views about their personal worth. They thought it unlikely that middle-class women would tolerate the living conditions they had experienced. They only stayed because there appeared to be no alternative that would be entirely safe. Belle felt that the underlying attitude of staff was that "Women like me deserve no better". Fleur, commenting about the Women's Aid refuge, felt "Is this all we're good for? Is this all we can expect?". Belle's immediate reaction on being asked what she had thought of the black women's refuge where she had stayed was "They're disgusting! Whoever provides them? Really! It makes you feel ... that you're being punished for the choice you've made".

Fleur spoke of women who had returned to violent partners rather than live in "dirty" conditions with staff "who didn't like their jobs". She had found it difficult to share a bedroom with her two teenage sons, a situation made worse by an acute shortage of sheets for residents during her stay. Some women and their children slept on the floors. Black women's refuge staff were viewed critically: variously described as "useless", "unmotivated" or "authoritarian", in sharp contrast to previous research (for example, see Rai and Thiara, 1997). There was conflict between residents and staff over rubbish and cleaning rotas, and cookers in the shared kitchen were damaged and unsafe. Cooking pans were often missing, and personal food and equipment was often stolen.

Staff appeared to provide little or no help with housing applications. Fleur commented that Women's Aid staff only helped women with their housing applications when they were asked to help. No advice was given about particular areas of the city. She felt that some women had little or no confidence and would not ask for help because they thought that they were imposing on staff. Rai and Thiara (1997) noted this tendency in older women. Belle received some help from the staff in the black women's refuge to complete housing applications but six weeks later discovered them still on the desk of the refuge worker who had helped her. When challenged, the worker had said that she "had not got round to doing them". Zahrah had missed two appointments to see a Housing Manager because she had relied on refuge staff. Staff only sporadically collected the residents' post from a post office address and she received an appointment letter too late for her to attend. On another occasion, a Refuge Worker forgot that she had arranged to act as an interpreter in an interview and got to work too late for them to get there in time.

One of the potential difficulties with a 'self-help' approach to organising advice and building women's confidence emerged clearly here. If assistance from refuge staff depended on women asking, a number of women who needed help would not receive it, especially if they were particularly lacking in confidence. The way women in this study described asking for help seemed more akin to the supplicant role discussed in Chapter Five.

Zaahirah moved to a women's hostel from the black women's refuge and could compare them. She described her Support Worker in the black women's refuge as "useless". By contrast, the staff in the women's hostel were described as "very helpful and friendly". Even though they did not speak Urdu or Mirpuri, staff got an interpreter. Some staff went with her to local offices and shops. In this directly-run association hostel, each woman was limited to a stay of six months. They were helped to apply for housing from a range of possible landlords. Support workers checked progress regularly with women and additional help was provided when necessary. This approach was nearer to the rights-based style where staff expertise was built up and actively made available to residents.

Women's comments illustrated what was important to them in the services provided by refuges and hostels. Having left violent partners/ex-partners, they needed a secure, clean and supportive environment and help from trusted staff, preferably in their own first language. It appeared that the problems experienced in refuges by the women in this study were largely the result of poorly motivated and managed staff. The standard of services provided was different from the usual account of the work of refuges (see Charles, 2000, pp 135-55 as an example). For this reason, particular issues were raised in the interviews with refuge staff. They confirmed that the issues which women had raised in this study had been significant problems. One refuge was later transferred to another managing agent: staff became redundant. The other decided to employ staff to clean and do the laundry.

Housing interviews

Despite the recommendations in the *Code of Guidance* about how to conduct interviews, women who have become homeless because of violent men have sometimes been interviewed insensitively by local authority housing staff (Binney et al, 1981; Malos et al, 1993). A number of local authorities have adopted policy guidelines on how to handle these situations appropriately (including the local authority in this study). Nevertheless, there might be differences between the intention of formal organisational policy and the actual practice of frontline staff (Lipsky, 1980). The women in this study made comments that illustrated divergence between local authority policy and practice and differences between individual local authority staff.

A member of the central homeless team had interviewed each of the women (with the exception of Rose). The women were generally satisfied with these interviews. Detailed comment was reserved for the interviews they had later when their papers were forwarded to the local authority neighbourhood offices or housing associations. Formal housing waiting lists might prioritise domestic violence, but women identified issues that illustrated a more complicated reality. Three features of the application process were important to them: the extent to which women were personally able to push their applications forward; whether staff were sympathetic or indifferent to their situation; and whether or not women should provide supporting evidence or proof of the violence they had experienced.

Pushing their applications to the forefront of staff attention

Research has shown that obtaining appropriate and useful help from agencies has not been straightforward for women who have left violent partners/ex-partners. It has often involved contacting a large number of different organisations (Binney et al, 1981; Homer et al, 1984; Rai and Thiara, 1997). As far as finding a new home was concerned, all of the women (except Zahrah) had applied to the local authority *and* housing associations to increase their chances of being rehoused quickly. Each landlord had to be approached separately. Fleur, Belle, Rose and Iris dealt with housing staff themselves. Lily, Raihaanah, Zahrah and Zaahirah were helped by an advice worker or support worker (employed by the local authority, an advice centre, the black women's refuge and the women's hostel respectively).

Having applied for housing, most women in this study were reluctant to push themselves forward to emphasise the urgency of their application to staff. This was because their confidence was low as a result of their experience of violence (Mullender, 1996, pp 23-26; BMA, 1998, pp 30-2). Only Belle thought that it was important for women to keep drawing the attention of staff to their housing applications:

> "They're all bits of paper with a name on and they don't know really what's going on unless you are there, jumping up and down." (Belle)

Having to tell people about the violence that they had experienced was a personal strain, especially when the likely response was unpredictable and might be critical (Binney et al, 1981; Homer et al, 1984; Mama, 1989; Kirkwood, 1993; Malos et al, 1993). A large amount of emotional energy was used in following up housing applications. Several women described this. Belle and Fleur's comments illustrated two different perspectives although both feared personal criticism from staff. Belle commented:

"One thing I found very hard is that you need to mention all the time that you've suffered domestic violence. Then you feel as if you're harping on about it.... You feel like you need to be going 'Hello, I've been abused. *I've been abused!*'. You need to mention it every time.... You might seem like you're being a nuisance and that's a hard thing because you've been conditioned into not wanting to bother anybody and to be quiet. You know, don't disturb, don't rock the boat – but *rock* the boat. You know these are people that aren't going to turn around and beat you up because you've got on their nerves...." (Belle)

Fleur found it too upsetting to talk about the violence she had experienced and had been relieved that staff had not wanted too many details. She did not want to "open up" about the violence and then "get kicked" (criticised) by staff.

Women who regularly visited associations' offices risked being considered negatively by staff: they took up time that might be better used on other applicants. For example, the Housing Services Officer in Foxglove HA (see Chapter Six) had characterised women as very vocal and adept at obtaining support. They were "all too happy to go everywhere to get supporting letters because they know the system". They might also be seen as trying to challenge the supplicant role which some staff by implication expected of applicants (see Chapter Five; also Lambert et al, 1978).

How sympathetic were staff?

The nature of the approach of staff who interviewed women was important because of the difficulty which women might have in talking about violence. Women's experiences of housing association staff were mixed. At one end of the scale, Belle believed that she had talked to a member of staff in Tulip HA who was sympathetic because she received an offer of the last vacant house on a desirable new consortium estate where she wanted to live. She had only been interviewed four days before and felt that she must have convinced the Housing Officer how desperate she was after eight months to leave the black women's refuge. Some research has shown the tendency in merit schemes to allocate high-demand vacancies to applicants whose circumstances appear the most urgent (Niner, 1985). Belle's approach would have helped as Tulip HA staff considered *all* relevant and high-point-scoring applications when allocating vacancies (see Chapter Six). This approach would not have suited Foxglove HA who only chose applications to consider strictly by points total and date order. At the other end of the scale, Lily, Fleur and Iris felt that some staff had treated them very impersonally, especially those who worked in local authority neighbourhood offices. Staff only appeared to be concerned about application form details and/or whether they had a nomination. Lily remarked that even though she had priority because she was homeless, one local authority Housing Manager who interviewed her "didn't seem as though she cared one bit, really".

The poor housing offers she received from that office reinforced her view. She "despaired" of the local authority.

Sometimes it was difficult for women to judge staff accurately, especially in cases where they had a sympathetic personal approach. Women sometimes needed skilled advocates to deal with what staff in associations *actually did* (or did not do) in relation to their housing applications. For example, Raihaanah believed that Tulip HA staff were "very nice people". They had always been courteous and helpful when she had telephoned, including the staff who did not speak Punjabi, and she felt that they had given her a chance of a "new life". The irony was that she was first offered a very poor property in a very unsafe part of the city. She would have accepted it because she was desperate to move but her advice worker/interpreter insisted that she refuse it on the grounds of unsuitability. Immediately, a second offer was made to her of a newly-built four-bedroom house. She attributed this change of fortune to Allah: "In our religion, God shuts one door for you and opens a hundred more. I thought that was true then". A more earthly interpretation would emphasise the role of the knowledgeable advice worker/interpreter!

Lily also had difficulties, although she did not recognise them as such. Bluebell HA staff expected *her* to sort out a muddle that had occurred in the local authority about her nomination to the association. This was despite the fact that she had already asked the local authority neighbourhood office – several times. It had been lost – several times – and she was clearly emotionally very vulnerable. She eventually asked her Support Worker to help, but it would not have been unusual in the past for a Bluebell HA staff member to deal with this problem directly. This was one area of work where the staff had shifted responsibility to applicants to save themselves time.

Housing management services in associations were being provided in increasingly pressurised and cost-conscious circumstances. Women were most likely to see the effects of this in interviews. As staff became increasingly hard pressed, they would be unlikely to spend more time talking to women applicants than was absolutely necessary to do their job. They needed sufficient detail on the application form and from the interview to write an assessment report and would expect women themselves to obtain a nomination from the local authority. Staff would be unlikely to offer support and/or advice unless they found themselves with someone who was distressed (like Lily) or determined (like Belle). Women in this study interpreted this contraction in service personally, as hurtful indifference.

Supporting evidence or proof

Excessive demands for proof had been used by authorities in some parts of the country to reduce the numbers of women accepted as homeless under the legislation (Binney et al, 1981; Malos et al, 1993). The local authority in this study was not one of them. Formally, it did not expect women to provide external corroboration of the violence they had endured before considering them to be statutory homeless. Belle, Lily and Rose commented on the need for supporting evidence or proof of violence. Ironically, they thought that providing extra information would have helped them.

Lily believed that neighbourhood office staff would have made better quality housing offers had they received letters from her psychiatrist, social worker and solicitor about the violence and her subsequent ill health. It was actually doubtful whether this was true, since the particular neighbourhood office she dealt with had few two-bedroom vacancies. Nevertheless, individual Housing Managers *could* exercise discretion in relation to the quality of accommodation offered if there were suitable vacancies (see Chapter Three). Belle and Rose felt that asking for supporting evidence was a protection against abuse of the system. Rose had been asked by Tulip HA to provide a letter from the Social Services Department confirming that her daughter had been abused. She thought that this was fair:

> "It's not a nice thing to say but people would so they could get moved."
> (Rose)

Mooney's (1993) study in London found that 45% of the women who had experienced domestic violence over the 12 months before they were contacted by researchers had told nobody about it. It was clear that some women would have no difficulty in providing letters, copies of injunctions/exclusion orders, support letters and so on, but some would. The comments of women in this study illustrate some of the difficulties. Asking for proof might reinforce women's position as supplicants. Not asking for proof might lead to perceived unfairness in the waiting-list system.

Housing offers

Each of the women was assessed as statutory homeless by the local authority except Rose. They were registered on the housing register and had been nominated to housing associations of their choice. The policy in this local authority was that one offer of accommodation would be made to applicants in these circumstances. If the offer had been turned down and staff felt that it had been 'reasonable', the application would be reassessed as 'not homeless' (that is, it would be downgraded so that the woman would be unlikely to be rehoused). This complied with the authority's minimum obligation in the 1996 Housing Act. Homeless people were likely to receive fewer offers and far less choice than other housing register applicants (see Niner, 1989, pp 73-4 for a discussion of this practice). The local authority also expected associations to make one offer, but associations had different policies about this: illustrating again the limits of the local authority's influence over association rehousing practices.

Offers of accommodation

Although council policy was to offer only one property to homeless applicants, council staff *could* make more offers than this were applicants able to convince them that an offer was unreasonable. The most usual reason women gave for refusing offers was the very poor state of repair of the property that was offered to them. Table 3 shows the number of housing offers from the local authority which women in this study refused. Women refused far fewer offers made to them by housing associations.

This local authority's policy on domestic violence might have given the impression that women received a sympathetic service. This view has to be tempered, especially when considering the allocation practices of neighbourhood offices. Women in this study had been exclusively offered poor property by local authority neighbourhood offices (see Prescott-Clarke et al, 1994, pp 96-7, for similar findings for homeless applicants in other local authorities). All of these houses had been turned down apart from the property that Zahrah accepted. It was large and her relatives lived nearby.

It was possible that homeless women were offered houses that were in serious disrepair because staff had no other vacancies. Alternatively, they might have been offered them because staff needed to let property quickly (to minimise rent loss) and thought that women would accept because they were desperate (CRE, 1984a; Henderson and Karn, 1987). Offering poor quality housing might also have been used to test women whose 'stories' were regarded as doubtful by housing management staff. The intention was to push a woman into providing more information about her circumstances to show how unreasonable a particular offer was (see the Contract Manager's comments in Chapter Three). Staff might justify using homeless applicants to fill otherwise unlettable voids by negatively stereotyping women who had left violence as potentially 'undeserving' or 'queue jumpers'. Women in this study did not directly encounter attitudes like this from local authority staff, although women

Table 3: Offers of housing that were refused

Name	Council offers refused	Association offers refused	Who rehoused?	The time it took (months)
Lily	7	0	Housing association	12
Iris	0	0	Housing association	5
Rose	Council transfer	0	Housing association	9
Zahrah	1	Did not apply	Local authority	12
Raihaanah	0	1	Housing association	4
Fleur	4	1	Housing association	18+
Zaahirah	1	0	Housing association	5
Belle	0	2	Housing association	8

interviewed for research in other areas have done so (Binney et al, 1981; Malos et al, 1993, p 50).

The impact of offers of poor quality council housing

Women in this study were shocked at the condition of houses they were expected to consider suitable for themselves and their families. Fleur, Lily and Belle wondered whether they were a reflection of how they were thought of by the local authority and housing association staff. Worse still, it made them question whether they had done the right thing in leaving their violent partner. For example, Zaahirah had two children aged under three years old. She was offered a boarded-up, semi-derelict council house in a street that formed part of a pre-clearance area. Other houses were boarded-up and the street was littered with bricks, rubble and wooden planks, where vandals had broken into property. Lily had similar offers:

> "They were appalling.... They were trying to put me in houses that were boarded-up on each side. Ten feet high of rubbish! You couldn't get round the back. Windows smashed and houses unoccupied in the street. I would have been a nervous wreck after one night.... I felt as if I had to make up an excuse to justify it [turning properties down] and I should not have had to justify myself." (Lily)

An equally important reason for turning down offers was personal safety. Fleur refused a house in an area that she discovered had a reputation for racist attacks. Zahrah turned down a council flat in a converted house where two male tenants lived because she would not have felt safe living there.

It was clear that constructing a domestic violence policy in the local authority which did not include advice/instructions to staff about the quality of the housing offers to be made was at best only a partial response to women trying to leave violent partners/ex-partners. Housing associations appeared less likely to make poor-quality offers. Having said that, Raihaanah's experience with Tulip HA was shocking, and illustrated that associations were also not immune to putting housing management interests first even when it blatantly disadvantaged women applicants.

Did women have a choice?

Researchers have spoken of homeless applicants making choices in relation to social rented housing and have identified the apparent paradox of applicants seeming to choose poor areas (English, 1975, 1979; Clapham and Kintrea, 1984, 1986). Whether the decisions made by women in this study can be called choices is very doubtful given the condition of the property offered and women's fears about being reassessed should they refuse them 'unreasonably'. The priorities of housing management staff were to fill vacancies quickly. The priorities of women were to find a safe, well-repaired home. These priorities sometimes contradicted one another.

Although association staff worked under similar constraints to the local authority staff, the way the two sectors meshed together was complicated and unpredictable in terms of housing offers made. Fleur refused four offers and was told by council staff that were she to refuse the next one her application would be reassessed. Then at the same time she received two separate offers of different properties from two associations. Nevertheless, she was very clear that she was not choosing between them. She was adamant that the threat of her application being downgraded forced her to accept one of them. For Belle, the pressure to accept an association offer derived from the desperation and frustration of having spent eight months in a refuge. For Raihaanah, the absolute priority was getting away from the danger of having to continue to live with a violent husband. For Iris, the rules of the 1996 Housing Act were the problem. Had the local authority offered her a reasonable property *before* Foxglove HA, she would have been obliged to accept it even though she only wanted a Foxglove HA house.

In this local authority area, the position of housing associations in the housing system, their stock holding compared to that of the local authority (especially their new consortium housing), and the way their allocation systems interacted with the local authority's, were distinctive. Research in the past has commented that housing associations have not housed many homeless applicants because they have fewer suitable vacancies (Niner, 1989; Malos et al, 1993). This study indicated slightly different issues because of the impact of new building by the associations and the targets they had to reach for nominations. The local authority could usually make offers first because of its size and turnover. Associations *might* provide an alternative if women were prepared to wait. They also had to be prepared to turn down unreasonable local authority offers and risk being reassessed. Some women were better placed to do all this. For example, Fleur and Lily were living in more secure and manageable temporary homes (a second-stage self-contained house and a son's home respectively) rather than shared and possibly stressful refuges.

A new home and new area

Conflicts between housing management priorities and women's particular requirements were seen in a number of other ways. Selecting applicants for vacancies was a time-consuming process in the case study associations (see Chapter Six), but each of them then expected applicants whom they had selected to decide *immediately* whether or not they wanted the property (even though they may have been waiting months with no news). Staff were managed closely in relation to 'void control' and were expected to maximise rental income by ensuring that properties were tenanted as quickly as possible. Women in this study were given the minimum of time to decide: if they wanted the house, they had to sign the tenancy agreement and become liable for the rent immediately. This had potentially serious ramifications for women.

The new home

Iris, Lily, Raihaanah and Zaahirah were shown properties by Housing Officers and Housing Services Officers from each of the case study associations. Staff retained strict control over the amount of time women had to look round. Zaahirah had ten minutes to look round and decide whether to accept a house from Bluebell HA in an area she did not know. Iris, who was rehoused by Foxglove HA, commented that she had noted the time it had taken on her watch. She had

> "never known somebody so arrogant in all my life.... He showed me round this house in three minutes – three minutes! That's the God's honest truth – three minutes. He was in the house a total of seven minutes from the moment we opened the door, to me signing up, to him getting into his car." (Iris)

Other women collected keys from the offices to view property by themselves. They had longer to look round, but if they wanted the property they also had to sign the tenancy agreement on the same day. Sometimes the staff wanted new tenants to move in quickly to prevent vandalism. Iris was offered a larger property on a consortium estate than her family size might have indicated but only on the condition that she move in immediately. Empty houses had been spray-painted by vandals and staff wanted to avoid further problems by having properties occupied.

It was clear that the priority for staff was to establish a rental stream for the association. They seemed to give little thought to whether this approach to managing property disadvantaged women. Women were affected by this sudden urgency for a decision in different ways. They had little time to think or find out much about an area or its local facilities. This created problems for women who were new to the city or the area, whose first language was not English or who could not obtain independent help quickly. Signing up for the tenancy meant that women who were living in refuges, hostels or second-stage homes were immediately liable for two rents from that day (for their current temporary home and their new permanent home). In cases where they were reliant on state benefits for an income, they often could not move until they had received a community care grant from the DSS for furniture. Housing benefit regulations prevented local authorities paying two rents for this period, so the delay of three or four weeks meant that many women moved into their new homes with considerable rent arrears. Some paid off the arrears with part of the DSS grant for basic household items.

Despite these difficulties, most of the women in this study were pleased with the association housing they had accepted. Many women spoke of being able to start "new lives" or lead "normal" lives because of their new home. When

Lily went to see her current home for the first time, she thought that it would be "another dump" similar to the seven council properties which she had rejected. She had been pleasantly surprised by the housing offered by Tulip HA's Housing Officer: "I was *so* excited when he brought me to see this that I gave him a hug! I've not seen the man since!".

Belle was even more enthusiastic:

> "I'm happy and part of that happiness is I love my house, my little back garden and my shed. I kept going on to my Mum, 'Mum, I've got *a shed* in the back garden!', and she sent me a card saying 'Welcome to your new home'. And then she said, 'Are you sure you're not actually *living* in the shed, Belle?', because I'd gone on about this shed more than anything. It's such a picture of normalness to me…. I've got my house. I've got my driveway. I've got my fence. I've got my shed. It's just such a picture of normalness. We are so lucky to have these houses." (Belle)

All of the women in this study now lived on state benefits (since they were unemployed, caring for small children or were very ill). They had only been able to accept their tenancies because they were entitled to full housing benefit to pay the rent. They all worried about how much the rent was, especially when compared to local authority rents. Two women had started working but their jobs were part-time and very badly paid (sewing and working in a fast-food restaurant). They had experienced problems with benefits payments because of their changing circumstances and were worse off in real terms than if they had stayed at home. Three women felt they would never find a job in the future which would enable them to pay the rent independently of the housing benefit system. Effectively, the case study associations were contributing towards women's continued reliance on state benefits as the main household income.

The new area and staying safe

The government's current interest in building communities in social housing and strengthening them through allocations practices had a potentially negative impact on the lives of women in this study (DETR and DSS, 2000). Their housing options may have been severely affected by housing staff anxious not to rehouse too many 'vulnerable' and homeless lone parents. The experience of women in this study also showed an aspect of 'social capital building', or building networks of people and knowledge of community services which was very constrained and limited. There were fundamental reasons for this. They needed to ensure their family's personal safety through limiting contacts and maintaining anonymity. Most moved to areas of the city which were previously unknown to them and had little or no contact with neighbours. They did not like doing this and there were risks in being regarded as 'outsiders' in the area, but it was important as a way of protecting their privacy and ensuring their safety (Phizacklea and Miles, 1979; Charles with Jones, 1993).

Fleur's experience showed the wisdom of restricting contacts with neighbours. She had discovered that her new neighbour ("a gossip") had come from the same area where she had lived previously (see Chapter Six) and still visited friends there. Fleur thought that it was only a matter of time before her ex-partner heard about where she was. She was now fearful all the time, restricting herself to the back room during the day to avoid being seen through the front window and not sleeping because of anxiety at night. She blamed the Housing Officer for this. He "could not have been listening to her" when she had told him about her violent ex-partner. She was afraid that if she asked for a transfer the situation would "be thrown back in my face" and would then "turn into a shouting match". Some days she said that she felt paralysed by anxiety.

Women in this study used local shops, schools and surgeries as another way of maintaining their safety. Raihaanah and Zaahirah had difficulties shopping for Asian food and clothes, but they preferred to be further away from the community because of the privacy that they and their children had found. Other Asian families would be likely to ask questions about a woman living by herself with her children. These could potentially be very dangerous as well as ill-informed and hurtful (Khan, 1979).

Raihaanah and Zaahirah had moved to areas which they did not know and where few Asian families lived. In doing this, they had followed the advice given to them by advice workers who had correctly reassured them that they would be safe there from racist attacks. However, they did have problems in using some services because of language differences. Zaahirah was learning to speak English in order to cope with this, but Raihaanah relied on her older children to communicate with English speakers as she had several small children and no transport or time to go to English classes.

This illustrated more than anything else the importance of associations having staff who spoke the most common community languages. Of the three Pakistani women rehoused by different landlords in this study, only Raihaanah could contact the landlord's office herself and talk to a member of staff in Punjabi. Although Zaahirah and Zahrah were learning English, not being able to communicate directly with housing management staff created delays and difficulties (for example, in getting basic services like repairs) and increased their sense of isolation. It also meant that were they to experience serious problems such as harassment or violence, it would be very difficult for them to obtain help from housing staff easily and quickly.

Kirkwood (1993, pp 117-21) remarked on the anger that some women may feel in comparing their circumstances with their former abuser's, especially when they are going through difficulties or had been allocated poor-quality accommodation. Iris certainly felt angry, although her anger was directed at Foxglove HA. She had been rehoused years before by the association because of her partner's violence and had been safe until her landlord rehoused her violent ex-partner's mother opposite her home. Foxglove HA then effectively did nothing for months as his violence started again (see Chapter Six for comments about how transfers can get 'forgotten' in the association's allocation system). Iris was severely injured and her home was vandalised, but she refused to let him across the threshold. No association transfer offer had been forthcoming and after nearly a year of waiting she felt she had no choice but to leave for her own and her children's safety. She moved in with her parents. Eventually, she was rehoused by Foxglove HA, as a statutory homeless nominee, in a completely unfamiliar and distant area:

> "I think that the likes of me and the people like me get the short end of the straw because why should *we* move, isolate *ourselves* right over here…?" (Iris)

Keeping safe from families

Even when women had left years before, some men sought ways of finding or threatening them; so maintaining links with some family members might be dangerous. Fleur's sister had told Fleur's ex-partner where she lived because she had not known he had been violent. Now he was trying to find Fleur again even though she had left him nine years before. Belle had kept in contact with her ex-partner's mother who wanted to continue to see her only grandson. She had then put Belle at risk by telling her son the name of the city in which Belle currently lived. He now telephoned regularly, and alternated between "sweet talking" and threatening her. She felt that it was only the physical distance between them that ensured her continued safety. Her father had recently told her to come home to get more support and had stopped paying her telephone bill. Belle thought this was his unhelpful way of making an unrealistic point.

Hester and Radford (1996) found that 50 out of 53 mothers in their study had experienced violence from their ex-partners following arrangements made to continue contact with children after partners had separated. Belle's situation has already been mentioned. Zaahirah and Iris were both anxious about their ex-partners' intentions. Zaahirah's husband looked after the children at the weekends. She felt that he was trying to emotionally sway them in his favour to make it more difficult for her to care for them so that he could eventually take the children from her. Iris's ex-partner had recently used a solicitor to approach her about seeing their child. She thought that this was a ploy to find her because he had shown no interest in the child before.

While women were trying to rebuild their lives, some ex-partners were determined to find them to wreak vengeance or re-establish their authority. This was the grim reality for women in this study. It contradicted the view of the Team Leader in Foxglove HA (see Chapter Six) about women "needing" violent ex-partners and the neighbourhood office Manager (in Chapter Three) who believed that women "never learn" and always go back to violent partners. The women in this study had changed or modified their lives to avoid violence from these men (Stanko, 1985, 1994). The extent of their fear of being found depended on the physical distance between themselves and their ex-partner and their assessment of how difficult it might be for their new home to be discovered. Women had taken care over where they lived, their contact with neighbours, where they shopped and where and when they walked in public places, and the supervision of their children.

Throughout all of these emotional and practical difficulties, maintaining family ties could become dangerous or strained since other people might not understand the woman's particular situation. Women might not receive help or help itself might be conditional (further complicating their efforts to rebuild their lives). Belle, Iris and Fleur had relationships with new male partners and had started new families. This was a reflection of the years that had passed since they had left their violent ex-partner, although they were still being pursued (with greater or lesser determination). All of them felt that their current relationship had been adversely affected by past experience of violence. They found it difficult or impossible to fully trust their new partners. They had fears about whether he would also become violent. They worried about what he would do if their ex-partner found them. Would he protect them?

Conclusion

The ways in which women were able to find a new home involved housing application processes (applying, being assessed and being allocated property) that were inevitably affected by their personal experience of violence. Their intense fear of being found again and their lack of self-confidence and self-esteem meant that they were unsure of how people, including staff, would treat them. It was notable that they sometimes used language referring to their fear of being killed, beaten up, criticised or shouted at when they were talking about situations where they might have to ask for help or stand up for themselves. Association housing staff had little time to talk to them about what had happened and what they required, so they were often unaware of the continuing impact of fear on women's daily lives.

When they first left, the temporary arrangements which women made to enable them to leave their violent partner/ex-partner were severely restricted to what was *immediately* possible. This reflected their limited resources in what was often an urgent situation. If close members of their family could not help then the local authority was approached to provide safe temporary housing. Local authority homeless staff usually referred women to one of the refuges. Women had no choice or control over these arrangements: their main priority was safety.

The nature and range of comments which women made in this study about housing services, staff and housing offers were not unexpected. They have been identified before as important in 'good practice' reports, policy documents and research on this subject. The unexpected aspect of women's views was the way they interpreted the nature and quality of housing management services and property offers with people's views about what they were worth as women. The refuges and the local authority neighbourhood offices had a negative impact on the women in this study because of the quality of the service they received and the housing offers made to them. A women's hostel and the associations which had rehoused them had a positive effect. Within certain limitations, they had responded with what women wanted: sound advice and help and a good quality home.

The women interviewed had established themselves in their new homes for varying lengths of time – some for many years, others for a few months. It was clear that although they spoke of new lives, these were only possible when they felt completely safe from their ex-partner. The most noticeable feature of their accounts was the different ways in which some ex-partners still threatened the women and their children. Some women were able to speak more positively than others: they had a new home which they loved; they had a new job; the children were doing very well at school; they had a new relationship with a man who was supportive; their health had improved. Fear and isolation haunted the lives of some of the other women in this study. They also worried about the long-term damage of the violence on their children.

Rehousing women who had experienced violence required a more sensitive and appropriate housing management practice than appeared to be currently available from each of the case study associations in this research. Housing management staff appeared to be distant figures at the outer limits of women's helping networks. Only Iris had specifically talked to housing management staff about her safety (wanting reassurance that her address would be confidential). None of the women had seen a Housing Officer or Housing Services Officer since moving in. Women had to telephone the office when they wanted to talk to staff or report a repair. Housing Officers and Housing Services Officers had effectively withdrawn from day-to-day management of their estates and management areas because of management pressure on them to complete 'core' tasks such as arrears and void-control work. This meant that women were not given the opportunity to build up workable relationships with the staff who managed their home and management area. This might create difficulties in the future should their violent ex-partner reappear (especially for women who spoke no English) since staff would not be able to act quickly or with any knowledge of the woman's immediate circumstances. The associations' stance against domestic violence seemed very limited when looked at from a service-wide perspective. It barely extended beyond prioritising domestic violence within waiting lists and rehousing women. Once they had moved into their new homes, housing management staff appeared to let women sink or swim.

EIGHT

Conclusions

Housing associations are becoming increasingly important as providers of social housing. If the present government's stock transfer plans proceed (DETR and DSS, 2000), they will take over the role of being the main provider of social rented housing from local authorities by 2004. This increasing privatisation of social housing stock is paralleled by the continuing fragmentation of public housing policy. The present study illustrates what this may mean in practice for homeless women who have left violent men and need to find a new home.

The primary homelessness legislation in force at the time of this study was the 1996 Housing Act. This has now been superceded by the 2002 Homelessness Act, which provides local authorities with new duties as well as amending some of those originally found in the 1996 Act. The aim of the new legislation is to provide a more constructive response to homeless people than was possible before. The new legislation will reinforce the practice of local authorities which have been offering a sympathetic response to homeless women who have escaped domestic violence, including the local authority in this study.

The 2002 Homelessness Act expects local authorities to review homelessness in their areas and prepare a strategy every five years to respond to it. This strategy should cover preventative measures, temporary accommodation and support. The 1996 Act has been amended so that 'priority need' status has been extended to single people who have experienced or who are at risk of violence and who are considered to be vulnerable. The restriction of two years for the provision of temporary accommodation has been abolished: temporary accommodation is to be available for as long as it takes the applicant to be provided with permanent accommodation. The local authority duty to consider private sector alternatives before acting itself is also abolished. Part VI of the 1996 Act is amended by the 2002 Act so that more groups are included that must be given reasonable preference within local authorities' allocation schemes, including homeless people.

The local authority in this study will be able to build on the sympathetic approach that it provided despite the restrictions of the 1996 Act. The 2002 Homelessness Act also gives it another opportunity, via the strategy it must prepare, to be more proactive in relation to housing association policy and practice in relation to homelessness, domestic violence and housing. Another important opportunity for change is that it will now have to indicate in its allocation scheme how applicants (including homeless people) will be able to exercise choice over the accommodation offered to them. How this will work in practice remains to be seen, but it may enable homeless people to have more control over where they live. Traditionally, they have had little or no choice with 'one offer only' policies in the majority of local authorities (including the authority in this study).

So what may be identified from this study that has continuing general relevance? Are there insights into what may happen in the future for homeless women looking for a new home?

There are three main areas in which important issues emerged. The first concerns the different futures of local authorities and housing associations as managers of social rented housing. The second is the nature of the relationship between the enabling or strategic local authority and housing associations. Finally, the nature of housing management services provided by associations (access, assessment, allocation, management and support) is the third and crucial area affecting women's opportunities of finding alternative accommodation.

The local authority in this study implemented the 1996 Housing Act in a way that protected its sympathetic approach to homeless women who had left domestic violence. About one third of all the statutory homeless households whom it rehoused each year were women leaving domestic violence. This was partly due to the positive effects on staff of its domestic violence policy, despite its introduction and implementation, which arguably could have been more consistently managed. It also helped that vacancies were available which could be offered to statutory homeless households, although again there were issues about quality, location and choice of council housing that could have been better handled.

The unexpected discovery in this research, however, was that the local authority in this study was able to quite radically distort the intentions of the 1996 Act, especially in relation to lone parents. This should give pause for thought about the prospects of the 2002 Homelessness Act. Local authorities will still be able to interpret the legislation more or less sympathetically in ways that have been largely illustrated in the history described in Chapter Two. It is also worth recalling that only one in five of a total of 50 homeless services investigated by the Audit Commission have been judged to be good, and only one has been judged to be excellent (Audit Commission, 2003).

However, local authorities may not be the main providers of social rented housing for much longer. Indeed, in over 140 authorities, they no longer manage rented housing (the stock having been transferred to housing associations). Concern has been expressed that in some of these, the local authority no longer has sufficient access to rented social housing as the stock transfer association has introduced barriers to rehousing homeless households (Bennet, 2001). Some other local authorities have also contracted out homeless assessment work to an association, and problems have arisen. Many other local authorities, which have no intention of transferring stock, have taken steps to set up 'arms-length' housing organisations to manage their council housing, but what the nature of the service to homeless households will be remains to be seen. It is for this reason that the enabling or strategic role of the local authority may grow in importance. The local authority in this study had some way to go in improving its enabling or strategic functions, including its ability to monitor and influence associations' work.

For example, nominations were very important for homeless women who wanted to be rehoused by associations in this study. Le Grand and Bartlett (1993) conceptualised nominations as vouchers through which the local authority purchased accommodation that was provided and managed by associations. But the reality of this type of 'arms-length' rehousing was more complicated than theory implied. There was considerable variation in the nominations performance of the three case study associations and dissatisfaction from many senior local authority management staff about who associations were actually rehousing. Yet the authority itself had not developed detailed organisational monitoring to discover whether it was getting the vacancies it was entitled to, and council neighbourhood Managers relied on their own personal knowledge to judge individual associations. This lack of information made it impossible for the local authority to monitor the extent to which homeless women who had left violent men were being rehoused by associations across the city, the specific ethnic breakdown of the women rehoused, and the type/quality/location of accommodation they were offered.

Although the local authority itself had a domestic violence policy, it had not influenced policy development within associations. Most staff in associations did not know about the local authority's own policy or the NFHA 'good practice' guide (Davis, 1993). The multi-regional Foxglove HA had developed its own harassment policy (which included responding to domestic violence) independently of the local authority. Bluebell and Tulip HAs had not developed a policy and seemed unlikely to do so, in the short term at least. They believed that they had more pressing housing management concerns. Unless this issue becomes part of the regulatory requirements of the Housing Corporation or the Audit Commission, this situation will continue. The patchy response to homeless women from local authorities will be replicated many times over by housing associations.

Associations in this study rehoused direct waiting-list applicants, those who had been nominated by the local authority, and those who had applied for a transfer internally. Nationally, 11% of households rehoused by associations were statutory homeless in the first year of this study (1997/98), a figure far short of the high point of 22% for 1993/94. This decline has since continued annually. Although the policy emphasis in the association sector in the first half of the 1990s had been to rehouse more homeless households, towards the end of the decade the associations in this study had difficulty rehousing sufficient nominated applicants including statutory homeless households, to reach their nominations targets. In the first year of this study this was partly because the local authority nominated insufficient homeless applicants for association vacancies. Even so, the case study associations varied considerably in the rate and numbers of women they rehoused because of domestic violence. Very surprisingly, Tulip HA, the smallest association with the least resources, rehoused far more homeless women than the other two associations. This may have been because Tulip HA was the only association that maintained close working links with the local authority's central homeless teams, the hostels and the refuges. The consortium property (with its higher nomination rate) formed a more significant part of its stock than the stock of the other two associations, so it made more effort to increase the number of households it rehoused who were nominations. It appeared that the other two associations were not under such pressure. It is worth noting here that although many women rehoused by Tulip HA were black or Asian, the association also rehoused white women in these circumstances. Associations' practice also influenced this variable picture. Some homeless women would not consider associations because their rents were too high. Others were rejected by associations because they lacked sufficient proof of violence, had outstanding rent arrears or other apparent misdemeanours, even if they had been nominated.

It has been argued in the past that women's role in relation to the family – the nuclear family especially – was the key to understanding their access to council housing, particularly through the homeless legislation. The influence of familism in relation to women's access to associations' housing could be identified in a number of ways, but none of them was straightforward. The influence of managerialism on housing management practice in associations – and particularly the increasing importance of financial priorities – was far more dominant in these settings. This more complex set of relationships was illustrated in this study. Attitudes towards the women themselves, the nature of the violence that they had experienced, and whether or not they were suitable for a particular vacancy, were all considerations in association assessment and allocation processes. Nevertheless, some of the ways in which women's applications were considered had more to do with reducing financial risk for the association. This was the reason for not accepting some women with rent arrears and/or women whose previous homes had been damaged or abandoned.

Many women applicants already had the highest priority nomination. Even so, customer services staff in the associations (who were usually untrained and poorly managed) exercised considerable discretion in relation to what they expected women to provide by way of proof with their applications. The customer services staff in Foxglove HA would register an application only when a woman could supply such evidence from organisations or professionals. Tulip HA staff would consider letters from organisations and family and friends (although the latter were given less weight because staff thought that they would be biased). Bluebell HA on the other hand did not require such documentation. This varying requirement for support letters illustrated a number of organisational and attitudinal features in relation to homeless women who had left violent men. From an organisational point of view, it showed the current limitations of the local authority's enabling role. It also revealed staff attitudes. Some staff felt that protecting the association's waiting list from potential abuse was more important than responding to individual women's circumstances. Expecting support letters also showed that women were not trusted to tell the truth and would only be helped if they could prove that severe physical violence had occurred.

In deciding which applicant should be offered a vacant property, staff considered and used a woman's formal 'housing need' combined with commonsense views about their lives. These were often compared to those of an idealised nuclear family. Lone parents who had left violence were not regarded as "problem families". They were more likely to be regarded as "vulnerable". It seemed likely that these assumptions were also used in relation to single women in this situation. By contrast, women living with men in nuclear families were regarded as protected (because of the presence of the man), although statistically this was far from the case (Mooney, 1993).

Automatically regarding women who had experienced domestic violence as 'vulnerable' was sometimes detrimental to their chances of being offered housing in locations where staff thought that lone women would be at risk of harassment or violence. These attitudes were in part intended to protect women, but they also signalled a failure by staff in their day-to-day management of estates. This had come about because of the impact of competition on associations and the overriding requirement to increase the efficiency and reduce the cost of housing management services. Housing Officer jobs had been reduced in scope (to dealing with arrears, voids and antisocial behaviour) but increased in volume (the numbers of properties managed) and speediness of response (letting properties). Their increasing workloads pressured staff into offloading work where they could. It was either no longer done or 'customers' were sent to the local authority or advice centres for help. Staff had no time to help new tenants move into their new homes or provide any assistance once they had done so. Similarly, they appeared to have minimal capacity to deal effectively with violence and harassment, hoping to avoid contributing to tenants' difficulties by making reasonably careful allocation decisions. Nevertheless, Housing Officers' knowledge of estates and people had faded as they had to concentrate on 'core' service provision. There were a number of instances in this study where they had inadvertently created an unsafe environment for women whom they had rehoused in the past by not exercising enough care over other allocations made to property nearby.

The services provided by the case study associations did not provide a consistently accessible service for black and Asian women. The nature of staffing (especially the gender and ethnic composition of the service), and whether or not staff spoke the main languages of black and Asian people in the city, was important here. It seemed odd that the multi-regional, financially strong Foxglove HA was rehousing so few black and Asian applicants, including women. One reason might have been that it was a white association with white staff working in customer services. Would black and Asian women want to be rehoused by an association which did not employ black and Asian staff, and where customer services staff appeared unwilling to help or give them much time? Bluebell HA represented a more varied staff profile, but black and Asian women might prefer Tulip HA because many of the association's staff spoke the different community languages. Whether black and Asian applicants were exercising a choice or were in effect being 'channelled' to Tulip HA because of this is debatable.

Some commentators have spoken of the housing association sector being 'racialised'. Many associations in the 1970s and early 1980s concentrated on improving homes in inner-city areas. Inadvertently, this restricted the opportunities of tenants who aspired to live in areas with better-quality accommodation and a more desirable environment, including black and Asian tenants (Henderson and Karn, 1987). This also had implications for black and Asian women who had left violent men and who needed to live in areas where they could maintain their privacy and safety. The location of new housing was as important to them as the nature of association housing management services. Not all of the associations' newly-built property was popular with black and Asian applicants because they feared isolation and racial harassment in these new areas.

Women who had fled violence had additional and different concerns. Asian women often felt safer living away from the main settlement areas of different Asian communities, but only if they found a home in an area where the existing white community was not known for harassment. White women with black children also had to be careful. In predominantly white neighbourhoods, black children might be racially harassed. The family might be more likely to be found by an ex-partner because children were black. The problem for women was that they were rarely given information or time by Housing Officers to find out about these areas when they were offered property. Housing Officers' concern to reduce rent losses on empty property by letting it quickly took precedence over women's concerns about their own safety.

Women who were rehoused by associations saw little or nothing of housing management staff once they moved into their new homes. When women were indeed vulnerable, they might obtain support through outreach services from refuges, the local authority or voluntary organisations rather than the associations. The new Supporting People regime may lead to more intensive and coordinated support services for vulnerable people, although the women in this study largely sorted out problems for themselves even when they had previously lived in refuges.

The housing management service in local authorities and housing associations has become imbued with management ideas and practices derived from the private sector: new public management in various forms. This was clearly evident in the service to homeless women who had left domestic violence. Nevertheless, there were important tensions in the management service in the local authority and in the three case study associations. For staff at different levels, these focused around differing priorities and concerns about the quality of service now offered. For women applicants, these tensions focused around the nature of the service they received. They might be treated in ways which were essentially paternalistic (the 'supplicant' role), customer oriented, or rights-based.

In considering the housing management practices of the three associations, it became clear that applicants and tenants were most usually called customers but treated as supplicants. This was happening within management services that were becoming much more limited in scope than they had been in the past, as associations (and the local authority) strove to become more financially efficient. Calling applicants and tenants 'customers' was the ideological accompaniment to privatisation. This was most clearly seen in Foxglove HA, but there were signs of it in the other associations too. Far from exercising choice or rights, the women in this study, along with most applicants and tenants, had little idea of how their applications were considered by staff and how the management service was changing in nature and diminishing in scope. 'Customer' services to a large extent hid the procedures and processes through which inequalities were constructed and maintained in housing assessment and allocation.

The current government has shown no sign that it wishes to reverse these trends. The privatisation of public investment in housing is due to continue. For example, the government's annual local authority stock transfer programme of 200,000 council homes being transferred to associations and housing companies from 2001/02 continues, although it is beginning to falter (DETR and DSS, 2000). From 2000, Best Value replaced compulsory competitive tendering in local authority service evaluation and housing associations voluntarily participate in this approach (DETR, 1999). This entails five-yearly reviews of in-house services, comparing their competitiveness and financial efficiency with that of other providers in the private sector.

There has been some discussion about constructing a new "public service management" to provide an alternative to the "new public management". At its heart would be the recognition that applicants and tenants are people with rights who pay to receive a service, tailored to what they require in their particular circumstances, rather than receiving a diminishing core service which a local authority or housing association is prepared to provide (see Clarke and Newman, 1997, chapter seven, and Newman, 1998, for useful summaries of the issues). There may be possibilities of developing approaches that give greater emphasis to service quality, equity issues and accountability. Certainly, more priority recently has been given to race equality policies and targets across the range of their functions. Issues relating to governance and accountability also are a growing concern. Whether these will combine to produce a coherent and different management culture remains to be seen.

The government has limited its short-term options for change in social housing management by simply suggesting that allocations in social housing should be based more on choice than on a 'take it or leave it' basis (DETR and DSS, 2000). A number of pilot schemes are investigating the ways in which this might be achieved and 'choice' is being introduced in various ways by many local authorities and housing associations across the country. However, this barely touches the wider issue of the nature of the public role of local authorities and housing associations in protecting and supporting people who are in the weakest positions in society (through their class position, their relationship to the family and/or through the impact of racism).

This study shows how far the housing management service in associations needs to change in relation to one group of applicants and tenants who have become homeless because of domestic violence. Other applicants and tenants equally need a more responsive housing management service. Only by acknowledging this can associations begin to consider how their management services may positively assist some applicants and tenants in the difficult personal task of rebuilding their lives.

References

Abrahams, C. (1994) *The hidden victims – Children and domestic violence*, London: NCH Action for Change.

AMA (Association of Metropolitan Authorities) (1990) *Homelessness: Programme for action*, London: AMA.

AMA with the Association of District Councils (1995) *Fair and seen to be fair: A survey of local authority housing allocations practices*, London: AMA.

Anderson, I., Kemp, P. and Quilgars, D. (1993) *Single, homeless people*, London: HMSO.

Arden, A. and Hunter, C. (1997) *Homelessness and allocations: A guide to the Housing Act 1996, Parts VI and VII*, London: Legal Action Group.

Audit Commission (1989) *Housing the homeless: The local authority role*, London: HMSO.

Audit Commission (2003) *Homelessness: Responding to the new agenda*, London: Audit Commission.

Austerberry, H. and Watson, S. (1983) *Women on the margins: A study of single women's housing problems*, London: Housing Research Group, City University.

Bailey, R. and Ruddock, J. (1972) *The grief report*, London: Shelter.

Barron, J. (1990) *Not worth the paper...? The effectiveness of legal protection for women and children experiencing domestic violence*, Bristol: Women's Aid Federation England.

Batsleer, J., Burman, E., Chantler, K., McIntosh, H.S., Pantling, K., Smailes, S. and Warner, S. (2002) *Domestic violence and minoritisation – Supporting women to independence*, Manchester: Women's Studies Research Centre, Manchester Metropolitan University.

Bennet, J. (2001) *Out of stock. Stock transfer, homelessness and access to housing*, London: Shelter.

Binney, V., Harkell, G. and Nixon, J. (1981) *Leaving violent men: A study of refuges and housing for battered women*, Leeds: Women's Aid Federation England.

Blau, P.M. (1963) *The dynamics of bureaucracy: A study of interpersonal relations in two government agencies*, Chicago: University of Chicago Press.

BMA (British Medical Association) (1998) *Domestic violence: A health care issue?*, London: BMA.

Borkowski, M., Murch, M. and Walker, V. (1983) *Marital violence – The community response*, London: Tavistock.

Borland, M. (ed) (1976) *Violence in the family*, Manchester: Manchester University Press.

Brailey, M. (1986) *Women's access to council housing*, Occasional Paper 25, Glasgow: Planning Exchange.

Bramley, G. (1993) 'The enabling role for local authorities: a preliminary evaluation', in P. Malpass and R. Means (eds) *Implementing housing policy*, Buckingham: Open University Press, pp 127-49.

Bryan, B., Dadzie, S. and Scafe, S. (1985) *The heart of the race: Black women's lives in Britain*, London: Virago.

Bull, J. (1993) *The housing consequences of relationship breakdown*, Department of the Environment, London: HMSO.

Burney, E. (1967) *Housing on trial: A study of immigrants and local government*, Oxford: University Press for the Institute of Race Relations.

CHAC (Central Housing Advisory Committee) (1949) *Selection of tenants and transfers and exchanges. Third report of the Housing Management Sub-Committee of the Central Housing Advisory Committee*, Ministry of Housing and Local Government, London: HMSO.

CHAC (1955) *Unsatisfactory tenants. Sixth report of the Housing Management Sub-Committee of the Central Housing Advisory Committee*, Ministry of Housing and Local Government, London: HMSO.

CHAC (1969) *Council housing, purposes, procedures and priorities. The Cullingworth Report*, Ministry of Housing and Local Government, London: HMSO.

Charles, N. (1994) 'Domestic violence, homelessness and housing: the response of housing providers in Wales', *Critical Social Policy*, vol 14, no 2, pp 36-52.

Charles, N. (2000) *Feminism, the state and social policy*, Basingstoke: Macmillan.

Charles, N. with Jones, A. (1993) *The housing needs of women and children escaping domestic violence*, Cardiff: Tai Cymru (Housing for Wales).

Clapham, D. and Kintrea, K. (1984) 'Allocation systems and housing choice', *Urban Studies*, vol 21, pp 261-9.

Clapham, D. and Kintrea, K. (1986) 'Rationing choice and constraint: the allocation of public housing in Glasgow', *Journal of Social Policy*, vol 15, no 1, pp 51-67.

Clapham, D., Kemp, P. and Smith, S.J. (1990) *Housing and social policy*, Basingstoke: Macmillan.

Clarke, J. (1998) 'Consumerism', in G. Hughes (ed) *Imagining welfare futures*, London: Routledge with The Open University, pp 13-54.

Clarke, J. and Newman, J. (1997) *The managerial state: Power, politics and ideology in the remaking of social welfare*, London: Sage.

Cloke, P., Milbourne, P. and Widdowfield, R. (2000) 'Change, but no change: dealing with homelessness under the 1996 Housing Act ', *Housing Studies*, vol 15, no 5, pp 739-56.

Cole, I, Gidley, G., Ritchie, C., Simpson, D. and Wishart, B. (1996) *Creating communities or welfare housing? A study of new housing association developments in Yorkshire/Humberside*, Coventry: Chartered Institute of Housing.

Cole, I. and Furbey, R. (1994) *The eclipse of council housing*, London: Routledge.

Committee on One-Parent Families (1974) *Report of the Committee on One-Parent Families. Finer Report*, Cmnd 5629 (also 5629-1), London: HMSO.

CRE (Commission for Racial Equality) (1984a) *Race and council housing in Hackney. Report of a formal investigation*, London: CRE.

CRE (1984b) *Race and housing in Liverpool. A research report*, London: CRE.

CRE (1985) *Walsall Metropolitan Borough Council: Practices and policies of housing allocation. Report of a formal investigation*, London: CRE.

CRE (1989a) *Race and housing in Glasgow: The role of housing associations*, London: CRE.

CRE (1989b) *Racial discrimination in Liverpool City Council. Report of a formal investigation into the housing department*, London: CRE.

CRE (1993) *Housing associations and racial equality. Report of a formal investigation into housing associations in Wales, Scotland and England*, London: CRE.

Damer, S. (1974) 'Wine Alley: the sociology of a dreadful enclosure', *Sociological Review*, vol 22, pp 221-48.

Daniel, W.W. (1968) *Racial discrimination in England. Based on the PEP Report*, Harmondsworth: Penguin.

Davies, J.G. (1972) *The evangelistic bureaucrat: A study of a planning exercise in Newcastle upon Tyne*, London: Tavistock Publications, cited in P. Malpass and A. Murie (eds) (1987) *Housing policy and practice,* London: Macmillan.

Davis, C. (1993) *Women and violence at home: Policy and procedures for housing associations*, London: National Federation of Housing Associations.

Dennis, N. and Erdos, G. (1993) *Families without fatherhood*, London: Institute of Economic Affairs.

DoE, DH and WO (Department of the Environment, Department of Health and Welsh Office) (1977-96) *Homelessness: Code of guidance for local authorities* (1st edn, 1977; 2nd edn, 1983; 3rd edn, 1991; 4th edn, 1996), London: HMSO.

DETR (Department of the Environment, Transport and Regions) (1999) *Relationship breakdown: A guide for social landlords*, London: DETR.

DETR and DSS (Department of Social Security) (2000) *Quality and choice: A decent home for all*, London: HMSO.

Dhillon-Kashyap, P. (1994) 'Black women and housing', in R. Gilroy and R. Woods (eds) *Housing women*, London: Routledge & Kegan Paul, pp 101-26.

Dibblin, J. (1991) *Wherever I lay my hat: Young women and homelessness*, London: Shelter.

Digby, P.W. (1976) *Hostels and lodgings for single people*, London: HMSO.

Dobash, R.E. and Dobash, R.P. (1979) *Violence against wives: A case against the patriarchy*, London: Open Books.

Dobash, R.E. and Dobash, R.P. (1992) *Women, violence and social change*, London: Routledge.

DoE (Department of the Environment) (1974) *Homelessness*, Circular 18/74, London: HMSO.

DoE (1987) *Housing: The government's proposals*, London: HMSO.

DoE (1989) *The government's review of the homelessness legislation*, London: HMSO.

DoE (1994) *Access to local authority and housing association tenancies. A consultation paper*, London: HMSO.

DoE (1995a) *Our future homes: Opportunity, choice and responsibility. The government's housing policies for England and Wales*, London: HMSO.

DoE (1995b) *More choice in the social rented sector. Consultation paper linked to the housing White Paper 'Our future homes'*, London: HMSO.

DoE (1996) *The allocation of housing regulations*, London: HMSO.

Drake, M., O'Brien, M. and Biebuyck, T. (1981) *Single and homeless*, London: HMSO.

Edwards, R. (1995) 'Working with interpreters: access to services and to user views', in G. Wilson (ed) *Community care: Asking the user*, London: Chapman Hall, pp 54-68.

English, J. (1979) 'Access and deprivation in local authority housing', in C. Jones (ed) *Urban deprivation and the inner city*, London: Croom Helm, pp 113-35.

Evans, A. and Duncan, S. (1988) *Responding to homelessness: Local authority policy and practice*, London: HMSO.

Field, F. (1998) *Losing out: The emergence of Britain's underclass*, Oxford: Basil Blackwell.

Flett, H. (1979) 'Bureaucracy and ethnicity – notions of eligibility to public housing', in S. Wallman (ed) *Ethnicity at work*, London: Macmillan, pp 134-52.

Flett, H. (1984) 'Dimensions of inequality: Birmingham Council housing allocations', in R. Ward (ed) *Race and residence in Britain: Approaches to differential treatment in housing*, Birmingham: Economic and Social Research Council, pp 81-96.

Ford, J. and Seavers, J. (1999) *Housing associations and rent arrears: Attitudes, beliefs and behaviour*, Coventry: Chartered Institute of Housing.

Freeman, M.D.A. (1979) *Violence in the home: A socio-legal study*, Farnborough: Saxon House.

Gayford, J.J. (1975) 'Wife battering: a preliminary survey of 100 cases', *British Medical Journal*, vol 1, January, pp 194-7.

Gayford, J.J. (1976) 'Ten types of battered wives', *Welfare Officer*, vol 1, January, pp 5-9.

Gilbert, J. (1986) *Not just a roof: Single homeless women's housing needs in Birmingham*, Birmingham: Birmingham Standing Conference for the Single Homeless.

Gill, O. (1977) *Luke Street: Housing policy, conflict and the creation of the delinquent area*, London: Macmillan.

Glastonbury, B. (1971) *Homeless near a thousand homes: A study of families without homes in South Wales and the West of England*, London: Allen & Unwin.

Goodlad, R. (1994) 'Conceptualising enabling: the housing role of local authorities', *Local Government Studies*, vol 20, no 4, pp 570-87.

Goss, S. (1983) *Working the act: The Homeless Persons Act in practice*, London: SHAC.

Gray, F. (1976) 'Selection and allocation in council housing', *Transactions of the Institute of British Geographers (New Series)*, vol 1, no 1, pp 34-46.

Greve, J. (1964) *London's homeless*, Welwyn: The Codicote Press.

Greve, J., Page, D. and Greve, S. (1971) *Homelessness in London*, Edinburgh: Scottish Academic Press.

Griffiths, M., Park, J., Smith, R., Stirling, T. and Trott, T. (1996) *Allocation policies in practice*, York: Joseph Rowntree Foundation.

Hague, G. and Malos, E. with Dear, W. (1996) *Multi-agency work and domestic violence: A national study of inter-agency initiatives*, Bristol: The Policy Press.

Hague, G. and Wilson, C. (1996) *The silenced pain, domestic violence 1945-1970*, Bristol: The Policy Press.

Harrow, J. and Shaw, M. (1992) 'The manager faces the consumer', in L. Willcocks and J. Harrow (eds) *Rediscovering public services management*, Maidenhead: McGraw Hill.

Henderson, J. and Karn, V. (1984) 'Race, class and the allocation of public housing in Britain', *Urban Studies*, vol 21, pp 115-28.

Henderson, J. and Karn, V. (1987) *Race, class and state housing: Inequality and the allocation of public housing in Britain*, Aldershot: Gower.

Hester, M. and Radford, L. (1996) *Domestic violence and child contact in England and Denmark*, Bristol: The Policy Press.

Hester, M., Pearson, C. and Harwin, N. (2000) *Making an impact: Children and domestic violence: A reader*, London: Jessica Kingsley.

Home Office (2000) *Domestic violence: Break the chain. Multi-agency guidance for addressing domestic violence*, London: Stationery Office.

Home Office and Welsh Office (1995) *Domestic violence: Don't stand for it. Inter-agency co-ordination to tackle domestic violence* (Interagency Circular), London, HMSO.

Homer, M., Leonard, A.E. and Taylor, M.P. (1984) *Private violence: Public shame*, Cleveland and Bristol: Cleveland Refuge and Aid for Women and Children/ Women's Aid Federation England.

Hood, L. (1991) 'A public management for all seasons?', *Public Administration*, vol 69, pp 3-19.

Housing Corporation (1989) *Performance expectations*, London: Housing Corporation.

Humphreys, C. and Thiara, R. (2002) *Routes to safety: Protection issues facing abused women and children and the role of outreach services*, Warwick: Centre for the Study of Safety and Well-Being, University of Warwick.

Hunter, C. and Nixon, J. (2001) 'Taking the blame and losing the home: women and anti-social behaviour', *Journal of Social Welfare and Family Law*, vol 23, no 4, pp 395-410.

Imam, U.F. (1994) 'Asian children and domestic violence', in A. Mullender and R. Morley (eds) *Children living with domestic violence*, London: Whiting & Birch Ltd, pp 188-99.

IoH (Institute of Housing) (1988) *Who will house the homeless? An Institute of Housing Report*, London: IoH.

IoH (1990) *Housing allocations: Report of a survey of local authorities in England and Wales*, Coventry: IoH.

IoH (1995) *One-parent families – Are they jumping the housing queue? A survey from the Institute of Housing*, Coventry: IoH.

Joint Charities Group (1978) *The implementation of the Housing (Homeless Persons) Act 1977: An appraisal after four months*, London: Women's Aid Federation England.

Karn, V. and Henderson, J. (1981) 'Housing atypical households: understanding the practices of local government housing departments', in A.W. Franklin (ed) *Family matters: Perspectives on the family and social policy*, Oxford: Pergamon Press, pp 71–86.

Kelly, L. (1988) *Surviving sexual violence*, Cambridge: Polity Press.

Kennedy, C., Lynch, E and Goodlad, R. (2001) *Good practice in joint/multi-agency working on homelessness*, Edinburgh: Scottish Executive Central Research Unit/Stationery Office.

Khan, V. (ed) (1979) *Minority families in Britain: Support and stress*, London: Macmillan.

Kirkwood, C. (1993) *Leaving abusive partners: From the scars of survival to the wisdom of change*, London: Sage.

Lambert, J., Paris, C. and Blackaby, B. (1978) *Housing policy and the state: Allocation, access and control*, London: Macmillan.

Law Commission (1992) *Family law: Domestic violence and occupation of the family home*, London: HMSO.

Le Grand, J. and Bartlett, W. (eds), (1993) *Quasi-markets and social policy*, London: Macmillan.

Levison, D. and Robertson, I. (1989) *Partners in meeting housing need: Local authority nominations to housing associations in London. Good practice guide, LHAC and ALA/LBA Homelessness Working Party*, London: National Federation of Housing Associations.

Lindblom, C.E. (1959) 'The science of muddling through', *Public Administration Review*, vol 19, pp 79–88.

Lindblom, C.E. (1979) 'Still muddling, not yet through', *Public Administration Review*, vol 39, pp 517–26.

Lipsky, M. (1980) *Street level bureaucracy: Dilemmas of the individual in public services*, New York: Russell Sage Foundation.

Local Government Association (1998) *Domestic violence and child abuse: Policy and practice issues for local authorities and other agencies* (Circular 748/98), London: Local Government Association.

LFHA (London Federation of Housing Associations) (1995) *Managing vulnerability*, London: National Federation of Housing Associations.

London Research Centre Housing Group (1987) *London borough policies on the acceptance of homeless households*, Paper presented to Association of London Authorities/London Boroughs Association Joint Working Party on the Homelessness, London: London Research Centre.

Malos, E. and Hague, G. with Dear, W. (1993) *Domestic violence and housing: Local authority responses to women and children escaping violence in the home*, Bristol: Women's Aid Federation England and School of Applied Social Studies, University of Bristol.

Malpass, P. and Mullins, D. (2002) 'Local authority stock transfer in the UK: from local initiative to national policy', *Housing Studies*, vol 17, no 4, pp 673–86.

Malpass, P. and Murie, A. (1987) *Housing policy and practice*, London: Macmillan.

Mama, A. (1989) *The hidden struggle: Statutory and voluntary sector responses to violence against black women in the home*, London: London Race and Housing Research Unit.

Mann, K. (1992) *The making of an English 'underclass'? The social divisions of welfare and labour*, Milton Keynes: Open University Press.

Marcovitch, A. (1976) 'Refuges for battered women', *Social Work Today*, vol 7, no 2, pp 34–5.

Marsden, D. (1969) *Mothers alone: Poverty and the fatherless family*, London: Allen Lane.

Marsden, D. and Owens, D. (1975) 'The Jekyll and Hyde marriages', *New Society*, vol 8, May, no 32, pp 333–5.

May, M. (1978) 'Violence in the family: an historical perspective', in J.P. Martin (ed) *Violence and the family*, Chichester: John Wiley & Sons, pp 135–68.

Maynard, M. (1985) 'The response of social workers to domestic violence', in J. Pahl (ed) *Private violence and public policy*, London: Routledge, pp 125–41.

McCarthy, P. and Simpson, B. (1991) *Issues in post-divorce housing: Family policy or housing policy?*, Aldershot: Avebury.

McGibbon, A., Cooper, L. and Kelly, L. (1989) *What support?*, London: Hammersmith and Fulham Council Community Police Committee Domestic Violence Project, Polytechnic of North London.

Melville, J. (1977) 'In search of a refuge', *New Society*, vol 25, August, no 41, pp 389-90.

Miller, N. (1975) *Battered spouses*, London: G. Bell.

Modood, T., Berthoud, R., Lakey, J., Nazroo, J., Smith, P., Virdee, S. and Beishon, S. (1997) *Ethnic minorities in Britain: Diversity and disadvantage*, London: Policy Studies Institute.

Mooney, J. (1993) *The hidden figure: Domestic violence in North London. The findings of a survey conducted on domestic violence in the north London borough of Islington*, London: Centre for Criminology, Middlesex University.

Morley, R. and Pascall, G. (1996) 'Women and homelessness: proposals from the Department of the Environment. Part II: domestic violence', *Journal of Social Welfare and Family Law*, vol 18, no 3, pp 327-40.

Mullender, A. (1996) *Rethinking domestic violence: The social work and probation response*, London: Routledge.

Mullender, A. and Morley, R. (eds) (1994) *Children living with domestic violence: Putting men's abuse of women on the child care agenda*, London: Whiting & Birch Ltd.

Mullins, D. and Niner, P. (1996) *Evaluation of the 1991 Homelessness Code of Guidance*, London: Department of the Environment.

Mullins, D. and Niner, P. (1998) 'A prize of citizenship? Changing access to social housing', in A. Marsh and D. Mullins (eds) *Housing and public policy: Citizenship, choice and control*, Buckingham: Open University Press.

Murray, C. (1990) *The emerging British underclass*, London: Institute of Economic Affairs.

National Assistance Board (1966) *Homeless single persons: Report on a survey carried out by the National Assistance Board, with the co-operation of other government departments and voluntary bodies between October 1965 and March 1966*, London: HMSO.

National Audit Office (1990) *Homelessness: Report by the Comptroller and Auditor General*, London: HMSO.

Newman J. (1998) 'Managerialism and social welfare', in G. Hughes and G. Lewis (eds) *Unsettling welfare: The reconstruction of social policy*, London: Routledge, pp 333-74.

NFHA (National Federation of Housing Associations) (1982) *Race and housing*, London: NFHA.

NFHA (1983) *Race and housing: Still a cause for concern*, London: NFHA.

NFHA (1987) *Standards for housing management*, London: NFHA.

NFHA (1989) *Joint statement by the NFHA, AMA and ADC on local authority nominations to housing associations*, London: NFHA.

NFHA (1994) *Department of the Environment Consultation Paper: Access to local authority and housing association tenancies. Response of the National Federation of Housing Associations*, London: NFHA.

Niner, P. (1989) *Homelessness in nine local authorities: Case studies of policy and practice*, London: HMSO.

Niner, P. in collaboration with Karn, V. (1985) *Housing association allocations: Achieving racial equality. A West Midlands case study*, London: The Runnymede Trust.

Norman, P. (1975) 'Housing allocation procedures in slum clearance areas – a comparison of departmental styles', *Social Research*, no 11, Glasgow: University of Glasgow.

ODPM (Office of the Deputy Prime Minister) (2002a) *Allocation of accommodation – Code of guidance for local housing authorities. A consultation paper*, London: ODPM.

ODPM (2002b) *Homelessness: Code of guidance for local authorities*, London: ODPM.

ODPM (2002c) *Statutory homelessness: England, Quarterly Returns for 2002* (and access to previous homeless data for DTLR, DETR and DoE).

Page, D. (1993) *Building for communities: A study of new housing association estates*, York: Joseph Rowntree Foundation.

Pahl, J. (1978) *A refuge for battered women: A study of the role of a women's centre*, London: HMSO.

Pahl, J. (1980) *Matters of money management within marriage*, Canterbury: Department of Sociology, University of Kent.

Pahl, J. (1985) *Private violence and public policy: The needs of battered women and the response of the public services*, London: Routledge & Kegan Paul.

Parker, J. and Dugmore, K. (1976) *Colour and the allocation of GLC housing: The report of the GLC lettings survey, 1974-75*, Research Report 21, London: Greater London Council.

Parker, J., Smith, R. and Williams, P. (1992) *Access, allocations and nominations: The role of housing associations*, London: HMSO.

Pascall, G. and Morley, R. (1996) 'Women and homelessness: proposals from the Department of the Environment. Part I: Lone mothers', *Journal of Social Welfare and Family Law*, vol 18, no 2, pp 189-202.

Pawson, H., Levison, D., Third, H., Parker, J. and Lawton, G. (2001) *Local authority policy and practice on allocations: Transfers and homelessness*, London: DETR.

Phizacklea, A. and Miles, R. (1979) 'Working-class racist beliefs in the inner city', in R. Miles and A. Phizacklea (eds) *Racism and political action in Britain*, London: Routledge & Kegan Paul, pp 93-123.

Phoenix, A. (1996) 'Social constructions of lone motherhood: a case of competing discourses', in E.B. Silva (ed) *Good enough mothering? Feminist perspectives on lone motherhood*, London: Routledge, pp 175-90.

Pizzey, E. (A. Forbes, ed) (1974) *Scream quietly or the neighbours will hear*, Harmondsworth: Penguin.

Pollitt, C. (1990) *Managerialism and the public services: The Anglo-American experience*, Oxford: Basil Blackwell.

Potter, J. (1988) 'Consumerism and the public sector: how well does the coat fit?', *Public Administration*, vol 66, pp 149-64.

Prescott-Clarke, P., Clemens, S. and Park, A. (1994) *Routes into local authority housing: A study of local authority waiting lists and new tenancies*, London: Department of the Environment and HMSO.

Rai, D.K. and Thiara, R.K. (1997) *Re-defining spaces: The needs of black women and children in refuge support services and black workers in Women's Aid*, Bristol: Women's Aid Federation England.

Randall, G. (1989) *Tackling homelessness*, London: National Federation of Housing Associations.

Rao, N. (1990) *Black women in public housing: A report on the housing problems of black women in the London Boroughs of Wandsworth and Southwark*, London: Black Women in Housing Group.

Richards, J. (1981) *The Housing (Homeless Persons) Act 1977: A study in policymaking*, Bristol: School for Advanced Urban Studies, University of Bristol.

Roberts, M. (1991) *Living in a man-made world: Gender assumptions in modern housing design*, London: Routledge.

Roseneil, S. and Mann, K. (1996) 'Unpalatable choices and inadequate families. Lone mothers and the underclass debate', in E.B. Silva (ed) *Good enough mothering? Feminist perspectives on lone motherhood*, London: Routledge, pp 191-210.

Runnymede Trust (1975) *Race and council housing in London*, London: Runnymede Trust.

Scott, S., Kintrea, K., Keogham, M., Pawson, H. and Currie, H. (2000) *Review of housing management practice in Scotland*, Edinburgh: CRU/Scottish Executive.

Scottish Education Department (1982) *Violence in the family: Theory and practice in social work* (Social Work Services Group, Scottish Education Department), Edinburgh: HMSO.

Shelter (1976) *Blunt powers – Sharp practices*, London: Shelter.

Simpson, A. (1981) *Stacking the decks: A study of race, inequality and council housing in Nottingham*, Nottingham: Nottingham Community Relations Council.

Smith, D. and Whalley, A. (1975) *Racial minorities and public housing*, London: Political and Economic Planning.

Smith, S.J. (1989) *The politics of 'race' and residence: Citizenship, segregation and white supremacy in Britain*, Cambridge: Polity Press.

Smith, S.J. (1990) 'Income, housing wealth and gender inequality', *Urban Studies*, vol 27, no 1, pp 67-88.

Smith, S.J. (1993) 'Residential segregation and the politics of racialization', in M. Cross and M. Keith (eds) *Racism, the city and the state*, London: Routledge, pp 128-43.

Stanko, E. (1985) *Intimate intrusions: Women's experience of male violence*, London: Routledge & Kegan Paul.

Stanko, E. (1994) 'When precaution is normal: a feminist critique of crime prevention', in L. Gelsthorpe and A. Morris (eds) *Feminist perspectives in criminology*, Milton Keynes: Open University Press, pp 173-83.

Stewart, J. (1993) *Local government today: An observer's view*, Luton: Local Government Management Board.

Sutton, J. (1978) 'The growth of the British movement for battered women', *Victimology*, vol 2, nos 3-4, pp 576-84.

Thomas, A. and Niner, P. (1989) *Living in temporary accommodation: A survey of homeless people*, London: HMSO.

Thompson, L. (1988) *An act of compromise. An appraisal of the effects of the Housing (Homeless Persons) Act 1977 – Ten years on*, London: SHAC/Shelter.

Timms, N. (1975) 'Battered wives: a study in social problem definition', in K. Jones (ed) *The year book of social policy in Britain*, London: Routledge & Kegan Paul, pp 119-30.

Tucker, J. (1966) *Honourable estates*, London: Gollanz.

Walker, R. (1998) 'New public management and housing associations: from comfort to competition', *Policy and Politics*, vol 26, no 4, pp 71-87.

Walker, R. (2000) 'The changing management of social housing: the impact of externalisation and managerialism', *Housing Studies*, vol 15, no 2, pp 281-300.

Watson, S. (1986) 'Housing and the family – the marginalisation of non-family households in Britain', *International Journal of Urban and Regional Research*, vol 10, pp 8-28.

Watson, S. (1988) *Accommodating diversity: Gender and housing*, London: Allen & Unwin.

Watson, S. with Austerberry, H. (1986) *Housing and homelessness: A feminist perspective,* London: Routledge & Kegan Paul.

Weir, A. (1977) 'Battered women: some perspectives and problems', in M. Mayo (ed) *Women in the community*, London: Routledge & Kegan Paul, pp 109-20.

Welsh Women's Aid (1986) *The answer is maybe...and that's final!* (revised 1989), Cardiff: Welsh Women's Aid.

Wilkinson, M. and Craig, G. (2002) *New roles for old: Local authority members and partnership working,* York: York Publishing Services.

Withers, P. and Randolph, B. (1994) *Access, homelessness and housing associations,* London: National Federation of Housing Associations.

Wynn, M. (1964) *Fatherless families: A study of families deprived of a father by death, divorce, separation or desertion before or after marriage*, London: Michael Joseph.

New challenges and good practice

The points listed in this appendix are drawn from the different chapters in this book, so they are not comprehensive. More detailed guidance and information is available from the Office of the Deputy Prime Minister, Home Office and Shelter.

The local authority

Homelessness

- Homeless decisions in relation to people leaving domestic violence should be made sympathetically. The 'intentionality' and 'local connection' provisions in the legislation should not be relevant in these circumstances. The new *Code of Guidance* (ODPM, 2002b) should be the guideline.
- A domestic violence policy would be useful, giving staff guidance about what to consider in assessing applications from homeless and other applicants. It should include information about the role of other agencies including housing associations. It needs to be backed up with sufficient resources, regular training and consistent management.
- The local authority needs to ensure that a range of safe temporary accommodation is available to meet the variety of needs of homeless applicants in this situation. For example, homeless families should not have to deal with the extra trauma of their children of different ages having to live separately because there is no suitable emergency accommodation for them all to stay together.
- A range of temporary and permanent accommodation needs to be available for women who have serious mental health problems because of the impact of violence on them. Support services need to be aligned to assist them in the search for alternative accommodation and to help them settle permanently.

The 'strategic' role

- The local authority's 'strategic' role should be developed to give greater emphasis to the nature of housing management services provided by all social housing landlords in the area. The local authority should take the lead, whether or not it is the main housing provider. 'Good practice' in relation to responding to homelessness and domestic violence should be expected and promoted by the local authority.

- Nominations should be made of statutory and non-statutory homeless applicants who have left domestic violence. Rehousing by housing associations should be effectively monitored to ensure that applicants with different backgrounds and from different circumstances are assisted. Monitoring needs to be able to identify the type and quality of property offered, its location, and whether it is accepted or refused (with the reasons for this). Monitoring like this will help ensure fairness.
- The local authority should develop various multi-agency and specific initiatives. This could include encouraging training and policy development in associations as part of its 'enabling' or 'strategic' role.

Housing associations

General points

- A domestic violence policy should be introduced with practice guidelines for staff, outlining (where appropriate) the local authority's role and backed up by sufficient association procedures, resources and management commitment to enable better services to be provided.
- Staff need to be trained to understand domestic violence and its effect on the way they do their jobs, especially in relation to reception work ('customer services'), assessment and allocation practices.
- Associations need to ensure that women (and men) made homeless because of domestic violence obtain the highest waiting-list/transfer-list priority for rehousing.
- Senior management needs to ensure that staff have enough time to interview safely, confidentially and appropriately. This is an 'efficient' use of time.
- Associations need to publicise their commitment to rehouse women (and men) who are not necessarily 'local'. Information for residents and councillors about allocation practices may need to be clarified.

Applying for housing

- Associations need to ensure that staff who speak the local community languages are employed across the housing management service, and especially in customer services reception. Professional interpreting arrangements should also be in place and be well known to staff. Care should be exercised over the selection of interpreters to work in this field to ensure that they are acceptable to the person being interviewed.
- Associations should publicise the possibility that applicants or tenants who have left home because of domestic violence (or are still living with violence)

have a choice of interviewer to discuss their circumstances and are guaranteed a private, confidential interview. These services can be publicised in relevant languages in application literature and on posters or leaflets available in reception areas.

- Interviews about people's housing circumstances should only be undertaken in private interviewing rooms where they cannot be seen or overheard.
- There should be clear guidelines to the public and for staff about personal applicant information obtained during the housing application process. Will it remain confidential to the association or might it be obtained legally at a later date by the police, social services or the courts?
- Answering enquiries, interviewing and record keeping needs to be done so that confidentiality and safety are ensured. Staff should not be so pressured in their working environment that they accidentally reveal information.
- 'Proof' or 'supporting evidence' should not be necessary for housing applications to proceed. It is difficult for applicants to approach the local authority or housing associations for help because of the continued stigma associated with domestic violence. When nominated by the local authority, they should not need to be re-assessed by association staff. If they are direct or transfer applicants, a signed statement should be sufficient.

Assessing applications and allocating homes

- An applicant's long-term safety needs to be carefully considered by the association in relation to housing assessment and allocation. In protecting the applicant, the association is also helping to minimise the possibility that they will be found by the violent ex-partner and/or family members.
- Staff should ask for information that will help them make housing offers that are appropriate and safe. This may include information relating to transport use, shopping requirements, the need for health services and schooling, as well as details about the location of family members and friends. Information about the ex-partner's whereabouts and that of their family/ friends also needs to be recorded (if known).
- The safety features of vacant properties need to be assessed before they are offered to applicants who have left domestic violence. This should include consideration of the immediate location and area.
- Specific consideration needs to be given by staff to where members of the ex-partner's family are currently living (if this is known) and whether the vacancy is likely to be too near to them.
- When allocating property, any application where violence is involved should be considered the most urgent application.
- Applicants should have sufficient time to view a property and the area, especially in cases where it is unfamiliar to them. Information about local organisations should be made available. They will then be in a better position to judge whether or not the property is suitable.

- Applicants should not be further disadvantaged by being offered poor-quality accommodation in unsafe areas: good-quality accommodation will enable them to concentrate on re-establishing their family's stability.
- Associations should not be so focused on reducing voids and maximising rental income that they seriously financially disadvantage people who have no furniture and few possessions but want to accept an offer of housing. It should be possible to be flexible about tenancy commencement dates to allow the DSS time to process applications for social fund grants or loans.
- If an applicant has been rehoused because of violence, care needs to be exercised by housing management staff to ensure that they do not rehouse a member of the ex-partner's family nearby at a later date. These situations need to be avoided to protect the original applicant's safety.
- Housing officers need time to build workable relationships with tenants in the areas they manage. This will increase the confidence of new tenants in their association landlords. This could be part of the 'building communities' type work of associations. This is a far more positive and realistic approach than trying to regulate and/or restrict the 'type' of household rehoused into particular areas.

Index

A

advice, provision of 23, 57, 63, 75, 92, 54
African Caribbean community 79
age limits 17
alcoholism 49
allocation meetings 114-18
anti-social behaviour 65, 66, 149
anxiety 129
application forms 88, 90, 92
applications for housing 15-18, 79-97, 99, 112-13, 102, 143
  comparing and contrasting 113
  housing staff attention and 132-3
'arm's-length' rehousing 146-7
arrears, *see* rent arrears
Asian people 16, 29, 60, 62, 84, 86, 97, 99, 112, 121, 122, 141, 148, 149, 150
assessment 92-5, 99-122, 159, 169
Association of District Councils (ADC) 33
Association of Metropolitan Authorities (AMA) 33
asylum seekers 40
Audit Commission 8

B

bad practice 42-3
balanced communities 9
battered women 25
bed and breakfast accommodation 10, 30, 125, 127
bedsits 34
beneficiary associations 59
best practice 87
black people 15,16, 17, 29, 60, 62, 84, 86, 97, 99, 112, 121, 122, 150
black women 21, 27, 53, 129-30, 148, 149
blind people 86
boarded-up properties 137
budgets 62
building 4, 6, 8, 9, 59

C

Campaign for the Homeless and Rootless (CAHR) 31
Canterbury Women's Centre 20

case law 3, 49
central homeless teams 44-5, 54, 75, 76, 132, 148
Central Housing Advisory Committee (CHAC) 14
child density 119
children 1, 17-25, 31, 34, 36, 47, 68, 75, 76, 80, 112-16, 123, 125, 142, 144, 167
  abuse of 23, 125
  difficulties in refuges 130
  impact of violence on 125
choice 13, 50, 76, 77, 79, 137-8, 145-6
class distinctions 15, 16
cleanliness 130-1
Code of Guidance 3, 23, 24-5, 27, 49, 50, 84, 131, 167
Commission for Racial Equality 33
communication 53, 65, 71
community building 140, 170
community care 7
competition 58, 61, 63, 149
competitive regimes 63
competitive tendering 46
complaints 10, 16, 44, 64
confidentiality 88-90, 169
consultation 48
consumerism 79, 96
Continuous Recording (CORE) 34, 99
cost-conscious environments 134
cost control 9, 76, 83, 149
councillors 29, 30, 39, 42, 44, 52-3, 58, 60, 67, 68-70, 115
court work 63
cultural needs 130
'customer care' 57, 74, 77, 79, 90, 96, 151
customer service 148
  officers 81-3
  teams 64

D

damage to belongings 48
day centres 30
deaf people 86
decision making 40-1, 48-52, 100, 111
decorating standards 108-9
democratic deficit 68

statutory 4, 18, 41, 49, 58, 59, 90, 99, 135, 168
teams 44-5, 54, 75, 76, 132, 148
homelessness
  stress areas 34
  causes of 19
  decision making and 40-1
  domestic violence and 20, 21, 35-6
  government policy on 4
  housing associations and 32-6
  in 1970s 21
  in London and the south 5
  inter-agency work on 7
  local authorities and vii, 44, 145, 167
  nature of 19
  preventative measures 145
  prioritisation and 47-53
  structural 19
Homelessness Act (2002) 1, 18, 145, 146
homeless service, organisation of 43-7
honesty 107, 110-11
hostels 10, 20, 22, 25, 25, 30, 44, 67,106, 110, 115, 125, 127, 129-31, 139, 144
house types 15
housekeeping standards 17, 108-9
Housing (Homeless Persons) Act (1977) 1, 13, 18, 20, 22, 23, 25, 40
Housing Act (1980) 4
Housing Act (1985) 1, 14, 25,29
Housing Act (1988) 2, 4, 7, 8, 57, 59, 60
Housing Act (1996) 1, 3, 4, 5-6, 10, 13, 18, 36-7, 40-1, 45, 47-8, 57, 135, 145, 146
Housing Action Trusts 4
housing allocation 15-18, 37, 52, 111-22, 145, 169-70
  process 113-18
  selective 9
Housing and Planning Act (1986) 25-6
housing applications, *see* applications for housing
housing associations
  alternatives to local authority housing 5
  applications 15-19, 79-97, 112-13
  as providers of housing 145
  building programmes 9
  change in 2
  consortium schemes and 46
  councillor intervention with 68-70
  domestic violence policy 70-5, 168
  'enabling' and 53-7
  financial priorities of 148
  future of 146

homeless people and 7,8, 9, 14, 32-6
  in 1970s 32
  management of 8-9
  priorities 138, 139, 148
  relationship with local authorities 75-6, 104-5, 121
  relationships with tenants 96, 120
  role 4, 7-9, 59-77, 167
  staffing levels 62
  statutory responsibilities 95
  targets 58
  track record of 2
  women's views of 2, 9-10, 123-44
housing benefit 107, 140
Housing Committee 41, 42
housing companies vii, 4
Housing Corporation, the 8, 32, 33, 68, 72
Housing Investment Programme (HIP) 34
housing location 17, 50, 100
housing management service 46, 63-7
housing offers 135-8
housing quality 10, 17, 20, 44, 50, 99, 105, 135, 136-7, 146, 170
housing registers 5, 40, 135, *see also* waiting list
housing staff
  attention of 132-3
  attitudes 9, 16, 24, 27, 29, 51, 60, 66, 104, 118-19, 139, 148
  class and 14
  complaints from 44
  customer service 148
  fear of criticism from 132-3
  generalist 43, 92
  influence of senior 95, 101
  insensitivity 96, 131
  job satisfaction 64
  judgements 92, 93, 100, 110, 113, 114
  lack of help from 123
  local 86-7
  morale 62
  moral judgements of 14, 15
  motivation and management of 131
  multilingual 85
  organisation of 83-4
  pay issue 65
  practices 3
  priorities 65, 139
  professional autonomy of 63
  specialist 43, 92
  sympathy of 133-4
  tensions 61, 95

new homes, attitudes to 123
nominations 33-4, 40, 54, 59, 69, 70, 75,
     92, 96, 99, 101, 103, 104, 112, 113,
     117, 122, 133, 147, 148, 168, 169
nuclear families 13, 15, 117, 148, 149

O

organisational pressures 39
outreach services 150
outsiders 8, 30, 68
overcrowding 128
owner occupiers 127

P

panic 70
parental conflicts 31
payment records 107
performance indicators 53
performance targets 46
permanent accommodation 5, 37, 40,
     167
physical violence 41, 48, 91, 92, 94, 108
Pizzey, Erin 22
points assessment scheme 92
policy documents 71
political opportunity 70
political support 53
post, difficulties with 131
poverty 10, 107
prioritisation 47-53, 55, 68, 72, 76, 91,
     94, 117-18, 121, 133-4, 144, 168
priority need 35, 40, 145
privacy 87-8, 121, 141, 169
private sector 6, 16, 22, 24, 37, 40, 145,
     151
privatisation 60
problem families 16, 66; *see also*
     irresponsible families
professional boundaries 53
proof of violence 24, 31, 37, 41, 42, 49,
     51, 73, 93-6, 103, 121, 122, 123,
     134-5, 148, 169
property abandonment 67, 109
psychological violence 41, 48, 91
Public Accounts Committee 33
public management 8

Q

quality of housing, *see* housing quality

R

race issues 2, 9, 14, 16, 21, 27, 33-4, 35,
     79-88, 151
Race Relations Amendment Act (2002)
     79
racial attacks 62, 137
racial discrimination 16, 33, 100, 112
racial harassment 67, 68, 72, 73, 87, 91,
     150
racialisation 150
racialisation of space 100
racist attacks 141
reception services vii, 80-90
references, taking up 107
refuges 3, 10, 23, 25, 30, 32, 35, 41, 67,
     125, 127-31, 138, 139, 143
refusal of offers 135-8
relationships 52, 53, 56, 57, 58, 60,
     68-70, 75-6, 107, 120, 170
   breakdown of 9, 17, 28, 115
religious issues 27, 28, 128, 130
rent
   arrears 41, 58, 63, 64, 65, 66, 67, 83,
       91, 107-8, 120, 148, 149
   collection 58
   cost of 8, 34, 35, 55, 68, 69, 148
   difficulties in paying 16
   payment record 107
repairs 58, 81, 83, 141
reproduction of workforce 15
respectability 14, 15, 16, 17, 30
response times 42
right to buy 4
rooflessness 126
rudeness 32
R v LB Ealing, ex parte Sidhu [1982] 3

S

safety 10, 70, 87, 96, 121, 125, 137, 140-
     4, 169, 170
secrecy 126
security 81, 131
self-blame 129
self-confidence 132, 143
self-esteem 143
self-help, problems with 131
sexual violence 31, 41, 48 108-9, 124-5
shelters 22
shopping requirements 169
single people 18, 30, 145
single women 21-3, 25, 30-2, 68, 119
social status 126

Also available from The Policy Press

Women and homelessness in Europe
Pathways, services and experiences
Bill Edgar and Joe Doherty
Paperback £15.99 US$28.95
ISBN 1 86134 351 5
234 x 156mm 296 pages
September 2001

Challenging violence against women
The Canadian experience
Gill Hague, Liz Kelly and Audrey Mullender
Paperback £15.99 US$25.00
ISBN 1 86134 278 0
297 x 210mm 76 pages
March 2001

Social work, domestic violence and child protection
Challenging practice
Catherine Humphreys
Paperback £12.99 US$23.50
ISBN 1 86134 190 3
297 x 210mm 56 pages
January 2000

Domestic violence and health
The response of the medical profession
Emma Williamson
Paperback £14.99 US$26.95
ISBN 1 86134 251 2
234 x 156mm 228 pages
December 2000

From good intentions to good practice
Mapping services working with families where there is domestic violence
Catherine Humphreys, Marianne Hester, Gill Hague, Pam Lowe, Hilary Abrahams and Audrey Mullender
Paperback £13.95 US$25.00
ISBN 1 86134 245 4
297 x 210mm 68 pages
August 2000

Managing public services innovation
The experience of English housing associations
Richard Walker, Emma L. Jeames and Robert O. Rowlands
Paperback £16.99 US$31.00
ISBN 1 86134 294 2
234 x 156mm 144 pages
April 2001

Changing places
Housing association policy and practice on nominations and lettings
Hal Pawson and David Mullins
Paperback £19.99
ISBN 1 86134 507 0
297 x 210mm 152 pages
March 2003

Housing, social policy and difference
Disability, ethnicity, gender and housing
Malcolm Harrison and Cathy Davis
Paperback £17.99 US$29.95
ISBN 1 86134 187 3
hardback £45.00 US$75.00
ISBN 1 86134 305 1
216 x 148mm 256 pages
April 2001

Two steps forward
Housing policy into the new millennium
David Cowan and Alex Marsh
Paperback £18.99 US$29.95
ISBN 1 86134 229 2
Hardback £45.00 US$69.95
ISBN 1 86134 252 7
216 x 148mm 408 pages
July 2001

Home ownership in a risk society
A social analysis of mortgage arrears and possessions
Janet Ford, Roger Burrows ans Sarah Nettleton
Paperback £16.99 US$32.50
ISBN 1 86134 261 6
Hardback £45.00 US$75.00
ISBN 1 86134 262 4
216 x 148mm 212 pages
July 2001

The private rented sector in a new century
Revival or false dawn?
Stuart Lowe and David Hughes
Paperback £18.99 US$29.95
ISBN 1 86134 384 5
Hardback £50.00 US$130.00
ISBN 1 86134 349 3
234 x 156mm 240 pages
September 2002

Inclusive housing in an ageing society
Innovative approaches
Sheila M. Peace and Caroline Holland
Paperback £18.99 US$29.95
ISBN 1 86134 263 2
Hardback £45.00 US$69.95
ISBN 1 86134 345 0
216 x 148mm 280 pages
October 2001

For further information about these and other titles published by The Policy Press, please visit our website at:
www.policypress.org.uk

To order titles, please contact:
Marston Book Services
PO Box 269 • Abingdon • Oxon OX14 4YN • UK
Tel: +44 (0)1235 465500 • Fax: +44 (0)1235 465556
E-mail: direct.orders@marston.co.uk